sint subscripta, eadem omnino habenda erit fides, quae huic haberetur,
si ostenderetur. Quae Nostra decreta in universum si quis vel
spreverit vel quoquo modo detrectaverit, sciat se poenas esse subi-
turum, iis iure statutas, qui Summorum Pontificum iussa non fe-
cerint. Datum Romae, apud Sanctum Petrum, die XXV mensis De-
cembris, in Nativitate Domini Nostri Iesu Christi, anno MDCCCLXI,
Pontificatus Nostri anno quarto. = J. C. =

Ego Ioannes Catholicae Ecclesiae
Episcopus

+ Ego Eugenius Episcopus Ostiensis ac Portuensis et S. Rufinae
Cardinalis Tisserant, Sacri Collegii Decanus

+ Ego Clemens Episcopus veliternus
Cardinalis Micara

+ Ego Josephus Episcopus Albanensis
Cardinalis Pizzardo

Last page of the Bull with the Pope's signature

LETTERS FROM VATICAN CITY

Xavier Rynne

✠

LETTERS
FROM
VATICAN CITY

✠

VATICAN COUNCIL II (FIRST SESSION):
BACKGROUND AND DEBATES

New York
Farrar, Straus & Company

. . . Our sacred obligation is not only to take care of this precious treasure [the deposit of faith] as if we had only to worry about the past, but we must also devote ourselves with joy and without fear to the work of giving this ancient and eternal doctrine a relevancy corresponding to the conditions of our era. . . .

POPE JOHN XXIII

Contents

✠

List of Illustrations

Preface

✠

THE FIRST SESSION of Pope John's Vatican Council, from October 11 to December 8, 1962, has proved to be a religious event of great significance. The kind and generous reception of our two articles on the Council in *The New Yorker* has prompted us to complete the story in depth. This book is based on sources available to the general public, particularly *L'Osservatore Romano, La Civiltà Cattolica, Herder-Korrespondenz, La Croix, Informations Catholiques Internationales,* and *La Documentation Catholique,* as well as on accounts in many other newspapers and journals around the world that were derived from the news releases supplied by the official Press Office of the Council and the ingenuity of individual reporters.

It should perhaps be made clear that Xavier Rynne is not "a disgruntled Catholic clergyman,"[1] nor "a Roman student who after failing his final exams criticized the Roman educational system,"[2] nor "a fellow named Wilfrid Sheed, who used to write for *Jubilee*,"[3] nor "a mild Redemptorist professor of Church history,"[4] nor—as one or another of us has personally been told—"an American bishop," "an English Dominican," "a New York Jesuit," "a writer inspired by the Vatican Secretariat of State," nor finally, believe it or not, "Jack Kerouac."

This book is an essay in theological journalism. The aim has been to make it as accurate and complete as possible under the circumstances. Any good journalist will realize that turns of phrase and emphatic judgments will inevitably give rise to misinterpretation in the minds of some readers. It is difficult, for example, to characterize groups of men of differing opinions who follow the same line of endeavor, without having recourse to terms commonly used in political debate, such as "conservative," "progressive," "liberal," "middle-of-the-roader," "reactionary," "traditionalist," and so on. One theologian has suggested the terms "open door" and "closed door" to remove the discussion from political and personal connotations altogether. While in agreement with this most desirable end, we find that the terms are too awkward in actual usage: "Cardinal X, an open-door prelate, rose to disagree with Archbishop Y, of the closed-door school." We prefer the more familiar terms only for their convenience, but it should be made clear that the use of these terms is not intentionally tendentious.

The authors have no ecclesiastical, theological, or other ax

[1] *The Priest,* December 1962, p. 1026.
[2] *American Ecclesiastical Review,* January 1963, p. 62.
[3] Letter dated January 22, 1963 to *The New Yorker.*
[4] *Camden Star Herald,* February 15, 1963.

to grind. The book is an attempt to give the reader a meaningful account of the proceedings during the eight weeks of the first session of Vatican Council II, with enough background material to enable him to understand what the debates and discussion were all about. The Council was essentially a religious experience; it can be understood only as such.

—XAVIER RYNNE.

I

"A Council!"

ACCORDING TO POPE JOHN, it was towards the end of 1958, shortly after assuming the papacy, that he engaged the late Cardinal Tardini in a troubled conversation regarding the state of the world and the Church's role in it. Noting the agitation and anxiety in which the modern world was plunged, and the apparently hopeless repetition of clamorings for peace and justice, he asked his Secretary of State what might be done to give the world an example of peace and concord between men and an occasion for new hope, when suddenly there sprang to his own lips the words, "A Council!" Uncertain of his most intimate aide's reaction to such an idea, and expecting to be deluged with a torrent of objections from this seasoned statesman, the pope was overcome when Cardinal Tardini responded with an immediate and emotion-charged assent: *"Si, si! un Concilio!"*

About a month later, the pope received a strikingly different reaction to his inspiration. This occurred on January 25, 1959 and came from a group of close associates, following the celebration of a mass for Church unity in the Benedictine monastery at the basilica of St. Paul's Outside the Walls. The pope gathered round him the eighteen cardinals present for the occasion and talked to them intimately of the affairs of the Church. He first told them of his intention to hold a local Synod for the diocese of Rome, to renew the Christian way of life in the center of Christendom. Then turning his attention to world conditions, he painted a brief and vivid picture of the good and evil influences struggling to control the contemporary world. He pointed to the sanctity and the moral confusion that exist side by side in villages, cities, and nations throughout the world, and to the continual temptation facing modern man to make an idol of scientific progress. In order to proclaim the truth, he said, and to reanimate the faith of Christians, and thereby to contribute to the well-being of the world here and now, he had decided to call a Council of the Universal Church. Then he turned to the cardinals, and said simply: "I would like to have your advice." The cardinals to a man sat mute before him. Not a single word of response was uttered.

The pope has candidly recorded his disappointment: "Humanly we could have expected that the cardinals, after hearing our allocution, might have crowded around to express approval and good wishes." Yet he put the kindest and most charitable light on their unanimous failure to show any immediate reaction: "Instead there was a devout and impressive silence. Explanations came on following days . . ."

Cardinal Tardini's original response to the pope's inspiration regarding the Council was immediate and sincere; we have Pope John's word for it. It is probable that later the cardinal had serious doubts about the feasibility of so vast an undertaking as an Ecumenical Council and, more particularly, about directing it primarily at the reunion of Christians. It is believed to be Tardini who first broached the idea of the Roman Synod, perhaps as a delaying tactic, or more likely as a pilot-project to give the pope and the Curia some notion of the complexities involved in organizing a worldwide Synod. Little by little, Vatican officials began to face the pontiff with stiff objections to the idea of the Council, its objectives, and the possibility of holding it within a few years. Some serious-minded counsellors were convinced that ten, even twenty, years of preparation were necessary.

The result of these cautions was a maturing decision on the pontiff's part to hold the Council well within the first years of his pontificate. Being a realist, he had the normal fears of a man of his advanced age that his pontificate might not prove a long one. On the very day of his election as pope, his remark on his choice of name echoed this feeling: "Nearly all [the previous pontiffs named John] had a brief pontificate."

European clerics are of two minds regarding Pope John. In some Vatican circles it is thought that he will not go down in history as a great pope, although his regime will probably be recorded as having had critical significance for the Church. Yet others point to the fact that, for all his simplicity and humility, the pope has got important things done—things so far-reaching and profound in their implications that his pontificate may well outrank even those of his most notable predecessors in this century. Thus many Roman officials actually find the Holy Father an enigmatic personality. He has made no secret of the fact that he does not consider himself a theologian, but rather a pastor. He assured a Protestant minister whom he received in private audience that, although as head of the Church he was infallible when proclaiming matters of faith and morals, it was another matter when it came to abstruse theological questions. Then, said the pope, he had to consult his official theologian.

Actually there is a core of deep spiritual wisdom in almost everything Pope John says. Though it is easy to understand, it continually reaches into the profoundest mysteries of the faith. Pope John lives on a level that is close to the ground, able deftly to put rulers of nations quickly at ease when they visit him amidst the splendors of Vatican court procedure, and at the same time to talk familiarly to a group of fifty couples celebrating their twenty-fifth wedding anniversary, reminding them that while the love they bore each other was like the roses the women were wearing for the occasion, it had not been without the thorns that always accompany roses. Neither as adept at languages as his predecessor, nor as indefatigable in giving private and public audiences, he is perhaps a bit loquacious where Pius XII was judicious, but he is warm and intimate where Pope Pius was correct. Entering a room filled with priests to whom he is granting a semi-private audience, Pope John immediately searches the group for old friends and acquaintances. *"Ah, i miei amici!"* he exclaims, or cries *"I miei alunni!"* with unsuppressed joy. And after the formalities of listening to and delivering an address, he descends from his throne to allow visitors to kiss his ring and exchange words of friendly greeting, often to the annoyances of his secretaries who try gently to disentangle him and move him to his next appointment. In preparation for President Eisenhower's visit to Rome, the pope took lessons in English from huge Monsignor Thomas Ryan, the Irish counsellor on the staff of the Vatican Secretariat of State, and the few words of greeting he memorized came out with a bit of a brogue. On the well-known occasion* when America's First Lady arrived, he waited in the library trying to choose one of two alternative greetings suggested by his secretary, "Mrs. Kennedy, Madame; Madame, Mrs. Kennedy," but when the doors opened and he saw her, he extended his arms in greeting and exclaimed: "Jacqueline!" Pope John has expressed his philosophy of action in the French epigram: *"Il faut faire quelque chose; il faut faire faire quelque chose; il faut laisser faire quelque chose,"* that is, there are some things one must do himself, some things he must make others do, and certain things to be left alone.

From the moment Angelo Roncalli accepted his election to the papacy, a new style and a new direction were given to papal affairs. It is characteristic of this Italian countryman from the north—he was born on November 25, 1881, in the little village of Sotto il Monte, outside Bergamo on the Lombard plains—that as the voting in the conclave of October, 1958 began mounting in his favor, he prepared for this eventuality by selecting a name and writing out a short speech of acceptance that will stand in history as both prophetic and programmatic. Asked by the Dean of the Sacred College, Cardinal Eugène Tisserant, by what name he desired to be known, he said simply: "I will be called John." Then he brought out the piece of paper on which he had been writing and began to read:

The name John is dear to me because it is the name of my father. It is dear because it is the title of the humble parish church where we received baptism. It is the solemn name of innumerable cathedrals throughout the world, and first of all the blessed and holy Lateran basilica, our cathedral. It is the name which, in the long series of Roman pontiffs, has been most used.

* *Time*, January 4, 1963.

Indeed there have been twenty-two unquestionably legitimate supreme pontiffs named John. Nearly all had a brief pontificate.

We have preferred to shield the smallness of our own name behind this magnificent succession of Roman pontiffs. And was not St. Mark the Evangelist, the glory and protector of our dearest Venice, he whom St. Peter, Prince of the Apostles and first Bishop of the Roman Church, loved as his own son, also called John? But we love the name of John, so dear to us and to all the Church, particularly because it was borne by two men who were closest to Christ the Lord, the divine Redeemer of all the world and Founder of the Church: John the Baptist, the precursor of our Lord. He was not indeed the Light, but the witness to the Light. And he was truly the unconquered witness of truth, of justice and of liberty in his preaching, in the baptism of repentance, in the blood he shed. And the other John, the disciple and Evangelist, preferred by Christ and by His most Holy Mother who, as he ate the Last Supper, leaned on the breast of our Lord, and thereby obtained that charitable love which burned in him with a lively and apostolic flame until great old age.

May God dispose that both these Johns shall plead in all the Church for our most humble pastoral ministry which follows the one so well conducted to its end by our lamented predecessor of venerable memory, Pius XII, and those of his predecessors so glorious in the Church. May they proclaim to the clergy and to all the people our work by which we desire to "prepare for the Lord a perfect people, to cut straight the windings of every street, and make rough paths into smooth roads, so that all mankind shall see the saving power of God" (Luke 3:4–6). And may John the Evangelist who, as he himself attests, took with him Mary the Mother of Christ and our Mother, sustain together with her this same exhortation, which concerns the life and the joy of the Catholic Church and also the peace and the prosperity of all peoples.

My children, love one another. Love one another, because this is the greatest commandment of the Lord. Venerable brethren, may God in His mercy grant that, bearing the name of the first of this series of supreme pontiffs, we can, with the help of divine grace, have his sanctity of life and his strength of soul, unto the shedding of our blood if God so wills.

This was a fairly long Latin speech, but it was an excellent homily. It was a humble and sincere enunciation of his program: he intended to be a pastoral pope, one who would devote himself to spreading the word of God and the Church in the world. Thus he began his pontificate by giving the cardinals who had just elected him the assurance that their choice had been wise. It was as if the Holy Spirit had breathed an *Amen* to their prayerful and successful effort.

At once the new pope's personality began to emerge in a way that astonished his entourage. His first move was to ask the cardinals to remain in conclave until the following morning, demonstrating his dislike of being alone and his desire to be surrounded by those associated with him in the guidance of the Church. This unprecedented act gave rise to an incident that was to have a certain far-reaching effect within the Curia. For immediately after the pope had given his blessing *urbi et orbi* from the balustrade of St. Peter's, the then Msgr. Tardini and a number of Vatican officials who were not cardinals came rushing into the sealed rooms of the conclave to be the first to pay their respects to the new pontiff. They were met by the imposing Cardinal Dean, Eugène Tisserant, who as senior member of the conclave furiously accused them of breaking its inviolability. Turning to Msgr. Tardini in particular, the cardinal informed the officials that they were excommunicated.

The next morning, of course, Pope John with a certain mock seriousness lifted the penalty thus apparently incurred by these overzealous officials. But the relationship between *il francese* (as Cardinal Tisserant is known in Rome) and the man who within two months was created a cardinal and appointed Secretary of State, suffered an almost fatal shock. Because of this, the subsequent resignation of Cardinal Tisserant from his position as Prefect of the Oriental Congregation was attributed to pressure from Tardini. However, this resignation was in reality an act of deference to the wishes of the pope, by way of giving good example, for Cardinal Tisserant was at that time head of both the Vatican Library and of the Oriental Congregation. With the swelling of the number of cardinals in the Curia as a result of the four consistories held by Pope John (those of December 1958 and 1959, March 1960 and January 1961), there were not enough important positions to go round. It is said that at this juncture the pope spoke to four or five of the oldest cardinals, asking them to relinquish their positions as heads of Congregations. After the interview, the pope was seen standing in some amazement, shaking his head and saying out loud: "But they refused, they refused! Never in my life did I think anyone would refuse the pope . . ." It is in the light of this incident that Cardinal Tisserant's withdrawal from one of the posts is better understood.

Pope John worked strenuously at changing the atmosphere of quasi-adoration that surrounded his predecessor, Pius XII. He curtailed the length of ceremonies in St. Peter's and attempted to reduce the fulsome forms and titles used in the columns of *L'Osservatore Romano*. Speaking to Raimondo Manzini, the new editor of this newspaper whom he brought from Bologna, the pope is reported to have answered the question, "What is the new style to be, Your Holiness?" by saying: "When you speak of me in my official capacity, say the supreme pontiff; then write simply, the pope, for everything else." Nor has there ever been question in the pope's mind of giving titles of nobility or extraordinary honors to any members of his family. Speaking on this subject one day, and recalling the spartan attitude of his eighteenth-century predecessor, Benedict XIV, who forbade his relatives to come to Rome from Bologna during his pontificate, Pope John said it was sufficient honor for his brothers and family that he was pope. In fact they have been his guests in Rome on several occasions, but every effort has been made to keep these visits on a quiet and homely plane, as much to avoid embarrassment for these unobtrusive countryfolk as in deference to the pontiff's wishes.

From the day of his election, John XXIII acted primarily as a pastoral pope, and insisted more and more on his office as Bishop of Rome. Although he did not interfere in the actual administration of the diocese—he has a Cardinal Vicar and two auxiliary bishops to attend to this business —he began to make direct contact with his priests and people by personally visiting parishes, colleges and other institutions, and by paying courtesy calls on the sick, the orphaned, and the imprisoned.

In preparing for the Council, Pope John kept an invisible but firm hand on the 800 theologians and experts who were called to Rome to prepare the agenda. In less than three years, they sifted and codified a mountain of facts relating to ecclesiastical affairs in the modern world, covering everything from the rigid norms of canon law to the price of beeswax in Nigeria. The pope had announced the goal of the Council as an *aggiornamento,* or a "bringing up to date." Vatican ultra-conservatives hopefully interpreted this as a face-saving device whereby, after a great display of rhetorical debate and ceremonial pageantry, nothing would be changed. On the other hand it was understood by many, if not the majority, of the bishops as a decision in favor of major improvements in the Church's practices. The pope himself spoke of a renewal that would restore "the simple and pure lines that the face of the Church of Jesus had at its birth." Luther, Calvin and Melanchthon must have started in amazement in their graves to hear such words on the lips of the Pope of Rome. Alfred Loisy's cynical remark, "Jesus founded the Kingdom of God, and what came forth but the Church of Rome," seemed to have lost its bite. Pope John, of course, had no intention of changing any of the basic doctrines of the Church. In Catholic tradition there is no room for any reversal of position with regard to the articles of the creed or the obligations of the ten commandments. Yet Cardinal Augustin Bea, head of the Secretariat for Christian Unity, stated that while the Church may not reverse dogma, it may clarify it—in other words, reappraisal and reassessment were clearly in order.

For the most part, there were only obscure hints in the world press of the pressures from German, Dutch, French, Oriental and other Catholics for a modernization of the way in which the Church faces its internal problems. Some groups were openly agitating for a reorganization, if not abolition, of the Roman Curia. Others wanted changes in the laws and regulations affecting marriage and education, the mass, the sacraments, liturgical ceremonies, the inquisitorial and condemnatory procedures of the Holy Office, clerical dress and the unseemly pomp of prelatial vestiture, and a redefinition of the rights and prerogatives of bishops and laymen in the Church's structure.

Just as in the third and fourth centuries Clement of Alexandria, Origen, Basil, the Gregories, Jerome and Augustine gave an originally Semitic creed a Greco-Roman dress, and in the twelfth and thirteenth centuries Thomas Aquinas, Bonaventure, Duns Scotus and Bernard succeeded in adapting it to the complicated atmosphere of the medieval world, so it was now time for a rephrasing or restating of the Christian message in terms comprehensible to the educated, international-minded laity of today. The redistribution of responsibilities in the Church, including the proper functioning of the laity, depended upon recognition by the bishops of their rightful place in the Church. For though monarchical, the Church is not totalitarian in structure, and while the pope is supreme teacher and law-giver, since he functions in the place of Peter who in turn represents Christ, the head of the Mystical Body, the Holy Father's function is defined by Christ in the words, "And thou once strengthened, confirm thy brethren." (Lk. 22:32)

This notion of the pope's role is dignified in the Oriental Catholic Churches by regarding the pope as a gift of Christ to the Church. In designating Peter as the Rock upon which he was to build the Church, the Son of God was giving this institution a final safeguard against error and perversion, and a guarantee of its duration until the end of time. Roman theologians have unfortunately been tempted to interpret this metaphor-based fact too literally, not only accepting the idea of the Rock as the foundation or support of the Church's unity, but pushing it to its furthest logical development and considering the pope as thereby endowed with absolute and sole dominative power. This concept (quite distinct from the dogma of infallibility) seems to be a far cry from Christ's intention, Who organized His Church through the college of Apostles. He gave to each Apostle equally a commission to preach and teach and baptize all men everywhere, and then spoke of Peter's function rather as serving his brethren: "Feed my lambs and my sheep," and "Confirm thy brethren."

History indicates, unfortunately, that the Church in the West has frequently succumbed to the temptation that affects all worldly institutions. It has assumed features of the political society in which at various times it has found itself —in the fourth and fifth centuries imitating the legal structure of the later Roman Empire, and in the Middle Ages becoming a feudal power. In the fourteenth and fifteenth centuries it barely escaped falling into the trap of so exaggerating the collegial approach as to make a Council supreme over the pope. Together with the secular governments of succeeding ages, which were strongly opposed to movements favoring democratic theories, the Roman churchmen reacted against all types of representative government by so exaggerating the monarchical nature of the papal power that both in the later Middle Ages and in more recent times the members of the Roman Curia, the administrative arm of the Vatican, have frequently exercised absolutist powers. Acting, theoretically at least, on behalf of the pope, they have not infrequently gone far beyond his wishes on the excuse that they alone were able to cope with dangers to faith and morals presented by the complicated problems of the day, as well as by the intricate administrative functions of a world-wide Church.

This tendency reached its climax in 1870 at Vatican Council I, an event which by a weird series of historical occurrences proved clearly that the Church is both a human and divine institution. The necessity of clarifying the pope's position in the Church as supreme teacher and guide, as well as law-giver, arose from the centrifugal tendencies of French and Central European bishops, aligned in good part with their respective secular rulers. These anti-Roman movements, known as Gallicanism and Josephism respectively, were reactions against the absolutist tendencies of the Roman curialists. However, the dogma of papal infallibility in matters of faith and morals is one thing; the definition of papal supremacy as implying the *exclusion* of the rest of the episcopacy is another. The bishops who convened at Vatican Council I had no intention of separating the pope from the rest of the Church, particularly from themselves. Yet this almost happened when the constitution on papal infallibility was taken out of its context within the prepared schema dealing with the nature of the Church, and was defined separately. At this point the seizure of Rome and the outbreak of the Franco-Prussian war brought the Council to a premature halt. Its work remained unfinished.

The result was a curious development of theological thinking on the nature of the Church. The majority of Catholic theologians fell in with the triumphal reaction of the Roman theologians, who had unhesitatingly begun to push this one-sided view of the papacy to its farthest conclusions. Years later in a famous speech at Vatican Council II (see page 218) the bishop of Bruges, Msgr. Emile Josef De Smedt, would characterize this view as a childish display of "triumphalism, juridicism, and clericalism."

In recent years, despite Pope Pius XII's achievements in bringing the Church's doctrine abreast of the intellectual and moral problems of the age, the tendency toward one-man rule during his reign was carried so far that, in the interregnum, it was officially acknowledged that something had to be done "to restore the ecclesiastical organism." Exasperated in his later years with the backwardness of many of his Curial colleagues, Pius XII apparently decided to "go it alone" as regards doctrinal and moral teaching. This unfortunately left the Curia in almost complete control of administrative processes and gave rise to many of the evils connected with careerism, both within the Curia itself and externally on the part of bishops who hesitated to decide anything without first considering its possible effect in Rome.* Meanwhile Pius XII continued his brilliant critiques of such complex problems as

* To an American bishop whom he consecrated for a missionary diocese, the late Archbishop of Philadelphia, Cardinal Denis Dougherty, said in reference to a bishop's relations with Rome: "My dear young man, when you face Jesus Christ in eternity as one of His bishops He is not going to ask you how you got along with the Roman Curia, but how many souls you saved."

those connected with advances in genetics, medical and surgical procedures, discoveries in psychology and psychiatry, and socio-economic developments that have had effects in the areas of civil liberty and personal freedom. While outward adulation always greeted Pius XII's pronouncements, it was obvious that little serious attention was paid to what he was saying by his more intimate administrative collaborators. Hence they were not only unprepared to deal with his successor, who had been reading and absorbing these teachings, but were appalled when Pope John began quietly and firmly reducing theories to practice. It is hardly to be wondered at that, three months after his election, the Roman cardinals were stunned by his announcement of a Council.

As the Catholic Church is an organism, nothing happens within one sector of the body ecclesiastic without some effect in its other parts. Along with the juridical problems that have dogged its existence throughout its nineteen hundred years of history, the Church from its earliest days has been caught up short by outbreaks of heresy and schism. In fact, the difficulties in the later Middle Ages were the immediate consequence of a breakdown in solid theological thinking that resulted from the nominalistic* tendencies in philosophy. Thus it was that outright war against the various Manichean movements—Albigensians in France, Waldensians in Italy, the Cathars and Bayonnites in central Europe— plagued the so-called Age of Faith. When combined with the corruptive elements that subsequently arose from papal involvement with political and dynastic interests, the tragic and inevitable result was the great split in European Christendom, led by the Lutheran revolt. As a consequence of this new protesting deviation from Roman Catholic doctrine,

---

* Nominalism may be defined as the theory of knowledge which denies reality to universal concepts.

there was a tightening of procedures for thought-control within the Church and the re-employment of inquisitorial methods during the Counter-reformation.

By the nineteenth century, the Church found itself on the defensive before the intellectual attacks of the Enlightenment and the rationalist disdain for supernatural phenomena that accompanied the early emergence of the modern physical sciences. Some theologians, mainly those outside the Roman sphere of influence, attempted to combine Catholic teaching with the idealism of Kant and the evolutionism of Hegel. Thus the German theologian George Hermes and the Bohemian Anton Guenther had, despite their genuine piety, finally to be condemned. With their proscription, danger signals arose against every type of liberalism, with the consequent rejection of the social thought of the Abbé de Lamennais and the suppression of the philosophical theories of Don Antonio Rosmini, although neither of these men seem to have been properly read or fundamentally understood by their Roman-trained critics. This could also be said of the ecumenical studies of the German J. Adam Moehler and the preoccupation with the development of doctrine that brought into the Church the great English churchman John Henry Newman.

Two forces took possession of the Roman Curia—a fear-inspired ruthlessness in dealing with every semblance of non-conformity in theological thought, and a determination to explain the traditional doctrine of the Church only within a rigid and static framework. Such tendencies ran counter to the spirit of a new age searching for a dynamic philosophy to explain the great expanse of movements caused by the opening up of so many new avenues in the physical sciences—the theory of evolution in the development of the universe, the new life-prolonging discoveries of medicine, and the vast social and economic changes accelerated by the industrial revolution.

Astute Catholic theologians endeavored to find a solution to the Church's difficulties through the reapplication of the principles of Thomistic philosophy and a restatement of its theological thought along scholastic lines. But they were disconcerted by developments in biblical criticism which, on the Protestant side, reflected the rationalistic spirit of the century and gradually emptied the Bible of its supernatural content. Friedrich Christian Baur's *Life of Christ,* in German, which was paralleled in the French by the ex-seminarian Ernest Renan's *La Vie de Jésus,* rejected Christ's divinity, thereby ridiculing all supernatural happenings recorded in the New Testament, while Friedrich Schleiermacher and the German critics generally reduced the Old Testament to a series of folkloristic legends.

The Roman reaction was swift and thorough. A *Syllabus of Errors* was drawn up and published with condign condemnations under Pope Pius IX in 1864, seven years before the opening of Vatican Council I. This listing of modern errors was complete, including ideas in every field of nineteenth century interest, from political and social theory to scriptural and theological thought. The definition of papal infallibility in 1871 was considered the *riposte juste* to all danger of secular aberration by providing a supernatural safeguard against the demoniacal errors into which the world at large seemed determined to hurl itself.

By the turn of the twentieth century a second wave of Catholic thinkers, who had hoped to face up to the new ways of thought set in motion in all branches of knowledge by modern discoveries, was quickly suppressed by the condemnation in 1907 of the heresy of Modernism, with Pope Pius X's decree *Lamentabili* and his encyclical *Pascendi.* This drove a number of Catholic exegetes and apologists such as

Alfred Loisy of France, the English convert George Tyrrel, and the Italians Ernest Buonaiuti and Romulo Murri out of the Church, although the two main instigators of the movement, the lay theologian, Baron Friedrich Von Huegel, and the Abbé Henri Brémond survived in communion with her.

The condemnation of Modernism as such was justified, for it was a heresy which in its essential features emasculated Christian doctrine by holding (1) that man's only means of knowing anything about God was by internal, personal religious experience; (2) that there was no objective reality behind such concepts as the Trinity, the divinity of Christ, the Incarnation, and the Resurrection, although within the cultural milieu in which these notions had their origin, they were good and useful for focusing a man's attention on his religious experiences; and (3) that these dogmatic formulas were undergoing a constant, purely natural evolution (for example, they explained the dimensions and import of the movement launched by Jesus Christ as completely beyond the imaginative perception of that interesting first-century rabbinical genius Himself, whose intention was to stir the people of the time to religious fervor by announcing the nearness of the end of the world).

What attracted some people to Modernism were the half-truths that it embodied. It is true to say, for example, that personal religious experience, whereby man makes contact with God through prayer and meditation, is an essential element in the life of the Church. It is also a fact that doctrinal formulas do not represent adequately the spiritual objectivity that they define, simply because the subject of these dogmas is either God Himself who is infinite, or some aspect of God's dealings with man which by definition is a mystery. Divine revelation is not given to man merely to satisfy his desire for truth, or his curiosity about the mystery of God. It is meant as a means whereby man can make contact with his Maker and as a result of this encounter direct the dynamic forces of his entire being toward the fulfilment of his personality in knowing, loving and serving God with his whole heart and soul. Finally, it is certain that the divine message contained in the Bible has been unfolded in the Church gradually, at times in a painful dialectic that reached successive climaxes in the great councils of the Church and in the dogmatic definitions of the Roman pontiffs.

The theologians and thinkers who at first accepted the modernist theories were aware of these basic truths and considered their elaboration as a true response to the evolutionary doctrines and dynamic drives of the world about them. Unfortunately, such real Modernists as Loisy, Tyrrel and Buonaiuti went much further in accepting as a premise for these considerations the inner core of the Kantian idealism and the Hegelian evolutional dynamism, denying objective reality to anything beyond the sphere of natural phenomena.

The real misfortune within the Church brought about by the condemnation of Modernism was the creation of a terrifying atmosphere of suspicion and distrust. Every thinker and publicist within the Church who did not conform unhesitatingly to the static formulation of the Church's teaching, as expressed in Roman-controlled manuals, was suspected of heresy. An oath against Modernism was concocted that is still imposed on all newly-elected bishops and each year required of professors and lecturers in theology at pontifical and ordinary seminaries. A secret society referred to unpopularly as the *Sapinière** was formed for ferreting out and delating to

---

* The members of this society, *Sodalitium Pianum*, or "Pian Society," delated books, manuscripts, and even class notes to the Holy Office. Its coordinator seems to have been Msgr. Umberto Benigni (d. 1934), of whom the *Enciclopedia Cattolica* says: "It is premature to give a definite judgment with regard to various facets of his life, and his varied and often obscure activities." *EC,* v. 2 (1949), 1347.

the Holy Office the writings and teachings of Catholics in every field, but particularly in biblical studies, in history and philosophy, and in the theory behind the physical and political sciences. Thus works of such eminent and orthodox historians as Msgr. Louis Duchesne and Pierre Batiffol were put on the *Index Librorum Prohibitorum,* and numerous other prominent ecclesiastics were removed from their teaching positions. However, groups of determined churchmen rode out this tide of suspicion and condemnation. Fr. F. M. Lagrange, O.P., for example, retired to Jerusalem and founded the Dominican Biblical School, while working away at the essential problems of scriptural exegesis and preparing scholars who would be able with confidence to face the intellectual problems of the next generation. In church history, patrology and philosophy, likewise, Catholic scholars prepared by the solid training given at such universities as Louvain in Belgium, Nijmegen in Holland, Freiburg in Switzerland, Innsbruck in Austria, the Catholic faculty of Tübingen, Germany, and the Catholic Institutes in Paris, Lille and Toulouse, continued to do the spade work necessary to keep the Church abreast of modern research.

The two world wars slowed down the pace of these intellectual movements, but immediately upon the close of World War II, in France particularly and in the northern European countries gradually, a new theological ferment was discovered in full motion. Utilizing in particular the great advance made since the turn of the century in the study of scripture and the early Church Fathers, a group of younger Jesuit and Dominican theologians interested themselves in a return to the sources of the Church's doctrine. They sought to renew the vigor and deepen the impact of Catholicism in a world that had largely repudiated the old-fashioned faith of its fathers. These men included the Jesuits Henri de Lubac, Jean

Daniélou, and Henri Bouillard; and Yves Congar, M. D. Chenu, and A. M. Dubarle of the Dominican House of Studies at Le Saulchoir. Fathers Congar and de Lubac started a series of studies devoted to the nature of the Church. They spoke of "true and false reform in the Church," and of "soundings for a theology of the laity." Two books that caused a sensation were de Lubac's volume on the supernatural, and Le Chartier's *Essay on the Problem of Theology*, the latter of which was put on the *Index* on February 1, 1952. They thus provoked a controversy that brought charges of a "new theology" and accusations of a return to the modernist heresy of relativism against the main exponents of the new movement. They were further suspected of falling into line with the existentialist leanings of the lay Catholic philosophers, Emanuel Mounier and Maurice Blondel. In particular two Roman theologians, Reginald Garrigou-Lagrange, O.P. and Charles Boyer, S.J. attacked the scriptural exegesis and the implications for the development of doctrine in the "new theology." Delations to Rome, frequently consisting of the submission for condemnation by the Holy Office of mimeographed classnotes or typewritten monographs, had alarmed the Holy See as early as 1946. By 1950 rumors spread that Pope Pius XII was about to bring out a scathing condemnation of the new men and their theologizing.

In August 1950 that pontiff published his encyclical *Humani Generis,* which was hailed in conservative circles as a new *Pascendi,* intended to nip in the bud heretical tendencies in scriptural study and every approach to modern positivism in historical and theological research. (A story went around in Roman circles that on the day after the encyclical's publication, Fr. Garrigou-Lagrange was seen stalking through the cloisters of the Angelicum college with a brace of six scalps neatly tucked under his belt.) In actual fact, however, *Humani*

Generis is a well-balanced document, condemning outright obvious heretical tendencies and cautioning to prudence theologians and scriptural exegetes, but at the same time insisting that the Church's scholars utilize all the latest advances in scientific methods of research to deal with such difficult problems in theology as relativism in the expression of revealed truths, the employment of non-scholastic philosophy in the elaboration of Christian doctrine, the person of Adam and original sin, polygenism, evolution, the significance of the supernatural order, the real presence of Christ in the eucharist, existentialism and mysticism, and the objective value of dogma.

What was immediately noticeable about the document was its paternal spirit. It cited no one for condemnation; nor did ecclesiastical censure occur after the publication of the encyclical, although eventually several professors and two French provincials, a Jesuit and a Dominican, were relieved of their positions by being shifted to other assignments. Although certain tendencies and ideas had been proscribed, the encyclical made no attempt to stifle theological initiative; rather it encouraged a vital and existentialist investigation of modern problems, merely cautioning against bizarre attempts to accommodate Catholic teaching to contemporary philosophical fads and materialistic errors.

Meanwhile, in the practical sphere of the Church's life a far-reaching movement seeking ceremonial reform in the interest of spiritual apperception had been started. The movement began as far back as a century previous, with Dom Guéranger's books on the liturgical year. This reassessment of the outward manifestation of the Church's religious life —the celebration of the mass being the principal expression of Catholic worship, together with the seven sacraments from baptism to extreme unction—had been accompanied by attempts to deepen the spiritual awareness of the people, by insisting upon their active and intelligent participation in the liturgy and the official prayer-life of the Church. The Benedictines in the great European abbeys of Maria Laach and Beuron in Germany, of Einsiedeln in Switzerland, and of Solesmes in France, for example, had started schools for the renewal of methods for popularizing the Gregorian chant and enabling the layman to utilize the priestly character given him in baptism by taking an actual part in the cere- monies of the liturgy. This latter movement was strenuously opposed by many older Roman theologians and by a large number of bishops trained in Rome, on the score that it smacked of Protestant ideas whereby the distinction between laymen and priests was all but done away with. Hence the so-called "dialogue mass" and any suggestion that liturgical functions should be carried on in the vernacular languages were frowned upon, if not strictly banned. (The papal Master of Ceremonies, Msgr. Enrico Dante, for example, has been saying mass regularly for a convent of nuns for the past thirty years. As the Secretary for the Congregation of Rites, having full power in these matters, he has never once allowed them to have a dialogue mass.)

However, as these movements were accompanied by solid historical research and thorough-going spiritual and theo- logical advances, they gradually won favor in many parts of the Catholic world, causing Pope Pius X, at the beginning of this century, to acknowledge their existence and Pius XII, at midcentury, to attempt to both stabilize and justify them in his great enclyclical on the liturgy known as *Mediator Dei*. As discussion at Vatican Council II would bring out so clearly, the eastern branch of the Church, though treated in good part as a sort of step-daughter by the Roman Curia, had preserved almost intact the better features of the early Church's way of saying its prayers and worshiping God.

Hence the so-called "innovators" in the western half of the Church soon discovered that what they were so painfully trying to achieve through the liturgical movement and by a return to patristic theology was an everyday part of the religious heritage of their eastern brethren. Although these churches were also in the throes of attempting to modernize their liturgical practice, their requirements had more to do with abbreviating ceremonies that once occupied the whole morning, if not the whole day, for people in an agricultural society, and adapting them to the needs of the industrial age, where men have so many other distractions.

This rediscovery of the Eastern Church's teaching and practice in the liturgical and theological spheres had been made by many theologians and a small group of interested lay intellectuals in various western countries. It had been ignored, for the most part, by the bishops of the west. Hence, at the Council the latter were amazed to find the Oriental prelates taking such an active part in the debates, and coming out for solutions to the problems raised by the schemata on divine revelation, Christian unity, and the nature of the Church, which the western theologians had been years in discovering through hard research and fear, and for which they had had to fight strenuously with the authorities in Rome.

The notion, for example, of the collegial character of the organization of the Church based on the original body of Apostles was everyday doctrine among the Melchites, Greeks, Syrians, Chaldean and Lebanese Catholics. It was frowned upon by the Roman curialists. Actually this doctrine had been well stated and insisted upon at Vatican Council I, in the preparatory schema concerned with the nature of the Church. It was to have been considered in connection with the definition of papal infallibility, before that doctrine was ripped from its context by the maneuverings of a clique of cardinals and bishops, led by Cardinal Henry Edward Man-

ning with the assistance of Pope Pius IX. Yet this doctrine
of the collegiality of the bishops was hardly given recognition
by the Preparatory Theological Commission in its schema on
the Church prepared in 1961–62 under the chairmanship of
Cardinal Ottaviani.

Similar observations could be made with regard to the proposals prepared for Vatican Council II, dealing with the
nature of divine revelation. Here, in reaction to Protestant
insistence on the scriptures as the sole deposit and source of
Christian religious knowledge, the scholastic-minded theologians had gradually slipped into considering Christ's words
and deeds as having been recorded and handed down in the
Church through two virtually separate vehicles—the written
word of the New Testament, and Tradition. The latter was
then utilized as a deposit upon which the magisterium, or
teaching power, of the Church could justify some of the definitions of doctrine that took place in the development of
Catholic theology down through the centuries, and which
seemed to have only a tenuous (the technical word is *implicit*)
expression in the written scriptures. The very title of the
Theological Commission's proposal betrayed modern Roman-
bound thought on this subject, for it was announced as "On
the Two Sources of Divine Revelation." This idea was strenuously opposed in the Council by the Oriental bishops, who
were joined by a majority of the better informed western
prelates. They insisted that there was only one *source* of
divine revelation: God in the person of His Son Jesus Christ.
If a distinction were to be made between Scripture and Tradition, it should be done only by recognizing these as vehicles,
not sources, for the transmission of the originally revealed
teachings of Christ. Here again in turning his mind to these
problems, Pope John could see no other solution than by
calling his bishops together in a Council.

In the administration of the Church over the course of the last two hundred years and more—at least since the French Revolution—the Congregations of the Roman Curia have achieved a startling supremacy, so much so as evidently to have given many members of these administrative organs the impression that, for all practical purposes, they are the Church. The bishops, priests and faithful were dealt with as a sort of mass appendage to the Vatican. Many of these officials seem to have felt that they were the active participants in the pope's absolutist power over the clergy and faithful, and that their decisions should not only be law but that their opinions on doctrinal, moral and political matters were the manifestations of papal infallibility. In the appointment of bishops all over the world, the creation and apportionment of dioceses, the surveillance of faith and morals, the licensing and control of religious orders and congregations, the dispensing of Church funds for missionary enterprises, and the safeguarding of tradition, as well as orthodoxy, in the ceremonial and moral life of Catholics, they gradually came to have the final say. A network of apostolic nuncios and delegates accredited to the national governments or to the episcopate of various countries, as in the United States, provided them with information concerning the prelates and the religious status generally of the Church throughout the world. Personal contact with former Roman fellow-students as well as occasional trips to the Americas, to different parts of Europe, and even to Africa and the Far East, which were accomplished with a certain *éclat,* if not triumph—their local hosts were obviously highly honored to be entertaining a member of the Roman Curia—gave them a feeling that they understood better than anyone else, including the pope, the needs of the Church in the modern world. It is not surprising that they became legalistic-minded in the extreme, for the preservation of protocol and the regularity of legal procedures, as they quickly discovered, are simple means for exercising control in an institution as vast as the Catholic Church. Likewise a sceptical and suspicious attitude toward innovation of any kind, particularly in areas of doctrine, scripture and the moral aspects of psychological research and psychiatric practice also provided weapons in the interests of supreme control. Finally, the gentle but continual intimidation of bishops by procrastination in granting them the use of special faculties for the administration of the sacraments, the ordination and government of their priests and people, and the close surveillance of what was said and written, particularly by clerics all over the world, guaranteed their undisputed authority in church matters generally.

No reasonable man can deny, of course, the possibility of error in doctrinal matters and the need of caution and prudence in asserting religious truth. Yet a prudent mind is not a closed one, and caution and care are not identical with rigidity of thought and narrowness of view. The problem comes down to the question asked of Christ by Pilate, "What is Truth?" For Catholic theologians generally, religious truth is first a series of propositions that capture the facts of divine revelation regarding the nature of God and His dealings with mankind, as well as those historical happenings that have been preserved in the Christian "deposit of faith" as necessary for an understanding of the divinely revealed truths. And second it is a spiritual experience that comes in the confrontation with Jesus Christ, the Son of God, Who is present in His Church in the world and Who, through the graces of the Spirit, demands the full ordination of man's powers, intellectual, voluntary, and sensitive, in His service.

Difficulty arises, however, when any group of theologians attempts to force a univocal expression of these truths on the

Church, particularly if they wield directive power. For while
the strictly logical, Thomistic approach in theology is not
only useful, but necessary for the achievement of clear and
precise concepts of religious truth, it is not the *only* way these
ideas have been, or can be, expressed. There is the whole
tradition of Patristic, as well as of Oriental, theology which
St. Thomas himself sought to incorporate, in part at least, in
his thirteenth-century summation of Catholic truth, but
which has a technique and manner of expression all its own.

What is even more fundamental to an understanding of
this problem is the fact that men of a juridical persuasion
seem to have made the possession of certain religious truths
the final end of their religion. There is a saying in Rome that
any slip in moral, social, or political fields would eventually
be forgiven, but that even a minor doctrinal deviation was
fatal as far as an ecclesiastical career was concerned. It is precisely this attitude that is being combatted by the theologians
from beyond the Alps, who point out that Christ announced
that He was not only the Truth, but that He was also the
Way and the Life (Jn. 14:6). History proves over-preoccu-
pation with the niceties of theological expression to have
brought great evils upon the Church in the form of both
verbal and sanguinary conflict, and to have resulted in a falling away from the Church of the majority of modern intellectuals who have been appalled by the *odium theologicum*
that frequently has replaced the not-so-simple Johannine injunction: "Brethren, if you do not love your brother whom
you can see, how can you love God, whom you cannot see?"
(1 Jn. 4:20).

While the early Patristic churchmen were careful to ham-
mer out and protect the essential truths of the Christian faith,
they changed the concept of man's final end or purpose from
both the Platonic contemplation of the Good and the Stoic

philanthropy to eternal beatitude which man must earn here on earth, under divine stimulus, not only by believing certain truths with all his heart and soul, but by conforming his conduct to the way and the life of Christ in the here and now. One of the strangest paradoxes in history is that the died-in-the-wool Roman theologians, whose whole theology was aimed at combatting the older Protestant shibboleth of "justification by faith alone," have all but succumbed to the temptation of proclaiming a univocal religious orthodoxy as the foremost requirement whereby a Catholic participates in the Church. It is as though "justification by only the scholastic definition of religious truth" were the final test.

A factor in this attitude is certainly the fact that these men were born and brought up as Catholics, and have never really faced other religious experiences except by reading about them, disguised as straw-men types of propositions, to be demolished in a textbook. What is wrong with the Roman Curia is not the personnel as such. Its members are intelligent, cordial, progressive-minded as regards material advances, and pious. The main difficulty is presented by the four groups in charge of the Holy Office, the Congregation of Studies and Universities, and to a certain extent the Congregations of Rites and of the Sacraments. Here the old-fashioned, restrictive fears for both the integrity of doctrine and for uniformity of practice have saddled the Church with a backward and frequently ominous outlook on the modern world. These officials were perfectly characterized by Pope John XXIII himself in his opening discourse at Vatican Council II as "prophets of doom."

In the end what seems to have convinced Pope John of the necessity for calling a Council was not only the parochial outlook of most of the men about him in the Vatican, but the backward attitude of so many bishops in the stabilized dioceses of the Old and New World. Though good men and hard-working administrators of both the spiritual and corporal works of the Church, they knew nothing of the new spirit fermenting in the minds and hearts of many of the clergy, young and old, and made manifest in the writings of the more advanced theologians, lay intellectuals, and church scholars.

The pope decided then to bring the bishops of the whole world together to let them educate each other as to the true status of the Church in a suffering, morally confused world, poverty-stricken in two-thirds of its area amidst unprecedented plenty in the rest, living in fear of thermonuclear warfare and total destruction, and seemingly unable to disentangle itself. In a century which showed forth the reality of evil in the horrors of two world wars, in racist persecutions and genocide on a hitherto unimaginable scale, in the widespread successes of totalitarianism, the communist branch in particular, and in the spread of materialistic atheism, why was the Church not accomplishing more effectively the worldwide mission entrusted to it by Christ? In such a world, why was the whole family of Christ so disunited? Were not these internal quarrels and differences unworthy of Christians, and perhaps more emotional than real? It was time for the Church to go about reclaiming its own lapsed members, converting the modern pagan who hungered after justice, and drawing back into the fold of Christ *all* the flock, more particularly those separated mainly by historical prejudices and misunderstandings, such as the Eastern Orthodox and the more traditionalist Protestant bodies.

Pope John's knowledge of these problems and his interest in their solution is explained by one thing: his whole life. Though born a farmer, with his feet solidly planted on the soil of the Lombard plain, he quickly proved himself a

pilgrim in this world, from his teens travelling the length and
breadth of the European continent, and gaining considerable
knowledge of the Near East. He made his first trip to Rome
as a youthful seminarian of twenty, and immediately decided
to win himself a scholarship to finish his ecclesiastical training there. While neither his year of national service in the
Italian army in 1901 (he achieved the rank of corporal on
duty and was promoted to sergeant on returning to civilian
life) nor his stint as a chaplain during World War I enlarged
his geographical horizons, his career as a young priest, secretary to Giacomo Radini-Tedeschi, Bishop of Bergamo,
brought him into contact with currents of social thought and
the economic facts of life that had alarmed the whole of
Europe before the outbreak of the first world war. He trav-
elled in France and northern Europe frequently with Bishop
Radini, and through this extremely able and activist prelate
became acquainted with the men who were to rule the
Church in the next generation. He had also tasted the bitterness of ecclesiastical intrigue and Roman suspicion, when he
took a principal part in the attempt to bring up to date the
Church's social and economic thinking in accord with the
prescriptions of Pope Leo XIII's encyclical, *Rerum Novarum,*
and found himself under the shadow of the taint of radical-
ism for his troubles. His knowledge of men and their problems had been increased by his military career, as well as by
the work he did for the youthful intellectuals of Bergamo,
both as a seminary professor and as a university student-
counsellor before being summoned to Rome by Pope Benedict XV in 1921. There he took over the Italian presidency
of the Society for the Propagation of the Faith (a position
similar to that now occupied by Bishop Fulton Sheen in New
York for U.S. Catholic interests in the foreign missions). Although he came on the Roman scene as a new man at the age

of forty, he was personally instructed by Pope Benedict XV to break with the older ways of doing things and given sufficient authority to remove the center of the Society from France (Lyons) to Rome. He was given the task of revitalizing the financial arrangements of this organization, after he had personally visited every diocese in the Italian peninsula as well as its more effective centers in France, Germany, Poland, and the former Austro-Hungarian Empire. His success was two-fold: he increased the financial strength of the Society enormously, and while taking a superficial interest in ecclesiastical affairs on the periphery of Roman Curial society (his reputation as a *conférencier* won him invitations to lecture on the Church Fathers at the Lateran University), he created an organization which proved substantially effective in giving assistance to the Italian foreign mission efforts. In the wake of this success, he was created an archbishop in 1925 and sent to Sofia as Apostolic Visitor, with the task of patiently investigating the possibility of improving the position of Catholics in an Orthodox-dominated region and achieving some sort of amicable arrangement with governments and people inclined to be anti-Roman.* In 1934 he was shifted to Istanbul and made Apostolic Delegate for both Turkish and Greek Catholics. Since throughout his life he was primarily a pastor at heart, he interested himself in the practical prob-

---

* In October 1929 he was involved in the ecclesiastical arrangements for the marriage of King Boris of Bulgaria (Orthodox in religion) with the daughter of the King of Italy (Roman Catholic). Pope Pius XI granted permission for this mixed marriage on condition of a Catholic ceremony only, and a promise that the children would be baptized and raised as Catholics. This caused some difficulty for Archbishop Roncalli, who had the King's signature on a document agreeing to both conditions, because after the Roman ceremony Boris returned to Sofia and had the marriage repeated according to the Orthodox rite; and when their daughter was born her baptism was also performed in this rite. This incident may have misled *Time* in their excellent "Man of the Year" cover story in January, 1963 to assert that Angelo Roncalli had been frowned upon in Rome for his somewhat advanced ideas on mixed marriages.

lems of everyday Catholic life in all the countries of the Near East, acquiring facility in the local languages and encouraging the people to use their native tongues in many of the church's ceremonial functions, rather than the Latin of the liturgy. He also encouraged the production of spiritual and doctrinal treatises in native languages.

His post-war diplomatic experiences in Paris, as Apostolic Nuncio to de Gaulle's newly created Fourth French Republic, gave him an exceptional knowledge of the Church's needs in a new world whose political and spiritual foundations had to be rebuilt from the ground up. He was involved in the aftermath of the controversy over the "new theology." He was an interested though not a directly involved spectator of the experiment conducted by the worker-priests, and experienced with Cardinal Suhard and the French episcopate the anxiety of not knowing whether the Church in France, or in Europe for that matter, was to continue in the great decline or achieve a renaissance. Finally, he witnessed the birth of UNESCO and despite the anticlerical tendencies manifested by that institution's earliest organizers, forced the Holy See to take an active interest in its proceedings, having recognized at once the importance of this worldwide educational and cultural movement for Catholic missions throughout the world. In 1953, having been created a cardinal by Pope Pius XII, he was allowed to fulfill the ambition of his early days as a priest and to serve directly as a pastor of souls by being made Patriarch of Venice. In his sermon upon entering the diocese, he assured the Venetians that all his life he had wanted to be nothing other than a parish priest, and he said that he was happy, as old age came upon him, to have his wish fulfilled. He was then 72 years old, but manifested no senile characteristics whatever. He immediately set about visiting the whole of the diocese, quietly but effectively reorganizing it. Instead of condemning the annual Venice Film Festival, he gave it his blessing and acted as host to committees and participants. He arranged for St. Mark's Cathedral to be the setting of the world première of Igor Stravinsky's "Sacred Canticle to Honour the Name of St. Mark." On the very day he left for Rome as a member of the conclave to elect a successor to Pius XII, he was correcting proofs of a diocesan synod.

It is against this background that John XXIII, shortly after his election, was inspired to undertake the difficult if not perilous task of summoning an Ecumenical Council, the first such Council in almost one hundred years, and only the twenty-first in nearly two thousand years of history.

II

The Council's Four Stages

POPE JOHN HAS REFERRED to the Councils of previous ages as "shining lights" in the Church's annals. The phrase occurred in his opening discourse of October 11. In the same talk he also described the Church's "prophets of doom" as behaving "as though at the time of the former Councils everything was a full triumph for the Christian idea and life, and for proper religious liberty." Together, these remarks constitute another way of saying that the history of the great Councils is mixed. The official list, beginning with the Council of Nicaea in 325, is as follows:

	A.D.		A.D.
1. Nicaea I	325	3. Ephesus	431
2. Constantinople I	381	4. Chalcedon	451

	A.D.		A.D.
5. Constantinople II	553	14. Lyons II	1274
6. Constantinople III	680	15. Vienne	1311
7. Nicaea II	787	16. Constance	1414–18
8. Constantinople IV	869	17. Florence	1438–42
9. Lateran I	1123	18. Lateran V	1512–17
10. Lateran II	1139	19. Trent	1545–63
11. Lateran III	1179	20. Vatican I	1869–70
12. Lateran IV	1215	21. Vatican II	1962–
13. Lyons I	1245		

Not one of these ecumenical councils—and this does not exclude the latest—was convened without a clash of ideas (even, on occasion, of fists), as a result of which theologians and prelates got hurt, some finding themselves unceremoniously ushered into schism or heresy. None of the earlier Councils was wholly successful on what may be termed the political plane, though in the end they all managed to clarify theological doctrine. Summoned by the emperors of the Roman Empire, the first seven Councils dealt mainly with the doctrines of the Trinity and the two natures—divine and human —in Christ. But they ended in a situation of chronic tension between East and West, with the Byzantine emperors in virtual full control of the Church in the East and their subjects weaned away from any ecclesiastical loyalty to Rome. While in the west the papacy managed to preserve a great measure of independence, it got itself involved in political entanglements which have hampered its spiritual effectiveness ever since, from the days of Charlemagne and the Holy Roman Empire right down to modern times. (In 1903 the last of the Habsburgs in Austria exercised his so-called "Right of Exclusion" or veto power in the election of the pope himself, and the government of Spain, under a concordat, still has the right to approve or veto new bishops.) The great Councils of the Middle Ages, through their failure to bring about a true reform, contributed directly to the Protestant revolt and the subsequent fracture of western Christendom. At Trent, in the middle of the sixteenth century, the popes shook off the last enticements of the Renaissance and the mirage of the Crusades, and inaugurated a Counter-reformation. But the movement never got into orbit fully, owing to the inveterate politicking of many Catholic churchmen. A century ago, Vatican Council I (1869–70) proved to be a premature effort to face the problems of a revolutionary age. After having proclaimed the doctrine of infallibility (not unanimously: two bishops—one of them the Bishop of Little Rock, Arkansas—voted against it, and fifty-five out of six hundred prelates abstained), it disbanded when the Italians seized Rome on September 20, 1870. Vatican Council I thus remained unfinished. One of the first things Pope John did, once he had made up his mind to hold Vatican II, was to declare Vatican I definitively closed. In this connection it is said that each time a Vatican official approached John XXIII with a suggestion for postponing his new Council, the pope advanced the target date. His original plan had looked to the autumn of 1963 for the convocation. After their first incredulous reaction, some of his immediate collaborators were appalled at his dismissal of their objections concerning the time and the complex preparations needed for such a step.

Despite his advanced age (he celebrated his eighty-first birthday while the Council was in session), despite the hesitations of the preceding pontiff, a man admittedly far more astute than himself, despite his Secretary of State who died in the summer of 1961 without having deflected the pope from his original decision in the slightest degree, despite the precariousness of world conditions, Pope John opened Vatican II in St. Peter's basilica on October 11, 1962. If some advocates of postponement were prompted by the hope that eternity would spare them the ordeal of a Council, they had only themselves to blame for the fact that Vatican II was inaugurated one year earlier than planned.

What had helped to solidify the pope's determination to get on with the Council was the success he experienced with his Roman Synod, preparations for which had proceeded throughout the first year of his pontificate. In a single year he had hustled his procrastinating pastors and theologians through a mountain of socio-religious facts and legal documents to enact some 755 statutes that gave expression to his idea of how the life of a Christian should be pursued in today's world. As the setting for the Synod, whose sessions were held during the week of January 24–31, 1960, he naturally chose the basilica of St. John Lateran, which is his proper cathedral as Bishop of Rome. Instead of discussions by theologians and parish priests, he decided on a four-day reading of the prospective synodal Acts prepared by a diocesan commission, inviting proposals and emendations in writing from the priests and religious clerics belonging to the diocese of Rome. (Invidious comment, particularly on the part of foreign clerics in Rome, implied that this "rubber stamp" Synod would serve as an unfortunate precedent for the Ecumenical Council, yet a number of changes were made in the proposed statutes of the Synod as a result of these readings and the suggestions they provoked.) Knowing the propensity of his Italian clerics for long-winded oratory, Pope John had decided to do the talking himself. In five talks, three of which were delivered in the synodal sessions, and a fourth and fifth at the church of the Gesù to clerics and nuns living in Rome, he supplied a full commentary on the Synod Acts which were officially promulgated on June 28, 1960, the vigil of the feast of the apostles Peter and Paul. The pope's talks ranged over a wide spiritual field, touching on some of the most sublime mysteries of the Christian faith: belief in God as a Trinity of love; redemption from sin by the earthly sufferings and death of the Son of God become a man; the resurrection and the hope of seeing God "face to face," in the graphic phrase employed by St. Paul. They also touched on the pitfalls and dangers of life in the modern world that could lead one to damnation. But Pope John insisted much more on a positive approach whereby priest, seminarian, nun and lay person, putting their shoulders to the wheel of life, could achieve decency, stability, security and a touch of holiness no matter what the physical and social conditions in which they found themselves. This was the spirit which permeated the majority of the synodal regulations, though the structure and the wording of the document followed the usual style of canonical legislation.

In actual fact, canon law experts were disturbed by the principles enunciated in this document. "That's not law," more than one canonist commented openly. To which the Holy Father's reply was equally frank and simple: "It's not intended as a strictly legal document." If he had wanted to publish "pure" law, he would merely have reprinted verbatim sections from the current Code of Canon Law by which the Church Universal is governed. Some canonists disliked the fact that the pope had set a precedent that could easily lead to a new conception of law in the Church. Despite their legal trappings, these regulations were meant to be a sort of *vade mecum,* or way of life, for the Christian. Along with an assertion of the rights and obligations that flow from the free acceptance of the Church as the guardian and guide of one's relations with Almighty God, the Synod exhorted Catholics on such matters as the type of prayers to be said; the courage clerics should exhibit in defending their dignity and honor if attacked in public, without of course descending to unseemly exchanges; the respect they must show the guardians of public order, the attention they must pay traffic regulations, financial and tax obligations, old age pensions for employees, and even annual visits to the cemetery. Penalties for violations of the law were held to a minimum, and affected those principally in clerical orders. Of considerable disappointment to foreign priests in the Eternal City—and especially to Americans and Germans—were the requirements of wearing the cassock in the streets, and of the tonsure, or shaving of the back of the head, that in Europe generally marks all clerics (not only monks) as men set aside for the service of the Lord. Clerics likewise were forbidden to attend all public spectacles, from operas to races. (As more than one prelate remarked, if the priests in Rome were allowed to go to public concerts and the opera, or even only to the better cinemas, who else would be able to get in? For there are more than five thousand priests alone in the environs of the Vatican.)

One innovation that is certainly due to Pope John's thinking—it is reported that he personally wrote out the ordinance —concerned priests who had fallen away from their calling. Article 35 of the Synodal statutes reads: "Priests laboring under censure or other penalty, or who have perhaps unhappily left the Church, should never cease to confide in the mercy of the Lord and the humaneness and decency of ecclesiastical superiors. Other priests, particularly those who were joined to them in friendship, motivated by heavenly charity, should sedulously strive to cultivate this trust in their minds. Towards all these unhappy men who persevere in their defection that norm is to be used which Pius XI found so fruitful: The less we can speak to men about God, the more it behooves us to speak to God about men. In these matters then, which are truly pitiful, no one is to be deprived of the friendliness of his fellow priests, or of consolation in his adversities, or even of temporal assistance should the circumstances call for it." The revolutionary character of this regulation for the treatment of lapsed priests in Rome was brought out by the Jesuit Father Domenico Grosso, writing in *Civiltà Cattolica* (November 5, 1960), the best informed and most authentic of Italian ecclesiastical journals. "We should not marvel to learn," says Father Grosso, "that this article was actually dictated by the Holy Father. For it reflects the full pastoral solicitude with which John XXIII has marked his pontificate. 'Unhappy' is indeed the proper designation for those who were once part of the clergy and are now cut off. Until the present, the Church, for reasons obvious to everyone, has taken a position of great firmness in regard to such persons. Against no others has it perhaps employed equal measures, for while ever ready to receive the penitent, it has been inexorable in its conditions. Frequently, however, this attitude on the part of ecclesiastical authority has caused priests, influenced by considerations of a moral or psychological character, to break off all relations with these unfortunate colleagues, even those who were once their friends. As a result, the *infelices* not infrequently have ended up by losing their faith. The Roman Synod definitely placed such prejudices in their proper perspective. Everyone had a right to God's mercy, hence priests who had an obligation to approach souls in need of divine grace had also the same obligation toward their former colleagues. In fact, there is an even stronger title, for these men are in greater need of understanding and pardon. Many scandals could be avoided if this norm were followed in all cases." It had taken the courage and determination of Pope John to put this change on the books. It is known that Pius XII gave serious consideration to this problem and for a year or so forced the

Congregation of the Council and the Sacred Apostolic Peniteniary to grant dispensations allowing unfrocked priests to marry legally; but that once he got absorbed in other problems, the Curial officials returned to their former practices.

With the Synod a *fait accompli*—it went into effect November 1, 1960—John XXIII had demonstrated to his own satisfaction that it was possible to organize theologians and experts as a working team. He learned what had to be done in order to produce in a year's time a document as thorough and well-knit as the regulations of the Synod. He next turned full attention to his plans for the Ecumenical Council.

The proportions of this enterprise were staggering, for it meant the questioning of each one of the Church's 2,500 bishops and prelates, the heads of all men's religious orders, and the faculties of Catholic universities (of which there are some thirty-seven in different parts of the world) to discover what they considered the more important problems facing the Church today, and how they should be handled. A letter signed by Cardinal Tardini, Vatican Secretary of State and, by the pope's appointment, head of the Ante-Preparatory Commission for the Council, was despatched to the Church's prelates on June 18, 1959 by the Secretary General for the Council, Msgr. Pericle Felici, titular Archbishop of Samosata, and Cardinal Tardini's choice for this all-important administrative post, as one of the more intelligent and tougher prelates in the Vatican service.

The bishops were requested to cooperate fully with the preparations for the Council. Close to two thousand answers were received and catalogued in a short time. What gave particular significance to these replies was the fact that no limitations were placed either on the matters to be considered or the manner of dealing with problems or proposals. The pope made it clear from the start that he wanted to hear the

mind of the whole of the Catholic world on the condition of
the Church today.* The vast material thus accumulated (it was
eventually printed in book form) was examined and arranged in some two thousand files. After an initial analysis,
national reports were compiled and synthesized to give, with
facts and figures, a bird's-eye view of the situation of the
Church in each country, and an overall view of the common
problems confronting the majority of bishops in the Church
universal.

It was with this material that the Preparatory Commissions created by the pope on the feast of Pentecost (June 5,
1960) were busily engaged. These bodies† included a Central
Commission that eventually was to pass on and coordinate
the work of the others.

* It is known that the proposals regarding the relations between Church
and State, as well as those having to do with liberty of conscience, prepared
by the faculty of the Catholic University of America in Washington, D.C. for
submission to the Theological Commission were withheld by the university
authorities. This fact was brought to the attention of the Secretary of the
Congregation for Universities and Studies during the Council, who expressed
considerable annoyance over such arbitrary action. "The Pope," he said,
"made it clear that he wanted the faculty consulted, and not merely the
authorities."

† The Preparatory Commissions and Secretariats were as follows: (1) CEN-
TRAL COMMISSION—President, Pope John XXIII; Secretary, Archbishop Felici.
(2) THEOLOGICAL COMMISSION (properly Com. on Faith and Morals)—Pres.,
Cardinal Ottaviani; Sec., Fr. S. Tromp, S.J. (3) COMMISSION FOR BISHOPS AND
THE GOVT. OF DIOCESES—Pres., Cardinal Mimmi, later Cardinal Marella;
Sec., Fr. Berutti, O.P. (4) COMMISSION FOR DISCIPLINE OF THE CLERGY AND
FAITHFUL—Pres., Cardinal Ciriaci; Sec., Fr. Berutti, O.P. (5) COMMISSION FOR
RELIGIOUS—Pres., Cardinal Valeri; Sec., Fr. Rousseau, O.M.I. (6) COMMISSION
FOR THE SACRAMENTS—Pres., Cardinal Masella; Sec., Fr. Bigador, S.J. (7) COM-
MISSION FOR THE LITURGY—Pres., Cardinal G. Cicognani, later Cardinal Lar-
raona, Sec., Fr. Bugnini, C.M. (8) COMMISSION FOR STUDIES AND SEMINARIES—
Pres., Cardinal Pizzardo; Sec., Fr. Mayer, O.S.B. (9) COMMISSION FOR ORIENTAL
CHURCHES—Pres., Cardinal A. Cicognani; Sec., Fr. Welykyj. (10) COMMISSION
FOR MISSIONS—Pres., Cardinal Agagianian; Sec., Msgr. Mathew. (11) COM-
MISSION FOR APOSTOLATE OF THE LAITY—Pres., Cardinal Cento; Sec., Msgr. Glo-
rieux. (12) COMMISSION FOR CEREMONIAL—Pres., Cardinal Tisserant; Sec., Msgr.
Nardone. SECRETARIATS: (1) PRESS AND INFORMATIONAL MEDIA—Pres., Archbishop
O'Connor; Sec., Msgr. Deskur. (2) PROMOTING CHRISTIAN UNITY—Pres., Cardinal
Bea; Sec., Msgr. Willebrands. (3) ADMINISTRATION—Pres., Cardinal Di Jorio;
Sec., Msgr. Guerri.

Speaking at a solemn vespers in St. Peter's on that day, the pope summarized what had gone before and was to come after, stating that "an Ecumenical Council takes place in four stages: first there is an introductory, exploratory, ante-pre-paratory* and general phase, which has lasted till now. This is followed by a preparatory phase, properly speaking, which we have just announced. Thirdly, there is the celebration or general meeting of the Council in all its solemnity. Finally, there is the promulgation of the Acts of the Council, that is, what the Council has agreed to determine, declare, and propose with respect to and for the improvement of thought and life, a deeper increase in spirituality and apostolic fervor, and the glorification of the Gospel of Christ, as applied and lived by His holy Church."†

While the pope had appointed the heads of the various Congregations that make up the Roman Curia as chairmen and secretaries of these Commissions—thus Cardinal Ottaviani and Fr. Sebastian Tromp, S.J. were, respectively, chairman and secretary of the Theological Commission; Cardinal Amleto Cicognani and Fr. Athanasius Welykyj, chairman and secretary of the Commission for the Oriental Church—he made it clear that the Curia and the Council were two distinct entities. Speaking on the above occasion, the pontiff said:

The Ecumenical Council has its own structure and organization which cannot be confused with the ordinary functions of the various departments that constitute the Roman Curia. The latter will carry on as usual during the Council. The preparation of the Council, however, will not be the task of the Roman Curia but, together with the illustrious prelates and consultors of the

* Though the term "ante-preparatory" is both a neologism and redundant, it was used (*antipreparatorio,* in Italian) to distinguish clearly between the two preparatory phases.
† *Discorsi,* v. 2, p. 392.

Roman Curia, bishops and scholars from all over the world will offer their contribution. This distinction is therefore precise: the ordinary government of the Church with which the Roman Curia is concerned is one matter, and the Council another.

It was on this occasion likewise that he clarified the aims of the Council. He conceived it as a demonstration and living proof to the world of the Church in her perennial vigor of life and truth. He wanted her legislation and practice brought up-to-date so as to reflect modern circumstances; and he desired that her theology be made concrete and dynamic, in line with her divine mission to be ready to face the great problems of the contemporary world. "If after this is accomplished, our separated brethren wish to realize a common desire for unity," said the pope, "they will find the way open to a meeting and a return to the Church."

Behind the scenes at the Vatican, the Council was looked upon with mixed feelings, ranging from passive acquiescence to outright alarm. It is perhaps understandable that the pope's frequent talk of unity with the separated brethren in Orthodox and Protestant bodies might have given some officials nightmares. As they saw it, the pope did not understand fully the doctrinal issues involved in these matters; and in their view he was unwittingly encouraging those Catholic theologians and apologists who had been flirting with heterodoxy by minimizing Catholic truth during the last thirty years or so. It was feared likewise that a gathering of the bishops of the whole world in Rome could only result in the forcing of issues that some officials felt they themselves alone were truly competent to deal with. These men acted as if they believed the majority of the bishops throughout the world were not sufficiently informed to know what it was all about. There was also an uneasiness lest efforts be made to suppress certain powers exercised by Curial officials, or more particularly to reorganize their offices and shuffle their personnel.

They realized further that there was considerable unhappiness among groups of bishops with the whole system of apostolic delegates and nuncios, who are frequently considered as little more than Vatican informers and meddlers. The Irish and Australian bishops in particular have little use for Italian ecclesiastical diplomats; Cardinal Amleto Cicognani as apostolic delegate in the United States for twenty-three years, by way of exception, had the complete respect and affection of the American bishops and laity.

Members of the Holy Office understandably felt that they alone were competent to deal with matters of faith and morals, and to keep a tight hold on the theological traditions of the Church as expressed in the scholastic terminology of Roman textbooks. The liturgical movement, so strong in Germany, France, parts of Canada, the mid-western United States and in many mission territories, was flooding the Congregation of Rites with insistent demands that the use of the vernacular languages in the mass and other Church ceremonies be legitimized on a universal scale. Similarly the Holy Office and certain professors at the Roman universities were convinced that the "new" biblical scholars had sold their scriptural birthright for a mess of Germanic rationalism parading under such formidable and dangerous terms as *Formgeschichte, Redaktionsgeschichte* and *Heilsgeschichte,* but by means of admonitions and condemnations these Curialists felt that they could keep the situation in hand. The gathering of the bishops of the whole world in the Eternal City, pessimists feared, might precipitate theological differences that could militate against the unity of the Church as controlled from Rome.

The pope, of course, was of an entirely different opinion.

He hoped that, by assembling the bishops in Council, they would demonstrate the unity of the Church, assert its awareness of the world about it, and thus pave the way for a re-Christianization of modern man. The pope had announced the Council's goal as an *aggiornamento,* or a bringing up to date of the Church. The story was often repeated that the pope, asked by a visiting cardinal for a simple explanation of the Council, went to the nearest window, opened it wide, and let in the fresh air. A French bishop, on hearing this story, drily observed: "When the pope indicated that we were to open the windows of the Church, he meant the Curia windows." Many responsible non-Italian prelates (and not a few Italian ones too) had come to believe that the time was approaching to break the stranglehold on ecclesiastical thought and practices exercised by the self-perpetuating clique in the Curia which dictates Roman Catholic policy and, to a large extent, controls the pope himself. These men had thus far successfully resisted all but the most innocuous changes dictated by the exigencies of modern life. They had long been conscious not only of dissatisfaction on the part of churchmen outside their circle but of movements in the intellectual and spiritual life of the Church that were opposed to official Curial thought and doctrine. They would have been content to continue their forceful course, restraining the thinking of the Church within what they considered its ancient and sacred ways. To these men, the announcement of the new Council came as a severe shock. As for the majority of bishops, what they feared most was that the new Council would be a mere pageant, run off by the officials in rubber-stamp fashion. They felt that if the Council failed to come to grips with the really basic spiritual ills and moral issues of the day, it would destroy the hope that its proclamation had aroused in the hearts of thinking Catholics and non-

Catholics alike. It was obvious that when the curialists and the bishops met in Council there was bound to be a reverberating clash.

Although the new Council was the last thing in the world the above officials desired, once they were convinced of the pope's determination to go ahead, they proved themselves not without resources. Enjoying the advantage of being on the spot and in control of Vatican activities, they quickly rallied to dominate the commissions that were to organize the Council. They made their trusted friends the presidents and the secretaries, inviting at first only "safe" men from various parts of the world to sit in as experts. Gradually, as complaints mounted that some of the outstanding theologians of the Church in France, Germany, and Belgium had been excluded, they called these people to Rome, but it was then too late for them to have any effect on the proposals to be placed before the bishops in council. Unable to control the important Central Commission, which had the final say on the agenda and was composed chiefly of cardinals, they did the next-best thing and arranged to have the conservative cardinals—Ottaviani, Ruffini, Siri, Pizzardo, Marella—lead the discussions. What was more to the point, they saw to it that the reports of this commission's meetings published in *L'Osservatore Romano*, the Vatican newspaper, reflected their line of thought. The information contained in these generally dull, perfunctory news releases was for the most part merely a rehash of the doctrinal explanations to be found in the old, stereotyped larger Roman Catechism, buttressed by an appeal to the current code of canon law. About the only revolutionary proposal that was officially admitted to have been considered was the possibility of the Council's coming out for a stabilized, universal calendar.

It was a poorly kept secret, however, that this commission's meetings were far from harmonious. Several times, resolutions to abolish the Congregation of the Holy Office outright were brought to the floor. In the sessions that took place in June 1962, after Cardinal Ottaviani had ordered that the Italian translation of a pastoral letter on the Council written by the Dutch bishops be withdrawn from circulation, the Indian cardinal—vehemently supported by Cardinals Doepfner of Munich; Koenig of Vienna; and Liénart of Lille— came to the aid of Cardinal Alfrink of Utrecht, by informing the representative of the Holy Office that while ecumenical councils usually ended with someone in schism, this time, for once, it would not be the outsiders, because they happened to represent not merely the majority of the Church but the *sanior pars,* and they expressed their disdain for the freemasonry (a nasty word in European ecclesiastical circles) of those Italian prelates who have held the Church in thrall too long. So pointed did the debate become that the pope eventually sent for the leading figures to calm them down. He did not tell them to abandon their positions, however—a healthy sign of the possibility of the free discussion which was to follow in the Council.

A close look at the *Annuario Pontificio,* the official yearbook of the Vatican, reveals a curious fact that is at the heart of the present difficulties within the Church. The twelve Roman Congregations of the Curia, though each is headed by a cardinal, are controlled by an interlocking directorate of bishops and monsignors, all Italian. The assessor or administrative director of the Holy Office, for example, is Archbishop Pietro Parente, who has the right to investigate any matters dealing with faith or morals in the Church. At the same time, Archbishop Parente is a consultor of the Consistorial Congregation, which is entrusted with the creation of new dioceses, the nomination of bishops, and supervision of their activities. He is a member of the Congregation of the Council, which watches over the discipline of both clergy and laity and has the right to revise acts of national councils. (It also passes on disputes concerning legacies and bequests.) He is a consultor of the Congregation for the Propagation of the Faith, whose competence extends to the mission field, and a member of the Congregation of Rites, which deals with the Church's ceremonies and conducts the processes whereby a person is raised to the altar as a saint. He sits in on the Pontifical Commission for Cinema, Radio, and Television, and has a place in the pope's official Chapel. Finally, he is a member of the Commission for Latin America. (On one occasion, addressing a group of bishops from South America, together with the superiors of various religious orders that have missionaries there, he offended most of his auditors by remarking, "My subject has to do with Paraguay, Uruguay, and all the other *guai*"—the Italian for "troubles.") It is incredible that a man of Archbishop Parente's temperament could be appointed to so sensitive a position as his present post in the Holy Office, for his personal history hardly reflects the stability or civility one expects of Vatican officialdom. Born near Benevento in 1892, he was ordained a priest in 1916 and consecrated Archbishop of Perugia in 1955. In the 1930's, as rector of the Propaganda College in Rome, he managed to incur the anger of Pius XI and had to leave the Eternal City. Powerful friends persuaded Pius XII to recall him to grace and promote him to the archbishopric of Perugia, but he disillusioned both laity and clergy of that Umbrian city so much by his interference in political and social matters that in 1959 he was, as the *Annuario* tersely puts it, "translated" to the titular see of Ptolemais, and brought into the Holy Office as assessor. It was Archbishop Parente, along with another conservative, Archbishop Pericle Felici, who had the most to say as to who would, and who would not, be placed on the preparatory commissions for the Council.

Archbishops Parente and Felici are only two of a host of Italian names that appear on every other page of the part of the *Annuario* that is devoted to the Roman Curia. (Here and there, of course, one comes across such names as Martin O'Connor, Paul Maria Krieg, Romuald Bissonnette, Francis J. Brennan, and Thomas Ryan, but, with the exception of Archbishop O'Connor and Monsignor Brennan, these men do not head offices.) By the peculiar workings of ecclesiastical fate, these same Italian names appear toward the top of the lists of members of the preparatory commissions charged with the responsibility of proposing an agenda for the Council. Though, in all, some eight hundred bishops and theologians from every corner of the world were brought to Rome for consultation regarding this agenda, certain outstanding Catholic figures were excluded, or only invited as consultors toward the very end of the preparatory period. Among those excluded or invited late were the American Jesuits John Courtney Murray and John L. McKenzie; the French theologians Henri de Lubac, M.-D. Chenu, and Jean Daniélou; and Hugo and Karl Rahner, of Innsbruck. These men were apparently considered to hold wildly liberal views, and therefore to be dangerous.

Over the last few years, some officials would seem to have been devising a plan to give themselves absolute control over the Church's intellectual life. Disturbed no little by the independent thinking of Pius XII, who in his later years made it his business to reassess the Church's attitude toward many phases of modern thought, they counted on reasserting their safe theses and doctrines after his death. Pius XII had, for one thing, emancipated the scriptural scholars of the Church by giving them a mandate to employ every legitimate discovery to modernize the Church's understanding of divine revelation. It is known that he had also prepared a complete reorganization of the Roman Curia, but that when he fell sick in 1954 he had had to abandon the project. Consequently, when he died, in 1958, and the conclave elected the seventy-six-year-old diplomat and Patriarch of Venice who became Pope John XXIII, the men of the Curia must have breathed a sigh of relief. They were no doubt convinced that Divine Providence was on their side. The new pontiff was not an intellectual. He made no pretense of being a theologian. With a little careful maneuvering, they could have their way.

One of the first things they had decided to undertake, according to many observers, was a complete reorganization of ecclesiastical studies, whereby they could directly influence the teaching of theology in all the seminaries of the world. The fact, for example, that the Jesuits and the Dominicans had the two best schools of scriptural studies—the Biblical Institute, in Rome, and the Ecole Biblique, in Jerusalem, respectively—was alarming, particularly since the better students turned out by these faculties were imbued with the new approach to the Bible. The curial plan called for a vast agglomeration of all the Catholic universities in Rome—primarily the Gregorian, the Angelicum, and Propaganda—under the leadership of the Lateran University, which would eventually also absorb such schools as the Jesuit-run Biblical Institute, the Capranica, and the Ecclesiastical Academy. The first step in this direction was a move to bring the Lateran itself up to true university status. At the time, it was actually little better than a glorified seminary with mediocre graduate schools of law and theology. To justify its right to be called a university, it aggregated to itself the Carmelite school of theology and the Redemptorist institute of moral theology, organized a faculty of pastoral theology, and brought under its aegis two new schools—one for nuns and one for teaching brothers—whose objective was the issuing of a licentiate, or master's degree, in religion.

It was at this juncture that the thunderbolt of Pope John's announcement of the forthcoming Council struck. This was followed almost immediately by a severe setback to the plan for gathering up all the universities under the domination of the Lateran. The campaign had started with an attack on the Biblical Institute published in the December, 1960, issue of *Divinitas,* the journal of the Lateran University, by Monsignor Antonino Romeo, secretary to Cardinal Pizzardo, head of the Congregation of Seminaries and Universities. Quite clearly, it was intended that this would be followed immediately by action on the part of the Holy Office; the works of several professors of the Biblical Institute, as well as of individual French and German theologians, would be condemned and proscribed. The next move, it may be assumed, would have been to call for control of all the theological faculties in Rome, and eventually throughout the world, by a safe school of theology—the Lateran, for example. As things turned out, the plan overreached itself. Intending to confront Pope John with a *fait accompli,* the officials had seen to it that Monsignor Romeo's article was kept from his eyes, and they refused to print in *Divinitas* the reply of the rector of the Biblical Institute; instead, they sent a free copy of the original article to every bishop in Italy. This proved their undoing, for one of the Italian bishops, on a Vatican visit, unwittingly offered the pope his sympathies on the fell state of theological affairs as revealed by Monsignor Romeo's article. This was the first Pope John had heard of the matter. When he read the article, he gave vent to one of the few angry outbursts of his pontificate. He had his secretary call the rector of the Biblical Institute and assure him of the pope's complete confidence in the school's orthodoxy. Next, he required Cardinal Pizzardo to write a letter to Cardinal Bea, former rector of the Institute, in which Pizzardo disclaimed any responsibility for the article, or knowledge of it before it was printed. This was a double humiliation, for all Rome knew that the article could never have been written without the clearance, and even the encouragement, of Cardinal Pizzardo.

The matter did not end there, however. Returning to the attack at the beginning of the scholastic year 1961, the Holy Office informed the General of the Jesuits that two professors at the Biblical Institute, Stanislas Lyonnet and Maximilian Zerwick, were to be removed from the faculty as being under suspicion of teaching erroneous doctrine. Fortunately for the cause of fair play as well as that of academic freedom, the Jesuit General decided that it was time to take a stand. He informed the Secretary of the Holy Office that he had personally examined the teachings of these two professors and could find no fault in them. He asked proof of their errors. As it is against the principles of the Holy Office ever to justify its activities, the matter died there and the two men remained in their posts. In June, however, at the close of the school year, the Holy Office forced the Vatican Secretary of State to intervene and suspend the two professors in question.

Actually, what is happening in Catholic biblical scholarship seems to be fully in line with the *aggiornamento* proclaimed by Pope John as the aim of his new Council. Using discoveries in the archaeological, literary, and historical fields that relate to the time of Christ, the scriptural men hope to arrive at a closer appreciation of Christ's words and deeds through study of the context and atmosphere in which they occurred. They make a clear distinction between biblical theology—the systematic presentation of the religious truths revealed by Christ as these truths were understood by the Apostles and early disciples, and as they were embodied in the New Testament—and modern theology, which is the result of the elaboration of these truths under the guidance of the Church down through the ages. Since the Catholic Church is a living organism, its thinking about God and about man's relation to his eternal destiny must be something at once dynamic and evolving. It begins with certain basic truths about the nature of God and his dealings with man, which are revealed in and through the Church and whose principles are unchangeable. Yet the cultural atmosphere, in which these truths are appreciated and lived, is continually changing. In each age the Church must be alert to restate or even rephrase them, so that they will be understood by the current generation. On both counts, the Catholic thinker today runs headlong into a certain type of intransigent theologian.

This position is typified by Cardinal Ernesto Ruffini of Sicily, who, though he specialized in biblical research as a young priest, has turned against the modern trend. He feels that the Bible must be interpreted in what can only be termed a fundamentalist sense—that to admit of any change in our appreciation of the words and deeds of Christ is to betray the Church by acknowledging that its teachers have been wrong. In an article published on page one of *L'Osservatore Romano* in June, 1961, he demonstrated the lengths to which some Italian theologians are prepared to go. The subject was Pope Pius XII's emancipating encyclical on the study of the scriptures, called "Divino Afflante Spiritu" and published in 1943. In it Pope Pius had written:

In the words and writings of the ancient Oriental authors, the literal sense does not appear with as much clarity as it does in writers of our times. What they—the authors of the Bible—intended to signify by their words cannot be determined solely by the laws of grammar or of philology. It is absolutely necessary that the exegete go back to the manner of thinking of the Orient in those far centuries, so that, helping himself *with the resources of history, of archaeology, of ethnology, and of the other sciences,* he may discern and recognize what literary genres the authors of that ancient age wished to use or actually did employ. . . . The exegete cannot determine *a priori* what were the forms of speech and expression used by these authors. He can only do this by the attentive study of the ancient literatures of the Orient.

In direct contradiction and literally rejecting Pius XII's words, Cardinal Ruffini wrote:

How can one suppose that the Church has during nineteen centuries presented the Divine Book to its children without knowing the literary genre in which it was composed, if this is the key to exact interpretation? Such an assertion becomes all the more absurd when one takes into account that a large number of these superior-minded critics not only call for new applications of the theory of literary genres in regard to the inspired books but remit to the future a definitive explanation; that is to say, to the time when one will come to understand better, *through the study of history, of archaeology, of ethnology, and of the other sciences,* the manner of speaking and writing of the ancients, particularly the Orientals.

What bothers one about this attack, which called the teaching of Pius XII "absurd," is the fact that in Rome, under the pretense of defending orthodoxy in peril, it is possible publicly to criticize a solemn pontifical document—but only if you happen to be a member of the right team. The experiences of the Jesuit, Father Lombardi, who made some mild suggestions for a reform of the papal household and the internationalizing of the Curia, provide a case in point. His book was immediately withdrawn from circulation, and he was at once sent back to his Institute for "A Better World" in Marino and told to stay there. On the other hand, an outrageous pamphlet on the biblical question by Msgr. Spadafora was printed several weeks before the Council opened and widely circulated among those bishops known to be favorable to the intransigent position in this matter. The brochure, less articulate and much more confused than the original attack on the Biblical Institute by Msgr. Romeo, contained two articles originally published in Rovigo and a third prepared for (but never printed in) *Divinitas*. Despite its hysterical approach, it may be said to have done some good in that it inspired a clear-cut, precisely worded reply from the Biblical Institute in French, German, Spanish and English that was sent to the bishops gathered for the Council. As for the author, not a word of criticism of him issued from the Curial offices.

It has been said that the most important factor in the formation of the rigid or closed ecclesiastical mind is the conviction, explicitly formulated in Italian seminaries, that the function of the theologian is to preserve Catholic doctrine from the least taint of change or error. "No heresy has ever originated in Italy" is the erroneous but persuasive axiom used in inculcating this conviction. A second factor is a method of instruction that is essentially a lecture-memory exercise, the student being trained to absorb attentively the words of the professor, to analyze by a rigidly logical interpretation of the terms the significance of the doctrine being explained, and, finally, to repeat verbatim the text of the lectures or of the manual in use. While the accusation that the medieval Scholastic theologians spent their time arguing over the number of angels who could dance on the point of a needle is obviously absurd, since it confuses two orders of reality—the spiritual and the material—which those same Scholastics, as philosophers, carefully distinguished, it is indicative of the extreme use to which Aristotelian logic has been, and is still being, put by such theologians. They deal in propositions that must be either true or false. Having reduced the teachings of Christ to logical concepts, they proceed to draw conclusions—always on a logical plane, of course —that frequently take no account of the logic of facts and events. When they encounter scriptural passages or historical events that embarrassingly fail to accord with their logical conclusions, they blindly force the issue. Thus, in the matter of the seven sacraments, which is now an uncontroverted doctrine of Catholic belief, these theologians maintain that all seven sacraments were specifically instituted by Christ, and were given to the Church as instruments of grace in the very form and manner in which they are administered today. This thesis, however, is by no means undisputed. One school of thought, for example, is convinced that there is no certain evidence of the existence of the rite of the anointing of a dying person until about the sixth century. As a matter of fact, St. Leo the Great, in the fifth century, though he twice discusses the way in which a priest is to minister to the dying, says not a word about anointing—and he was a traditionalist, bent on promoting uniformity of practice. There was, indeed, no agreement on the number of the sacraments until the thirteenth century, when the Church set the number at seven. This view of events makes no impression on the Roman theologian, who to this day requires his students to memorize texts asserting that Jesus personally instituted all the seven sacraments of the Church in the way they are now administered.

To take some of the starch out of possible recalcitrants, the curialists insisted upon the use of Latin as the language of the Council. What was being aimed at, again, was a logical exposition or formulation of doctrine that could be nailed down tight and recorded in a dead tongue. But in actual fact Latin is only the language of the Western, Roman, or Latin Church. The Greek, Slavic, Coptic, and other Eastern rites each have their own language. And it became ironically clear as the Council sessions began, that Italian prelates were by no means as good Latinists as was commonly believed, and that the stilted style of purified Renaissance Latin used for official documents was not really much more than a cultured doggerel. When it came to Ciceronian or patristic Latin, many Northern Europeans made the Italians sound like stuttering chickadees.

One great unknown element in the preparatory stage of the Council was the part to be played by the North American bishops. They seemed at first, with few exceptions, to show little interest in or understanding of the issues at stake. In Europe they were regarded as a hard-working, ingenuous, but theologically deficient lot. Many of them seemed to feel, for example, that the current liturgical movement, which goes to the very heart of the attempt to renew the inner life of the Church, was for the most part merely a fad—a matter of introducing the dialogue mass, abolishing Latin in favor of the vernacular in ecclesiastical ceremonies, and allowing laymen to read the Epistle and the Gospel. A few of them even seemed to think that it was only a question of rubrics, or the rules to be followed in sacred ceremonies. Actually, the liturgical movement means much more; namely, a return to the great sense of mystery with which the Apostles and Fathers of the early Church announced the good news of the Kingdom of God established in the world by Jesus Christ. The early apologists of Christianity stressed the tremendously mysterious aspects of a religion that maintained that its founder was both God and man at the same time, that He had submitted to death on the Cross to redeem all mankind from sin, and that He had established an organization in which there were forgiveness of sins and participation in the life of God through the reception of Christ in the Eucharist. To the tough, cynical Greeks and Romans of the ancient world, such ideas were ridiculous, as St. Paul admitted, and they also proved a stumbling block to the adherents of Judaism, from which Christianity sprang. The modern Roman-trained theologian tends to teach these all but incredible truths as if they were everyday facts. He has simplified the life and teachings of Jesus so that any Sunday-school teacher can break them down into easily digested stories for children. Despite a great display of Latin learning, he apparently believes that these truths should be taught to modern man on that level, as if they were so many commonplace happenings.

The leading figure in the group of intransigents—or "prophets of doom," to use the pope's phrase—is Cardinal Alfredo Ottaviani. Born in 1890 in Rome, with the black dirt of Trastevere (as a local saying goes) beneath his feet, he was ordained a priest in 1916. A teaching career followed in Roman seminaries and universities. Learned in canon law, he taught this subject for 20 years at the Lateran University. He was made a domestic prelate while working in the Secretariat of State and became Assessor of the Holy Office in 1935, as a protégé of Cardinal Canali. In 1953 Pius XII elevated him to the rank of cardinal-deacon, and in the same year he became Pro-Secretary of the Holy Office. In 1959 he was appointed Secretary of the Congregation of the Holy Office by John XXIII (who is President of the same body). It was not until 1962, oddly enough, that Cardinal Ottaviani became a bishop —for in that year Pope John elevated all the cardinal-deacons to the episcopate. This brilliant career can be summed up in three words: a Curia man. Cardinal Ottaviani is astute, scholarly, and at times witty. For years he has run a school within the Vatican grounds, as well as a summer *colonia* at Frascati, for poor children from the *borgate* outside the Vatican walls. Like all his fellow-bishops throughout the world, he is a strong opponent of communism. He has published a first-class textbook on the Church and the public law, and in 1961 a book of addresses entitled *Il Baluardo* ("The Bulwark").

Two years ago he and his conservative colleague, Cardinal Siri of Genoa, were prevented by the Vatican from publicly interfering in local Italian politics. When the Christian Democratic Party first moved into coalition with the Nenni Socialists in 1961, the Vatican prepared for the reaction to this event by advising that no Italian bishops were to make public comments on the matter. Cardinal Ottaviani failed to heed this admonition and spoke out against the move. To his considerable surprise, he was told the very next day that, as an Italian prelate, he too was required to show greater forbearance with regard to Italy's political affairs. Apparently Cardinal Siri decided to show his disdain for this Vatican injunction by departing from his usual custom of publishing during the Lenten season a long commentary denouncing leftist trends in social and economic affairs in Italy. Instead he put out a pious epistle on "Visits to the Blessed Sacrament," which was so out of keeping with his usual line that its unexpected publication, prominently on page one of *L'Osservatore Romano,* was interpreted as a gentle if not pointed rebuke.

The third member of the group, Cardinal Ruffini, is an excellent Latinist, as well as a caustic and intelligent prelate. He is the kind of churchman who has forgotten nothing he was ever taught but, since becoming a teacher himself, has resisted learning anything more. He made his studies at the Pontifical Biblical Institute some forty years ago, and taught scripture before his elevation to the hierarchy as Archbishop of Palermo in Sicily. One of his pupils, who later became Cardinal Alfrink of Utrecht, disagreed with his former teacher at the Council in the debate on theology (see page 147). Other members of the intransigent group include Archbishop Dino Staffa, Secretary of the Congregation for Seminaries and Universities, Archbishop Pietro Parente, and Msgr. Antonio Piolanti, Rector Magnificus of the Lateran University.

In the last fifteen years, it is Cardinal Ottaviani who has taken the lead among these men and their like-minded associates in the role of what might be called twentieth century "hammerers of heretics." In their view, in preserving the great heritage of the Church it is more important to caution and to condemn, than to encourage and to persuade.* In an age in which religion has suffered unprecedented losses and depredations, the wisdom of their position is at least open to question. One fact is clear, however. Their view is not consonant with that of the present Visible Head of the Church, who summoned the Council to proclaim, as he said, not the Church's condemnatory or inquisitorial role, but its ecumenical and pastoral mission.

As the opening date of the Council neared, from the four corners of the world men of every breed and circumstance began to gather in Rome. They were the sons of peasants and

* In a radio interview (December 1962) Cardinal Ottaviani replied to a question regarding his position as leader of a "conservative group of Council fathers" as follows: "My personal position is that of a man who has, from the nature of his office, the duty to keep the deposit of faith intact and who, at the same time, must leave full freedom to the progress which is necessary to better clarify, understand and expose Catholic teaching. Let us never forget: not all that is new is true and good merely because it is new. There are some opinions in theology today which are, if not false, at least debatable. In this situation, it is a completely positive action to defend the basic data of Holy Scripture and of Tradition, to avoid permitting some truths of the faith to be obscured, under the pretext of progress and adaptation."

princes, of bankers and laborers, of tribal chiefs and trolley-car conductors. Emanuel Mabathoana, Bishop of Maseru, is the grandson of the "Lion of the Mountain," chief of the Basutos in South Africa; Bishop Dlamini of Umzimkulu is a member of the royal family of Natal. Cardinal Gracias saw the light of day in the slums of Karachi, Cardinal Siri's father was a Genoese longshoreman, and Archb. Kominek of Vaga was the son of a Silesian miner. The youthful-looking Philippe Nguyen Kim Dien worked as a street-cleaner and rag-picker before entering the seminary; since becoming Bishop of Cantho, Vietnam, he has given up the episcopal palace as too luxurious for a poor country. When a friend saw him driving his tiny 4-horsepower French CV, he remarked: "We do not know what he has sold or pawned to buy that, after all his charities, but you can be sure that in this land of mandarins the image he presents is revolutionary."

Bishop Botero Salazar of Medellín, Colombia, has turned his palace, a gift from his family, into a school for workers, installing himself in a shed in one of the *barrios* on the edge of town, while the auxiliary bishop of Lyons, Msgr. Alfred Ancel, lives with a group of priests in a *banlieu* of Lyons and supports himself by part-time work in a basket-factory. In Argentina, a group of prelates has become known as the "bishops with wooden crosses and croziers." In Lima, Peru in 1959, Bp. Dammert Bellido of Cajamarca declared: "One area in which, with the best of intentions, we still provoke scandal in some and disgust in others is in the lack of simplicity in the decoration of our churches and the riches with which we surround our ceremonies. In all innocence, we stretch our resources to obtain the costliest ornaments, which are in doubtful taste to begin with, while at the same time children of God are suffering from hunger, sickness, and misery. This is a true cause for scandal in the Church today. Sumptuosity is not in accord with the poverty of our age."

In Chile, Bishop Larrain of Talca has handed over 366 acres of his episcopal domain at Los Sillos to eighteen impoverished families. Cardinal Silva Henriquez of Santiago has a similar project in hand for slum-dwellers. Bp. Jobst, vicar apostolic of the Kimberleys in Australia has bought 400,000 acres of semi-desert land for the economic rehabilitation of the nation's aborigines. At Privandrum in India, Bp. Peter B. Pereira has visited every fishing village in his diocese on the coast of Kerala, in an attempt to introduce a program of technical, economic and social development. In San Antonio, Texas, Archb. Robert Lucey has become the champion of social justice for the *braceros* or Mexican "wetbacks" who come to the U.S. seasonally for farm work.

Of the intellectuals among the conciliar fathers, Cardinals Frings of Cologne, Liénart of Lille, Ruffini of Palermo, Alfrink of Holland and Meyer of Chicago have licentiates or doctorates in Scripture Studies. Cardinal Tisserant, who is dean of the Sacred College, has the distinction of having been elected a member of the French Academy. When Cardinal Montini left Rome to become the new Archbishop of Milan, it was noted with wonder that he transported ninety cases full of books. Bishop Wright of Pittsburgh and Archbishop Hallinan of Atlanta have given evidence of a deep culture and wide knowledge of the social and political problems of our day. Cardinal Koenig of Vienna is the author of a three-volume work on comparative religion. Bishop Weber of Strasbourg is noted for contributing frequent articles and scholarly reviews to French ecclesiastical journals. Cardinals Bea and Suenens are theologians in their own right, and so are Bishops George Dwyer of Leeds and William Philbin of Down and Connor.

The pastorates of the more than 2,500 bishops who attended the Council ranged from the smallest—that of Msgr. Johann Gunnarson, vicar apostolic in Holar, Iceland, where there are 806 Catholics cared for by one diocesan and 8 religious priests, and one seminarian to the largest—that of Cardinal Meyer of Chicago, who has 2,119,000 Catholics, 3 auxiliary bishops, 1,264 diocesan, and 1,549 religious priests under his care.

Under John XXIII, the more homely but universal aspect of the pope's responsibility as a pastor has come to the fore. Pope John has said frequently that his first love in the priesthood has always been for the pastorate; and it is becoming noticeable that more and more bishops are being appointed from positions as pastors of churches, unlike former times when the majority came from among seminary professors and diocesan administrators. In the actual ministry, greater attention is now being paid to what might be called a dynamic sociology of pastoral activity. In Bologna, infested after the war with a militant communist worker movement, Cardinal Lercaro organized his "flying squad" of priests and catechists. Similar efforts were made by Bishop Morcillo in Bilbao and by Archbishop Modrego in the down-trodden suburbs of Barcelona. Bishop Baccino of San José, Uruguay, devoted a pastoral letter to the need for "an awareness of modern reality in adapting our pastoral efforts to the necessities of the hour." On this score, bishops all over the world have been stirring themselves to prayerful activity, revolutionizing methods of catechetical instruction, injecting new life into the liturgy, and combining spiritual realism with the use of modern techniques in the lay apostolate.

On the strictly spiritual side, Bishop Joseph Kiwanuka of Rubaga in Africa himself presides at, and preaches, the annual retreats for his clergy; Archbishop Rayappan of Pondichery and Cuddalore travels through much of his native India similarly employed. In almost every diocese in the world special attention is being paid to the erection and guidance of seminaries, and specialists are engaged in attracting vocations to the priesthood and religious life. Bishop Raymond of Allahabad is an expert catechist and Archbishop Gopu is himself director of the catechetical center at Hyderabad. Bps. Raspanti of Morón and Kémérer of Posadas in Argentina have rivalled Cardinal Lercaro and Bishop Himmer of Tournai in publishing up-to-date directories for the celebration of mass and other liturgical functions. Archb. Angelo Fernandes, coadjutor bishop of New Delhi, himself serves as commentator for the Holy Week services being celebrated by his archbishop, Joseph Fernandes. In West Bengal, Bishop La Ravoire Morrow assists at the mass chanted in Bengali, while Bishop Van Bekkum of Ruteng in Indonesia is not only a theoretician of liturgical renewal, having taken a leading part in the Liturgical Congress at Assisi in 1956, but he has adapted the ceremonies of confirmation to the local *mangarraie* customs, and is greeted by baptized and unbaptized alike with immense joy. (They kiss his episcopal ring with their noses when welcoming him to the "parish councils," which have replaced the traditional tribal gatherings and are usually preceded by a chanted mass in the local dialect and two or three hours of religious-inspired dancing.) Bishop Zoungrana of Upper Volta has made a special study of the initiation customs for entrance on manhood in the local tribes, with the idea of eventually Christianizing them; and Bishop Chitsulo of Nyasaland has just completed a translation and adaptation of the Roman ritual into the Cinyanja language. Bishop Van Cauwelaert of Inongo in the Congo is the leader among African bishops determined to adapt the liturgy to local customs, beginning with a consecration of the new born to the Creator, prayers and supplications for the sick and dying, and a wake and funeral rites. "We are looking for courageous directions from the Council that will assure us of a true and realistic liturgical renewal," he wrote in his last pastoral letter before the Council met.

In the modern political arena, a number of bishops have had to take an active and dangerous part in insisting upon civil liberty for their people. Archb. Pérez Serantes and Bp. Boza Masvidal were expelled from Cuba, and Bps. Panal and Reilly were caught in the Trujillo reign of terror in the Dominican Republic. Bp. Ferreira Gomes was exiled from Portugal for supporting the right of workers to organize in political associations, as was Bp. Pildáin of the Canary Islands because he supported resistance to the state-controlled unions in Spain. In the foreground, of course, are the heroic figures of Cardinal Wyszynski and the Polish bishops, as well as the whole Catholic episcopate in the "Church of Silence" not only in Europe but the Orient. More recently too, in Moslem countries, new waves of persecution have broken out against the Church, requiring heroic courage and astuteness on the part of the bishops.

In the cause of social justice and peace on both a local and worldwide scale, Archb. Duval of Algiers has taken a particularly bold stand, while Cardinal Doepfner in Berlin, Bp. Gutiérrez Granier in La Paz, and Patriarch Meouchi in Liban have helped to pacify dangerous national crises. And in the new nations, both native and foreign-born bishops have played a part in encouraging and helping to direct the forces striving for independence. In South Africa Archbishops Hurley of Durban and McCann of Capetown; Archbishop Rummel in New Orleans and Archb. Leonard of Madhurai, have taken strong stands against governmental and local anti-racial drives.

Three outstanding bishops represent the Churches of the Ukraine in exile—Archb. Hermaniuk of Canada, Bp. Kornyljak of Germany and Archb. Senyshyn of the U.S., while Bp. Sipovič stands for the scattered Bielorussians and Bp. Brizgys the Baltic peoples. Among the thirteen Armenian bishops of Egypt, Liban, Turkey and Iran, Bp. Zohrabian is the outstanding leader, while Patriarch Meouchi not only represents the Maronites of Lebanon and Patriarch Maximos IV Saigh the Melchites, but they bring to the Council the solid, ancient traditions of the Oriental Church with its liturgy and theology reaching all the way back to apostolic times.

Side by side with the European and American bishops, whose present status, in spite of all the economic, social and political ills plaguing the western world, is both stable and assured, the vast throngs of African, Asian, and Oceanic prelates, both native and missionary, bring with them to the Council an experience and determination rivalling the enthusiasm and drive manifested by the first Apostles and their immediate successors. It was for this reason that Pope John's optimistic and increasingly positive predictions that the Council would renew the face of the Church were more than justified. As the great day of the solemn assembly's opening approached, he had reason to believe that his Council would indeed restore "the simple and pure lines that the face of the Church of Jesus had at its birth."

III

The Council Opens

To ANYONE who had the good fortune to be standing in front of the bronze doors leading into the papal palace, on the side of St. Peter's Square, at eight o'clock on the morning of Thursday, October 11, 1962, there was suddenly revealed a dazzling spectacle. At that moment, two papal gendarmes, resplendent in parade uniform of white trousers and black topboots, coats, and busbies, slowly swung the great doors open, exposing to a portion of the crowd row upon row of bishops, clad in flowing white damask copes and mitres, descending Bernini's majestic *scala regia* from the papal apartments. As brilliant television floodlights were switched on along the stairway, the intense light brought to mind Henry Vaughan's lines:

> "I saw Eternity the other night,
> Like a great ring of pure and endless light."

In rows of sixes, an apparently inexhaustible phalanx of prelates filed out of the Vatican palace, swung to their right across St. Peter's Square, then wheeled right again, to mount the ramplike steps leading into the basilica. Every now and then, this white mass was dotted with the black cassock, full beard, and round headdress of an oriental bishop, and here and there with the bulbous gold crown and crossed pectoral reliquaries of a bishop of the Byzantine rite. Toward the end came the scarlet ranks of the Sacred College of Cardinals. Finally, the pope appeared, carried, in deference to the wishes of his entourage, on the *sedia gestatoria,* and looking rather timid, perhaps even frightened—as he always does when first mounting this oriental contraption—but gradually warming to the mild acclamation of the overawed crowd, and gently smiling and quietly weeping as he was carried undulantly forward, blessing the onlookers. At the entrance to the Council hall in the basilica, the procession halted while the pope dismounted and walked the length of the nave to the Confession of St. Peter.

Before the high altar the pope had ordered the substitution of a simpler, more informal style of throne for the unwieldy, pretentious "doctoral" throne, with a red damask backdrop and canopy, that the organizers of the Council had devised. The significance of this was soon made clear by the pope's opening speech, which stressed the Council's pastoral, or ministering, role over the dogmatic, or condemnatory, approach. After the traditional hymn "Veni Creator Spiritus," a solemn mass of the Holy Spirit was celebrated, in which the Epistle and the Gospel were chanted in both Greek and Latin, to signify the unity of both parts of the Church, East and West. The celebrant was the elderly but vigorous Cardinal Tisserant, bearded dean of the College of Cardinals. A touch of Byzantine court ceremonial followed the mass, as the cardinals mounted the steps of the papal throne one by one, with their scarlet mantles trailing behind them, to make their obeisance to the See of Peter. After the bishops' solemn profession of faith in unison, recitation of the litany of the Saints, and more prayers from the Greek rite, Pope John began to deliver his sermon.*

In clear and resonant tones that could be distinctly heard throughout the basilica, the pope, after a few introductory remarks, said that he was tired of listening to the prophets of doom among his advisers. "Though burning with zeal," he said, these men "are not endowed with very much sense of discretion or measure." They maintain that "our era, in comparison with past eras, is getting worse, and they behave as though they had learned nothing from history, which is nevertheless the great teacher of life." They were, he said, under the illusion that "at the time of the former Councils, everything was a triumph for the Christian idea and way of life and for proper religious liberty," and he added, "We feel that we must disagree with these prophets of doom, who are always forecasting disaster, as though the end of the world were at hand," and continually warning him, "in the course of our pastoral office," that the modern world is "full of prevarication and ruin."

As the listeners heard these words, their attention focussed irresistibly on the face of Cardinal Ottaviani, Secretary of the

---

* The conciliar rites and ceremonies follow a special *ordo* or ceremonial drawn up by the Preparatory Commission for Ceremonial and are contained in a booklet entitled *Methodus servanda et preces recitandae in Concilio Oecumenico Vaticano II.* Typographia Polyglotta Vaticana, 1962. The oriental litanies are printed separately in another booklet. In accordance with custom, a description of the ceremonies on Oct. 11, 1962, in French, was prepared for the use of the diplomatic corps and special guests.

Congregation of the Holy Office, who was seated at the pope's immediate right; on the face of the recently consecrated seventy-eight-year-old Archbishop Enrico Dante, the Papal Master of Ceremonies, at the pope's left and half a step to the rear; on Cardinal Siri, of Genoa, and on Cardinal Ruffini, of Palermo, sitting in the tier reserved for the Sacred College along the main aisle of the basilica; on Pericle Felici, Secretary General of the Council; on Pietro Parente, Assessor of the Holy Office; on Dino Staffa, of the Congregation of Seminaries and Universities; on Pietro Palazzini, of the Congregation of the Council; and on the other Roman monsignors who stand on the various rungs of the ladder that constitutes the *cursus honorum* of the Curia. These were the faces of some of the prophets of doom of whom the Holy Father was speaking, since they are the advisers he sees regularly on purely pastoral matters. (It is well known that these doomlike sentiments are not shared by the Secretary of State, Cardinal Cicognani; by the Prefect of the Congregation for Propagating the Faith, Cardinal Agagianian; by the Secretary of the Congregation for the Oriental Church, Cardinal Testa; or by the Secretary of the Consistorial Congregation, Cardinal Confalonieri.) The pope then proceeded to outline, serenely and optimistically, what he expected of the Council and why he had summoned it. "Divine Providence," he said, "is leading us to a new order of human relations." It was imperative for the Church "to bring herself up to date where required," in order to spread her message "to all men throughout the world." While the Church must "never depart from the sacred patrimony of truth received from the Fathers," she must "ever look to the present, to new conditions and new forms of life introduced into the modern world, which have opened new avenues to the Catholic apostolate."

Then came the phrases, so pregnant with meaning, that

either alarmed or gratified his listeners, depending on their theological outlook. The pope said that he had not called the Council to discuss "one article or another of the fundamental doctrine of the Church . . . which is presumed to be well known and familiar to all; for this, a Council was not necessary." Thus were ruled out the hopes of those who had expected the Council to proclaim some new dogma, isolated from the rest of Christian doctrine, in the manner of the previous Ecumenical Council here, in 1869–70, which concentrated on the dogma of papal infallibility. No, said the pope; "the world expects a step forward toward doctrinal penetration and a formation of consciences." This must be "in conformity with authentic doctrine," of course, but it "should be studied and expounded through the methods of research and through the literary forms of modern thought." In other words, doctrine was to be made more intelligible to contemporaries in the light of scholarship in biblical, theological, philosophical, and historical disciplines.

He next touched on a subject that is almost taboo in traditionalist Catholic theological circles, saying, "The substance of the ancient doctrine of the *depositum fidei* is one thing; the way in which it is expressed is another." That is, Catholic doctrine remains the same in substance, but the formulations of it vary and are not to be regarded as unalterable ends in themselves. The task of the Council, he told the assembled prelates, was to find the best formulas for our time, without being too hidebound or showing a too slavish respect for those of a previous age. He further emphasized the pastoral, rather than the doctrinal, note by declaring, "Nowadays, the bride of Christ [the Church] prefers to make use of the medicine of mercy rather than that of severity. She considers that she meets the needs of the present day by demonstrating the validity of her teaching rather than by condemnation." This was an unmistakable disavowal of the inquisitorial and condemnatory approach of the Holy Office. Finally, the pope turned his attention to the problem of Christian unity. "The entire Christian family has not yet fully attained the visible unity in truth" desired by Christ, he said, and the Catholic Church "therefore considers it her duty to work actively so that there may be fulfilled the great mystery of that unity." He said that the key to "the brotherly unity of all"—embracing not only Christians but "those who follow non-Christian religions"—is "the fullness of charity," or love. Thus Pope John put his seal on the methods and goals of Catholic participation in the ecumenical, or worldwide, movement for reunion.

This inaugural address to the Council, carefully worded and balanced, and delivering a bold message of renewal and reform, marked the end of the closed mentality that has characterized not a few Catholic bishops and theologians since the sixteenth century. Whether this message reached all the prelates to whom it was addressed, or will be heeded by all it did reach, is another matter; one does not cease being a prophet of doom overnight. But the Council as a whole received the pope's message gladly. Whatever changes come must be made by the bishops themselves. In calling the Council and in addressing it as he did in his opening speech, the pope made the great and essential contributions, which no one else could possibly have made. After his address, John XXIII did not enter the Council hall again until the next-to-last day of the session. He watched and heard the daily proceedings on closed-circuit television in his private apartments.

Despite the brilliance of the opening ceremonial, it was felt that there was incongruity between the outward show, largely reflecting the court etiquette of a by-gone age, and

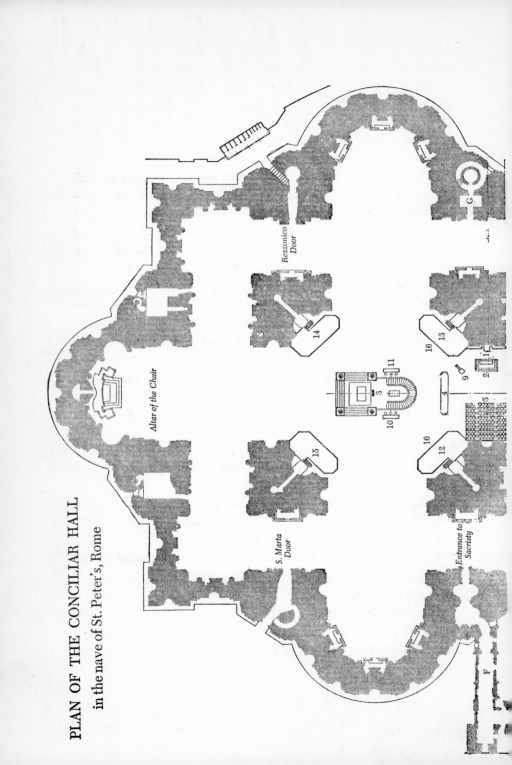

PLAN OF THE CONCILIAR HALL
in the nave of St. Peter's, Rome

Altar of the Chair

Rezzonico Door

S. Marta Door

Entrance to Sacristy

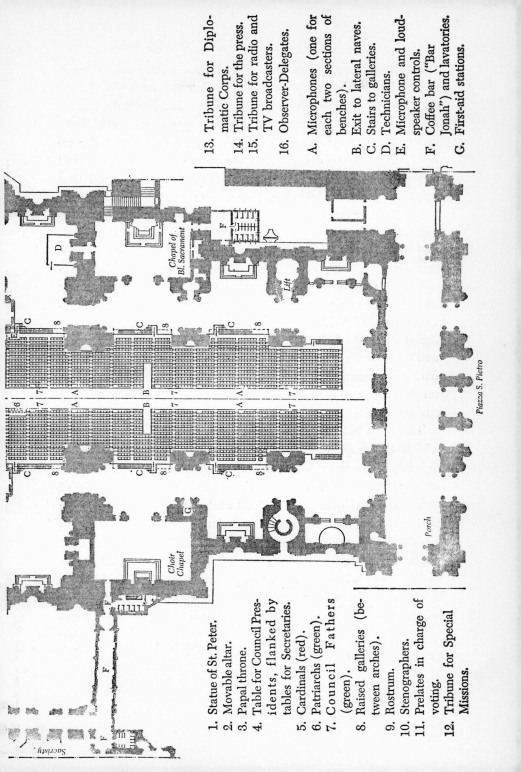

13. Tribune for Diplomatic Corps.
14. Tribune for the press.
15. Tribune for radio and TV broadcasters.
16. Observer-Delegates.

A. Microphones (one for each two sections of benches).
B. Exit to lateral naves.
C. Stairs to galleries.
D. Technicians.
E. Microphone and loudspeaker controls.
F. Coffee bar ("Bar Jonah") and lavatories.
G. First-aid stations.

1. Statue of St. Peter.
2. Movable altar.
3. Papal throne.
4. Table for Council Presidents, flanked by tables for Secretaries.
5. Cardinals (red).
6. Patriarchs (green).
7. Council Fathers (green).
8. Raised galleries (between arches).
9. Rostrum.
10. Stenographers.
11. Prelates in charge of voting.
12. Tribune for Special Missions.

the pastoral purpose of the Council. Some fathers regretted, in particular, that they were passive listeners to a polyphonic symphony, magnificently chanted as this was, instead of being allowed to join the celebrant in a mass that would have given better expression to the corporate feeling of the assembly.* As if to compensate for such defects and forestall any misapprehensions about a "rubber-stamp" Council that might have been forming, Pope John took great pains on the following days to create the "right atmosphere" by talking to the diplomatic corps and special missions, the press, and the observer-delegates, in a number of intimate gatherings held in the Sistine Chapel and the Hall of the Consistory. Speaking to the journalists (Oct. 13) before the great mural of Michelangelo's "Last Judgment," Pope John effectively reminded his hearers of their responsibility to report the truth and of the importance of the press in the modern world. Referring to the temptation of journalists to tamper with the truth, he departed from his text momentarily to remind them that he had said "temptation," and was not accusing them of actual fabrication.

The most touching encounter was unquestionably the one which the pope and Cardinal Bea had with the observer delegates, whose presence at the Council was unprecedented in the annals of Roman Catholicism. It was the fruit of months of delicate negotiations and a visible token of the new policy toward ecumenism and the problem of reunion which the pope had adopted. Departing from custom in a precedent-shattering move, the pope received the delegates in the Hall of the Consistory, appropriately, and then sat down with them in a square, in much the same way as he was accustomed to sit with the cardinals in consistory. It was

* Cf. Y. Congar, O.P., *Informations Catholiques Internationales*, Nov. 1, 1962, p. 1, and p. 7.

a small but significant detail that he sat on the same kind of chair as the delegates, rather than on his throne. The impression made by this brotherly gesture was immediate and lasting. After a few words by Msgr. Willebrands, Secretary of the Secretariat for Unity, who introduced the delegates as "our brethren in Christ," Pope John began his talk.

Speaking in French, he assured them of his heartfelt welcome and his hope that their presence would hasten the day when Christ's prayer, "That they may be one," might be fully realized. If they could read his heart, he said, they would perhaps have a better idea of what he was thinking than from his words. Charity was the key to progress in the ecumenical sphere, as his past experiences in Sofia, Istanbul and Athens had shown. He said it was pointless to engage in controversy. What was needed was mutual understanding and tolerance: "Though we did not discuss, we loved each other . . ." As for the ultimate goal of reunion, "the Christian virtue of patience must not be allowed to harm the virtue of prudence, which is equally fundamental." The important thing, he said, was that they had come and were there, for which he could only say, repeating the words of the Psalmist, "May God be blessed every day!"

On the following Monday (Oct. 15), Cardinal Bea, speaking before the observers at a reception in the Hotel Columbus, addressed them as "my brethren in Christ." This phrase, he said, reminded him of the immeasurable grace of Christian baptism, which has formed bonds that were "stronger than all our divisions." The awareness of these bonds had moved their parent bodies to send them to Rome where Pope John had created the Secretariat for Promoting Christian Unity so that non-Catholic communities could be in a better position to follow the work of the Council. It was to be regretted, of course, that not all were able to come, he said, referring to

the absence of the Greek Orthodox Church. But this should
be regarded as a mere temporary setback. Then, after explaining that the Secretariat was at their disposition, and
would arrange to see that the observers were kept abreast of
developments by periodic meetings, Cardinal Bea said that
he wanted the delegates to speak their minds freely with
regard to the course of the Council, letting the Secretariat
know their criticisms, suggestions, or desires. He could not
always guarantee a solution, but he assured them that he
would do whatever was possible to meet their wishes. Dr.
Edmund Schlink, observer-delegate for the Evangelical
Churches of Germany, replied to the cardinal in the name
of the delegates, stating that he had been particularly impressed, thus far, by two things: the insistence of both the
pope and the cardinal that a distinction must be made between revealed truth and its formulation, and the progress
already made by the Church of Rome in biblical studies.
Msgr. Antony, observer-delegate for the European exarchate
of the Russian Orthodox Church, associated himself with the
remarks of Dr. Schlink.

The observer-delegates were one of the pleasant surprises
of the Council. They represented all the important non-
Roman communions except the Greek Orthodox, the World
Baptist Alliance, and certain fundamentalist churches. They
held the status of honored guests in "the house of their
father," to use the pope's expression, being handed the same
secret schemata as the fathers, allotted the best seats in the
house, and provided with the translation service that was so
sorely missed by some of their hosts. They were admitted to
all the daily general congregations, and to as many meetings
of the commissions as they wished to attend. Nothing like
it had ever happened before in the history of the Catholic
Church. Though all this made the observers reluctant to say

anything that might embarrass their hosts, they were clearly grateful for the courtesy and attention shown them. Their sentiments were summed up, in part, by the famous Protestant theologian Oscar Cullmann, professor at the Sorbonne and the University of Basel, who disclosed in an interview (Nov. 23) that he was especially impressed by the freedom of the debates and the voicing of diametrically opposite concepts of fundamental religious positions. But he also noted the fathers' absolute agreement on the articles of the Creed, and their unanimous loyalty to the Holy See. He said he could see large areas for agreement between Catholic, Protestant, and Orthodox thought on many dogmatic issues. (Here, however, Dr. Cullmann was speaking mainly with reference to Continental Europe, where there are only two principal Protestant traditions, the Lutheran and the Calvinist.)*

The appearance, at the last minute on October 12, and contrary to everyone's expectations, of delegates from Moscow —the Archpriest Vitali Borovoi and the Archimandrite Vladimir Kotlyarov—in their long black robes and high-crowned hats, created something of a sensation.† Their arrival represented the first official connection between the Vatican and the Russian Church in hundreds of years. It was all the more remarkable in view of the fact that until very recently the Russians had been indulging in their usual innuendoes about the "power politics" of the Vatican. According to the Soviet news agency, Novosti, the Russian delegates expressed their pleasure at the "unaffected friendship" of the pope, but not everyone in Rome was pleased by their presence. The

---

* Full text of Dr. Cullmann's talk in *The Catholic Messenger,* Dec. 13, 1962.

† There have been a number of disclosures, since the above was written, regarding the background of their appointment, see *Catholic World,* Feb. 1963; ICI, Feb. 15, and *La Croix,* Feb. 16; also regarding the part played by them in effecting the dramatic release in February, 1963, of the exiled head of the Ukrainian Church, Archb. Slipyi, see report of Msgr. J. I. Tucek in *St. Louis Review,* Feb. 22, and *Time,* Feb. 22, 1963.

Ukrainian bishops of the Byzantine-Slavic rite outside Russia—active participants in the Council—met to formulate a
protest against Soviet persecution of the Church behind the
Iron Curtain. The Vatican Secretariat of State persuaded the
bishops to shelve the protest, but one of their number leaked
it to the Italian press, and as a consequence Msgr. Willebrands had to clarify the position of the Church (in a press
interview on Nov. 23) by stating that the Russians were most
welcomed, that there had been no dealings with the Soviet
government, and that their presence could not be interpreted
as a political maneuver.

The list of official observer-delegates who attended the
Council is as follows:

RUSSIAN ORTHODOX CHURCH (MOSCOW PATRIARCHATE): Archpriest
Vitaly Borovoy, professor at the Leningrad Theological Faculty, and Archimandrite Vladimir Kotlyarov, deputy-head of
the Russian Orthodox mission in Jerusalem.
COPTIC CHURCH OF EGYPT: Rev. Younna Girgis, and Dr. Mikhail
Tadros.
SYRIAN JACOBITE CHURCH: Rev. Ramban Zakka B. Iwas, and Rev.
Paul Varghese.
ETHIOPIAN CHURCH: Abbas Petros Gabre Sellassie, and Dr. Haile
Mariam Teshome.
ARMENIAN CATHOLICATE OF CILICIA: Archimandrite Karekin Sarkissian.
RUSSIAN ORTHODOX CHURCH OUTSIDE RUSSIA: Most Rev. Antony,
Bishop of Geneva, and Archpriest Igor Troyanoff.
OLD CATHOLIC CHURCH: Canon P. J. Maan, professor at the Seminary of Amersfoort, Holland.
ANGLICAN COMMUNION: Rt. Rev. Dr. John Moorman, Bishop of
Ripon, England; Rev. Dr. Frederick Grant, professor emeritus
of Union Theological Seminary, New York; Ven. Rev. Dr.
Harold de Soysa, Archdeacon of Colombo, Ceylon.
LUTHERAN WORLD FEDERATION: Dr. Kristen E. Skydsgaard, professor of systematic theology, University of Copenhagen;

Dr. George Lindbeck, professor of historical theology, Yale University.

WORLD PRESBYTERIAN ALLIANCE: Rev. Hébert Roux, of the Reformed Church of France; Dr. Douglas W. D. Shaw, of the Church of Scotland; Rev. Dr. James H. Nichols, professor at Princeton Theological Seminary.

EVANGELICAL CHURCH OF GERMANY: Dr. Edmund Schlink, professor at Heidelberg University.

DISCIPLES OF CHRIST: Rev. Jesse Bader, Secretary General of the World Convention of the Churches of Christ, N.Y.

WORLD SOCIETY OF FRIENDS (QUAKERS): Dr. Richard Ullmann, professor at Woodbrooke College, Birmingham, England.

INTERNATIONAL CONGREGATIONALIST COUNCIL: Rev. Dr. Douglas Horton, moderator of the Council, Cambridge, Mass.; Dr. George Caird, professor at Mansfield College, Oxford.

WORLD METHODIST COUNCIL: Bishop Fred. P. Corson, Philadelphia, Pa.; Dr. Harold Roberts, head of the Theological College, Richmond, England; Dr. Albert C. Outler, professor at Southern Methodist University, Dallas, Tex.

INTERNATIONAL ASSOCIATION FOR LIBERAL CHRISTIANITY: Dr. L. J. Van Holk, professor at Leiden University, Holland; Dr. J. L. Adams.

WORLD COUNCIL OF CHURCHES: Dr. Lukas Vischer, of the Council's Permanent Secretariat, Geneva.

SPECIAL GUESTS OF THE SECRETARIAT FOR CHRISTIAN UNITY: Most Rev. Bishop Cassian, rector of Orthodox Theological Institute of St. Sergius, Paris; Pastor Roger Schutz, prior of the Community of Taizé; Pastor Max Thurian, of the same Community; Dr. Oscar Cullmann, professor at the Universities of Basle and Paris (Lutheran); Dr. G. C. Berkouwer, professor at the Protestant University of Amsterdam; Rev. Dr. Joseph Jackson, president of the National Baptist Convention, Chicago, U.S.A.; Canon Bernard Pawley of Ely Cathedral, England, representative to the Secretariat of the Archbishops of Canterbury and York; Archpriest A. Schmemann, vice-dean of St. Vladimir's Orthodox Seminary, New York; Dr. Stanley J. Stuber, Jefferson City, U.S.A.

ALTERNATE DELEGATES: Dr. Vilmos Vajta, World Lutheran Federation; Dr. G. H. Williams, professor at Harvard University

(Congregationalist); Dr. F. Hildebrandt, professor at Drew University, Madison, U.S.A. (Methodist); Dean Robert E. Cushman, Duke Divinity School, Durham, N.C., U.S.A.; Reginald Kissack; Prof. V. Subilia, dean of the Theological Faculty of the Waldensian Church; Prof. Serge Grotoff; Dr. José Miguez Bonino.

Close to a thousand reporters were on hand for the opening days of the Council, and the coverage ranged from the world-wide news services to the Italian Communist daily *Unità*. Little by little, however, the number of journalists dwindled, owing to the nature of the Council and to the manner in which press relations were handled under the direction of Archbishop Felici, its Secretary General. The pope put at the disposal of the press a whole floor of the first building outside the Vatican on the Via della Conciliazione, but reporters were barred from the meetings and had to make do with distilled news contained in a daily bulletin prepared under the Secretary General's direction. Despite vociferous complaints from the press, this bulletin was often worded in such fashion that it seemed to be written in advance of the news it was reporting and dealt only in generalities, favoring the Curial line. Though the bulletin eventually became more informative,* it consistently disregarded the axiom that names and facts make news. As organized by members of the Curia, the Council was conducted in the strictest possible secrecy, but Italian commentators maintained that this only guaranteed the widest possible circulation for the Council's more intimate doings, and a pasquinade quickly made the rounds: "Why the great conciliar secrecy? Because secrets spread faster."

* The Holy Office threatened to excommunicate the Press Office for revealing the name of one of the Fathers in connection with a definite proposal—the only time that such a lapse occurred—in its bulletin relating to the 29th General Congregation on Nov. 28. The name in question was that of Cardinal Ottaviani. See *Irénikon*, 35 (1962) 540.

This challenge to journalistic enterprise was met by Paul Brindel, a free-lance American writer, who turned up in the back row of a choir during the Council mass on November 11, as official Vatican photographs later revealed. (He had been interviewing some young Califorians, protégés of Cardinal Agagianian, who were members of the Armenian choir, and he somehow obtained a cassock, joined their ranks, marched past three cordons of Swiss guards and Vatican plainclothes operatives, and entered St. Peter's through the sacristy door.) The London *Tablet,* one of the oldest and best Catholic weeklies, complained that the wording of one Council press release was couched in "English so peculiarly outrageous that one hardly knows whether to laugh or cry," and pointed out that in one document the word "condemn" appeared fifteen times in twenty-four pages, despite Pope John's inaugural address. It was not surprising that many applications for press credentials were lost, or that most reporters who obtained a blue leather *permesso* found it to be next to worthless; it did not even help them buy tax-free Vatican City cigarettes.

Perhaps the most striking moment at each day's meeting of the Council was the fifteen-minute period before the fathers came to order in St. Peter's and got down to the day's business. By that time most of the prelates were at or near their places in the two long banks of serrated benches covered in green, as well as in the six galleries between the central nave of the basilica. The episcopal purple contrasted here and there with a dash of the white, grey, brown or black religious habit worn by a Dominican, Franciscan, or Eastern-rite bishop, and with the brilliant scarlet of the cardinalatial robes.

Cardinals and bishops could be seen stopping one another in the aisles or on the benches, or being accosted by some eager ecclesiastic. Other prelates used this period for meditation and prayer, and many of them called this and the period which followed their favorite moments of the day. Precisely at nine, as the organ sounded, the fathers seemed to come to order simultaneously and were all at their places. When the mass, which was said each day in a different rite by the fathers in turn, was celebrated in Latin, the whole congregation of prelates and bishops answered the prayers in dialogue form. When mass was conducted by one of the Oriental bishops, a lector explained the diverse actions from the pulpit. Usually the Oriental liturgy required the assistance of a choir which was supplied by one of the appropriate colleges in Rome, such as the Russicum, the Maronite, the Greek, or Armenian.

During mass very few breviaries were in evidence, for the fathers realized that active participation in this official prayer of the Church was an essential part of their conciliar activity. On his return to the United States, Cardinal Ritter of St. Louis cited the 26 different rites used at these masses. Few bishops, he said, had any detailed knowledge of these different rites, let alone the opportunity to witness them. "And yet," he added, "the various rites have not only been tolerated but encouraged from Apostolic times." Cardinal Ritter called the Council "the grace of a lifetime."

The Council got under way at its first business session (1st General Congregation)* on Saturday, Oct. 13, under the presidency of Cardinal Tisserant. The agenda called for the election of members to the various conciliar Commissions, ten in all, the successors to the Preparatory Commissions, which were to present the draft proposals for decrees (schemata)†

---

* The term "Congregation" was officially used for the daily meetings, the word "Session" being reserved for the series of congregations from Oct. 11 to Dec. 8, as a whole. In addition to the plenary meetings of the Council, the various Conciliar Commissions also met to transact business.

† The Latin word *schema* (s. *schema*, pl. *schemata*) is customarily used for any kind of a documentary draft, especially the drafts of conciliar decrees or constitutions.

and consider the amendments proposed by the Council in the course of the debates. Sixteen members for each Commission were to be elected by the Council itself, while eight members would be appointed directly by the pope.

As soon as the Secretary General announced that the Council would proceed to the election, Cardinal Liénart of Lille rose and read a prepared statement in which he suggested that instead of voting immediately for the Commissions, the fathers meet in national or regional caucuses and attempt to agree upon slates of candidates for the different Commissions. He pointed to the fact that there were already some 47 episcopal conferences in existence, most of whose members were then in Rome, so that it would not be difficult to proceed in this way. He added that it would result in the choice of better candidates because the Council would have more time to consider qualifications, than if it acted immediately on the basis of a list of the members of the various Preparatory Commissions, distributed to the fathers at the beginning of the session.

Immediately Cardinal Frings of Cologne seconded the proposal of Cardinal Liénart and said that he was doing so in the names of the other German-speaking cardinals. The vigorous applause that greeted this unexpected move made it perfectly clear what the sentiments of the assembly were, and no vote was deemed necessary. After the Secretary General had consulted for a moment and informed the Council which cardinals could be elected to the ten Commissions, Cardinal Tisserant adjourned the meeting, after it had sat for only a bare fifteen minutes.

The repercussions and implications of this dramatic turn of events were endlessly commented on by the press. The French periodical *Informations Catholiques Internationales* (Nov. 1) characterized it as one of the three "curtain-raisers"

which set the tone of the first session of the Council in that
it expressed the Council's "courage to act"; the other two
being the pope's opening discourse ("courage to think") and
the Council's message to the world ("courage to speak").

Between Saturday and Tuesday, Oct. 16, when the Council
was scheduled to meet again to vote for the Commissions, the
fathers engaged in a feverish round of caucusing in an attempt
to agree upon lists of candidates. If the bishops had been
slow at first in getting to know each other, this consultation,
by breaking down barriers, served to fuse them into a real
corporate body. Different national or regional lists were
drawn up—Asian, African, Spanish, Italian, French, etc.—
but there was nothing exclusively nationalistic about them.
A serious effort was made to make them as international as
possible in fact, on the model of the Italian list which had
been compiled along these lines at the suggestion of Cardinal
Montini, seconded by Cardinal Siri. There were frequent
consultations between various groups with a view toward this
end, and in order to avoid the appearance of the formation
of exclusive national blocks. The combined list known as the
"Central and northern European" seems to have been the
most influential when the voting actually began on Oct. 16.

A difficulty arose when it was realized that the two-thirds
majority required by the regulations, in accordance with the
usual practice in canon law, would be difficult of attainment
and might prolong the elections unduly.* Accordingly Cardinal Ottaviani moved, on the 16th, that a simple majority
suffice for election. Since the Council was bound by the regulations, an appeal was made by the Council to the pope, who
ruled, before the first announcement of the results of the
balloting on Saturday, Oct. 20, that a simple majority would

---

* Art. 39 provided that a two-thirds majority was required for the first and
second balloting; only on the third balloting would a simple majority
suffice.

suffice, in accordance with the wishes of the majority of the Council. This proved to be the first of a number of significant papal interventions designed to speed the work of the Council in the sense desired by the majority.

Because the electronic computer was not capable of handling the ballots, the latter had to be counted by hand. This was done by pressing into service the seminarians who were attending the various ecclesiastical colleges and universities in Rome. When the Council reconvened on the 20th to hear the results, only the members of the first seven conciliar Commissions could be announced. The pope at once announced the appointment of the eight members for the Liturgical Commission reserved to him, so that that Commission could present the schema on the Liturgy which the Council was destined to take up on Monday, the 22nd. However, with respect to this and the other Commissions, he derogated from the rules by appointing nine instead of the required eight members, in order to give himself greater flexibility in controlling the composition of the Commissions. On the whole, the feeling was general that between the elected and appointed members, the Commissions turned out to be fairly representative of the Church, both as to schools of thought and nationalities, all things taken into consideration. The Council "did not vote for the Curia," although many of the same members served on both the Preparatory and corresponding conciliar Commission. The Italians felt slighted that they had not won better representation in the voting. The pope used his prerogative to redress this balance, to a certain extent, and also to round out the geographical distribution to the membership. It was noted that the ninth member the pope added to the Commissions in most cases turned out to be the Secretary of the corresponding Roman Congregation. The immediate purpose was apparently to pro-

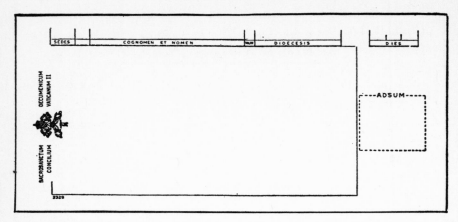

Ballots used by Council: for indicating attendance (*above*); for
voting on proposals (*below*)

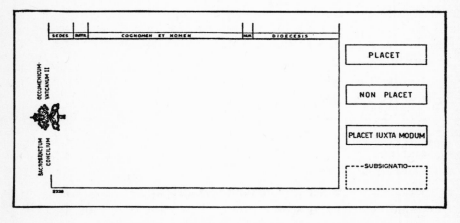

vide a certain continuity of experience. But as the course of
the Council proved, it was the majority of the Council itself
that would determine matters, not this or that member of one
of the auxiliary Commissions. (See page 90 for the complete
list of Commissions.)

After the results of the voting on the first seven commissions were made known to the fathers on Saturday, Oct. 20, at

SACROSANCTUM OECUMENICUM CONCILIUM VATICANUM II

SCHEDAE

**PRO ELIGENDIS SODALIBUS
COMMISSIONUM SACRI CONCILII**

(Subsignatio)

TYPIS POLYGLOTTIS VATICANIS — MCMLXII

Ballot for electing members of Conciliar Commissions

the third general congregation, a document was distributed to the fathers for their consideration. It was a "message to mankind" submitted by the Holy Father with the suggestion that it be amended, if necessary, and then proclaimed to the whole world as the first official act of the Council in ses-

Conciliar Commissions	Cardinal Presidents	Secretaries	Corresponding Congregation of Roman Curia
1. THEOLOGICAL (FAITH AND MORALS)	Cardinal Ottaviani	Fr. S. Tromp, S.J.	HOLY OFFICE
2. BISHOPS AND THE GOVT. OF DIOCESES	Cardinal Marella	Msgr. L. Governatori	CONGR. OF CONSISTORY
3. DISCIPLINE OF CLERGY AND FAITHFUL	Cardinal Ciriaci	Fr. A. Del Portillo	CONGR. OF COUNCIL
4. RELIGIOUS	Cardinal Valeri	Fr. J. Rousseau, O.M.I.	CONGR. OF RELIGIOUS
5. SACRAMENTS	Cardinal Masella	Fr. R. Bigador, S.J.	CONGR. FOR DISC. OF SACRA- MENTS
6. STUDIES AND SEMI- NARIES	Cardinal Pizzardo	Fr. A. Mayer, O.S.B.	CONGR. FOR SEMINARIES & UNIV.
7. MISSIONS	Cardinal Agagianian	Msgr. S. Paventi	PROPAGANDA FIDE
8. LITURGY	Cardinal Larraona	Fr. F. Antonelli, O.F.M.	CONGR. OF RITES
9. ORIENTAL CHURCHES	Cardinal A. Cicognani	Fr. A. G. Welykyj	CONGR. FOR OR. CHURCHES
10. APOSTOLATE OF LAITY, PRESS AND INFORMA- TION MEDIA	Cardinal Cento	Msgr. A. Glorieux Msgr. A. Galletto	Pont. Comm. for Cinema, Radio & TV
11. SECRETARIAT FOR PRO- MOTING UNITY (granted status of Commission, Oct. 19, 1962)	Cardinal Bea	Msgr. J. Willebrands	

sion. The fathers spent the whole morning considering
amendments that ran all the way from requests to insert a
clear and definitive condemnation of communism to an appeal not to say anything until the Council itself had produced its first accomplishment.

Bishop Guerry of Cambrai has revealed the true genesis of
this message of the Conciliar fathers to the world in an interview he gave soon after the Council's closing.* Early last September, several bishops wrote to the Cardinal Secretary of
State to draw his attention to the capital importance for the
Council to present a message to the world from its opening
and before the debates began on theological issues. They later
learned with considerable satisfaction that this idea had come
from two Dominican theologians, Fathers Chenu and Congar
who had drawn up a document with this end in mind, and
that they sent it to six cardinals in different countries. The
text was extremely interesting for it was based upon principles
of natural morality, thus rendering it proper for a dialogue
with non-Christians. But this would not suit a Council, as it
made no mention of Christ, the Savior. Hence it had to be
abandoned.

Four French bishops were then asked to prepare a suitable
text. They did so from an entirely different angle, namely, the
evidence for God's love of mankind. Their message drew attention to the Church's solicitude for the material and spiritual welfare of all people, their sufferings and aspirations. But
these cares and necessities were presented as a proof of man's
need for faithfulness to the Gospel of Christ and of Christ's
love for man. The announcement of the "good news" of eternal salvation for all corresponds to mankind's most profound
aspirations, and its deep longing for a Savior, Jesus Christ,
the unique Redeemer.

* *La Croix,* Jan. 10, 1963.

It was this message that was presented, at Pope John's insistence, first to the Cardinal Secretary of State, then to the Presidency of the Council, and finally to the fathers for their
discussion and approval. The only change admitted into the
original text was a reference to the Blessed Virgin, made on
the suggestion of Bishop Ancel, auxiliary to the archbishop of
Lyons.

During the remainder of this first session of the Council,
the pope went about his daily tasks almost as if nothing extraordinary were taking place in the great basilica below his
rooms. He issued a new constitution dealing with procedures
to be followed on the death of a pope, apparently to avoid the
kind of exploitation that seemed to have surrounded Pius
XII's death and burial. He appointed new bishops, apostolic
delegates and nuncios, and occasionally made a quick, unan-
nounced visit into Rome. Though he made frequent allusions
to his advanced age and the possibility of his passing on into
eternity soon (it was commonly being said in Rome that he
was to have an operation on December 10), his manner was
always cheerful and optimistic. He evidently felt that in summoning the Council, in addressing it as he did on the opening
day, and in starting the vast educative process for the bishops
that this great conciliar dialogue had become, he had carried
out the mandate given him by the Church. The rest was up to
the Holy Spirit.

SUMMARY

Jan. 25, 1959—Pope announces his intention to summon an Ecumenical Council at St. Paul's Outside the Walls.

May 16, 1959—Pope appoints an Ante-preparatory Commission, with Card. Tardini as President, to consult bishops about the agenda.

June 29, 1959—Encyclical *Ad Petri Cathedram* on the purpose of the Council.

June 5, 1960—Motu Proprio *Superno Dei nutu* announcing the appointment of the Preparatory Commissions and Secretariats.

Dec. 25, 1961—Pope signs the bull *Humanae Salutis* formally convoking the Council.

Feb. 2, 1962—Motu Proprio *Consilium* announcing that Council will convene on Oct. 11, 1962.

Sept. 5, 1962—Motu Proprio *Appropinquante Concilio* publishing Rules of Procedure for the Council.

Sept. 11, 1962—Pope broadcasts a message to the world one month before the opening of the Council.

Oct. 4, 1962—Pope's pilgrimage to Loreto and Assisi.

Oct. 11, 1962, Thursday—SOLEMN OPENING OF THE COUNCIL IN ST. PETER's, address by the pope.

Oct. 12, 1962, Friday—Pope addresses Diplomatic Corps and Special Missions to the Council.

Oct. 13, 1962, Saturday—Pope addresses journalists in the Sistine Chapel.

Pope addresses observer-delegates in the Consistory Hall.

1ST GENERAL CONGREGATION of the Council, voting on the Commissions postponed.

Oct. 15, 1962, Monday—Cardinal Bea receives the observer-delegates.

Pope receives Bishop Corson of Methodist Episcopal Church (U.S.A.).

Pope appoints 4 Under-Secretaries of the Council.

Oct. 16, 1962, Tuesday—2ND GENERAL CONGREGATION: voting for conciliar Commissions.

Pope receives ten members of Council of Presidents.

Oct. 17, 1962, Wednesday—Pope's weekly general audience.

Oct. 18, 1962, Thursday—Pope appoints Card. Wyszynski to Secretariat for Extraordinary Affairs, and names a fifth Under-Secretary of the Council.

Oct. 19, 1962, Friday—Secretariat for Promoting Christian Unity granted status equivalent to that of a conciliar Commission (announced 10/22, 1962).

Oct. 20, 1962, Saturday—3RD GENERAL CONGREGATION: Announcement of results of election of Commission Members; Council's Message to the World; papal appointments to Liturgical Commission.

IV

The Debate on the "Liturgy"

ON MONDAY, October 22, in the 4th General Congregation, with Cardinal Gilroy presiding, discussion of the schema on the liturgy was inaugurated by Cardinal Larraona, chairman of the Preparatory Liturgical Commission, who described how the Church must keep abreast of the times by adapting its ceremonies to the necessities of individual nations and peoples. The Secretary of the Commission, Fr. F. Antonelli, O.F.M., then gave a brief résumé of the eight chapters comprised in the schema.*

---

* SCHEMA ON THE LITURGY (*De Sacra Liturgia*): Preface; Chap. I: General principles concerning liturgical renewal and development; Chap. II: Mystery of the eucharist, the mass, con-celebration; Chap. III: Sacraments and sacramentals; Chap. IV: Divine office; Chap. V: Liturgical year and calendar; Chap. VI: Sacred ornaments; Chap. VII: Sacred music; Chap. VIII: Sacred art.

This chore accomplished, the fathers turned their attention to the schema itself. Its proposals were both praised by the progressive-minded bishops as an important step toward the modernization of the Church, and condemned by the traditionalist bishops as undesirable, with a number of them manifesting a determined opposition to any change in the ceremonies of the Church and insisting especially on the retention of Latin in the mass as a guarantee of the Church's unity.

The debate was initiated by Cardinal Frings of Cologne, followed by Cardinals Ruffini of Palermo, Lercaro of Bologna, Montini of Milan, Spellman of New York, Doepfner of Munich, Tatsuo Doi of Tokyo, Silva Henriquez of Santiago, Chile—all men of considerable experience, who in varying degrees had tried to adapt the Church's prayers and ceremonial practices to the requirements of a people whose outlook on life, preoccupation with social and economic problems, and emotional and intellectual interests, differed immeasurably from those of past ages. The present liturgical practice of the Church was formulated for the most part at a time when an agricultural society was dominated by a monastic spirituality.

It was pointed out by Cardinals Frings, Lercaro, Montini, Doepfner and Doi that the schema generally was in keeping with the necessities of the hour, for it reflected Pope John's admonition that the Council should concern itself with concrete facts, with the pastoral and practical aspects of the Church's mission in the world. It was likewise asserted that it had an ecumenical appeal. The document was essentially "Christo-centric" in character, based on a scriptural piety and spirituality. However, it was quickly noted by the two German cardinals that the original document prepared by the Liturgical Commission had been altered; certain important sections dealing with the biblical foundations of the liturgy had been suppressed, while an admonition had been inserted cautioning that the schema laid down only general principles, for the application of which direct recourse must be had to the Holy See. As the speakers pointed out, this latter insertion, "by unknown hands," could strip the conciliar decisions of their effect, leaving the reforms considered so essential by the bishops at the mercy of certain Roman officials, as had been the case up to the present. Hence they asked that the original text be introduced into the discussion.*

What a large number of bishops desired, and this was in accord with the first chapter of the schema, was that national or regional commissions be constituted that would have power to legislate the liturgical requirements of different nations; and that at Rome, a central commission made up of experts and representatives of the regional groups should meet periodically to coordinate and supervise the work of these local groups. In the end, of course, the approbation of the Holy See would be required since it is the pope's prerogative and duty to safeguard the doctrine and practices of the Church. In effect, such an arrangement would however greatly reduce the powers of the Sacred Congregation of Rites, which up to now has been the sole legislative body for the Church's liturgy.

Involved in this discussion was a much deeper problem, namely that of the extent of the power of bishops, both as individual governors of dioceses and as a collegiate body in succession to the college of Apostles. Roman officials had generally shown little liking for the national conferences of bishops that had been multiplying in various lands during the last fifty years. But as the recent constitution of such a body for the South American bishops, encouraged particularly by

---

* These changes were made *after* the text had been approved by the Central Commission and *before* it was circulated to the bishops. Cf. Henri Fesquet in *Le Monde*, Oct. 24, 1962.

Archbishop Samoré of the Vatican Secretariat of State, has proved, such an agency has become an essential instrument for coordinating the Church's efforts to safeguard the faith and win back the disaffected in large areas of the world. The debate on the liturgy was thus the occasion for a preliminary skirmish in what would prove to be one of the essential problems before the Council.

A large amount of conciliar interest was aroused by the apparently innocuous question of the use of Latin in the western liturgy generally. Cardinals Ruffini and Spellman were the first to broach this topic, commenting on the schema's preface which lays down the principle that the vernacular languages should be employed more generally in the mass and in the administration of the sacraments. The Cardinal of New York expressed his opinion that, for the sake of unity and uniformity, the mass in Latin as it is now celebrated in the Roman rite should be retained intact. But he favored the use of the vernacular in most of the other ceremonies of the Church.

The Apostolic Delegate to the United States, Archbishop Vagnozzi, condemned the schema as badly constructed and full of loose definitions. He suggested that it be reworked on the basis of Pius XII's encyclical *Mediator Dei* and referred to the Theological Commission presided over by Cardinal Ottaviani.

Msgr. Enrico Dante, the papal Master of Ceremonies and Secretary of the S. Congregation of Rites, rose to condemn the schema as both ill-conceived and too radical. In his opinion it should be reduced to a few simple principles. He stated that while the conferences of bishops in different countries might propose changes to the Holy See, it was only Rome that could decide what should and should not be done. He insisted that the mass must continue to be said in Latin, as well as the Breviary, by all those bound to recite the divine office daily.

He complained, finally, that the schema was incomplete for it said nothing about the veneration of relics. This latter point was seized upon by the Spanish prelate who followed him, Bishop García Martínez, who rose to ask how much longer the Church was to be embarrassed by such "relics" as Our Blessed Lady's milk and veil, St. Joseph's sandals, and the like. He had to be cut off by the President, Cardinal Gilroy, with *"Satis, satis,"* but not before he had managed to suggest that these things "be reverently buried and heard of no more" (*reverenter sepeliantur et deinceps nulla mentio fiat*).

The general discussion on the liturgy was continued on the following day, Oct. 23, in the 5th General Congregation presided over by Cardinal Spellman. In his first speech on this theme, Cardinal Ottaviani cautioned the fathers to be clear and precise in their employment of theological terminology. He questioned the propriety, for example, of the use of such terms as "the Paschal mysteries," and threw cold water on the notion that the liturgy ought to be a principal means of instructing the people, thus revealing his opposition to the whole tenor and purpose of the liturgical movement. He suggested that the schema ought to be referred to his own Theological Commission for an overhauling. Cardinal Ritter of St. Louis then spoke in favor of the schema, contenting himself with general observations about its implementation. He was followed by a succession of prelates (including Fares of Catanzaro, Italy; Argaya Goicoechea of Spain; and D'Avack of Camerino, Italy), who were critical of the schema.

At this point Cardinal Spellman allowed a narrator to speak for him, because the fathers were having difficulty in understanding him. The Council then turned its attention to Chapter I of the schema, and the discussion was led off by Cardinal Ruffini who felt that the schema as a whole should be reconsidered in the light of the principles enunciated by *Mediator Dei,* in particular by the thought that the Holy Father is to remain judge in these matters and that he alone (through the Curia, of course) was to decide; hence conferences or groups of bishops were to have no competence. Great prudence must be exercised in introducing the use of vernacular languages because of the danger to the Church's unity . . .

Cardinal Feltin of Paris then spoke on a more practical level. He made it plain that most people today knew little about the Church. If by chance the poorly instructed Catholic or even non-Catholic layman should find himself at mass, it ought to be immediately obvious to him that he was witnessing something tremendously significant, holy and profound. But, as things are at the present time, said the Cardinal, with the priest praying at the altar in Latin, accompanied by some of the congregation in a dialogue mass, or more commonly with the latter completely silent, the impression was easily given that the viewer was witnessing some kind of magical rites, good perhaps for those who understood them, but meaningless as far as the ordinary person was concerned. Actually the mass was the Word of God in action, bringing Christ to the hearts of the faithful by the prayers and lessons of the introductory or catechetical part, and then representing both the Last Supper and the sacrificial act of redemption on the Cross in the offertory, consecration and communion. The sanctification thus enacted should be immediately obvious to believer and unbeliever alike; but this could only be accomplished if both were fully aware of what was being said and done. For the actions as well as the words are sacramental signs. If the words have no immediate meaning for the people, they are failing in one of their primary objectives.

Cardinal McIntyre of Los Angeles spoke in favor of the unaltered retention of Latin in the mass and the Church's existing liturgical legislation. Cardinal Godfrey also opted for a conservative approach; as regards the use of Latin, he was for its retention *in toto* in the mass: *"Debemus levare linguam Latinam,"* he said, meaning, elevate it, increase its importance. Because *levare* in Italian means to pick up and throw away, Cardinal Godfrey was horrified to find himself reported next day in the Italian newspaper *Il Tempo* as having said that Latin should be abolished!

Quite apart from its use in the liturgy, Latin as a medium of communication at the Council proved to be less than a success. Experience showed that many of the fathers did not understand spoken Latin well enough to grasp what was being said. Cardinal Cushing, of Boston, is said to have informed the pope frankly of his feeling that a more realistic attitude was needed toward the use of Latin as the language of its sessions. (The story went around that at one of the preparatory meetings, when Cardinal Cushing started to speak in English and was admonished by Monsignor Felici, he asked a neighboring prelate to inform the gathering in Latin that he represented "the Church of Silence.") Even in discussions of simple procedural matters, some bishops came alive only when the proposals were translated into Spanish, Italian, French, English, German, or Arabic. Under these circumstances, it was practically impossible for an assembly of nearly three thousand prelates to "deliberate" or to absorb the more intricate speeches. The old saw that "Latin is the official language of the Church" was simply not borne out at the Council. The Secretariat for Promoting Unity, under Cardinal Bea, was farsighted enough to provide a fairly full translation service for the non-Catholic observer-delegates, and many of the bishops probably wished that the same had been done for them. In fact, long before the Council met, a simultaneous-translation system had been proposed. The pope is said to have suggested that the United Nations translation experts in Geneva be consulted, but Secretary General Felici never got around to it.

The matter is again under consideration, and it is reported that plans are being made for the installation of a simultaneous-translation system before next September.

One of the most interesting discourses at the Council was given by Maximos IV Saigh, Melchite Patriarch of Antioch, who in the last speech of this day (Oct. 23) ignored the Council's language barrier and spoke in French. The fathers were delighted by this eighty-four year old prelate from the East, who proved to be one of the most colorful figures at the Council. Desiring to focus attention on an old grievance whereby according to Vatican protocol the Oriental patriarchs have been ranked below the cardinals since the fifteenth century at least, whereas in antiquity and in the early Middle Ages they were traditionally regarded as coming immediately after the pope himself (Lateran Council IV under Pope Innocent III, decreed in 1215 that the order of precedence was: Rome, Constantinople, Alexandria, Antioch, and Jerusalem for the major sees), he had ostentatiously absented himself from the inaugural procession on the opening day of the council.*

Speaking in this day's debate the patriarch began by addressing, first, "their Beatitudes" the Patriarchs, and then "their Eminences" the Cardinals, a subtle maneuver that apparently escaped the attention of Cardinal Spellman who was presiding, but was caught by other alert fathers. Justifying his use of French instead of Latin, he said that the latter was not the language of the Eastern Church, and that as a consequence he felt it only proper to use a more universal tongue in addressing so Catholic a gathering:

> Even though this schema only concerns the Roman rite, I hope that I will be allowed to bring to the debate the testimony of a

* The pope has recently acted to rectify this situation, in part at least, by naming six of the patriarchs as members of the Congregation for the Oriental Churches. Hitherto only cardinals have been members of Curial congregations. *The Advocate*, Newark, N.J., Mar. 21, 1963.

patriarch of the East, who follows with great interest the progress of the liturgical movement in the Latin Church . . . I must say first of all that the schema is excellent taken as a whole, with the exception of a few amendments which the bishops concerned are not likely to fail to make. The schema does honor to the Commission which prepared it, and in a more general way, to the liturgical movement which inspired it.

I must admit, however, that the principle enunciated at the head of clause No. 24 appeared to me to be too positive: *latinae linguae usus in liturgia occidentali servetur.* It seems to me that the almost absolute value which this attempts to give to Latin in the liturgy, both in the teaching and in the administration of the Latin Church, is a sign of something which, to the Eastern Church is sufficiently abnormal. Christ, after all, talked in the language of His contemporaries. It was also in Aramaic that He offered the first sacrifice of the eucharist, in a language understood by all the people who heard Him. The Apostles and the Disciples did the same. It would never have occurred to them that, in a Christian assembly, the celebrant should deliver the scriptural lessons, or sing the psalms, or preach, or break bread, in a language other than that of the gathered faithful. St. Paul even tells us quite explicitly: "If thou dost pronounce a blessing in this spiritual fashion [that is to say, speaking an incomprehensible language], how can one who takes his place among the uninstructed say Amen to thy thanksgiving? He cannot tell what thou art saying. Thou, true enough, art duly giving thanks, but the other's faith is not strengthened . . . In the church, I would rather speak five words which my mind utters for your instruction, than ten thousand in a strange tongue" (1 Cor. 14:16–19). All the reasons quoted in favor of keeping Latin untouched—a liturgical but dead language—must give way before this clear, sound and precise reasoning of the Apostle.

In other respects, the Roman Church as well used Greek in her liturgy up to the third century, because it was the language used by the faithful of those times. And if then she started to abandon Greek in favor of Latin, it is precisely because Latin had become the language of the faithful. Why should the same principle not apply today? . . .

In the Western Church, it was only in the Middle Ages that

Latin was looked on as the only universal language of the Roman civilization and of the Holy Roman Empire, as opposed to the languages of the barbarian nations which dominated Europe. In addition, the Western Church made Latin her official and sacred tongue.

The East, on the contrary, never had a problem on the subject of liturgical language. Every language is, in effect, liturgical, for, following the advice of the psalmist: *laudate Dominum omnes gentes,* it is proper to glorify God, preach the Gospel, and offer the sacrifice in any language whatsoever. And we in the East never imagined that the faithful could be brought together to pray in a language which they do not understand.

The Latin language is dead; but the Church remains alive; and language, the vehicle of grace and of the Holy Ghost, should be clear and alive, for it is for men and not for angels; no language should be untouchable.

We all admit, though, that, in the Latin rite, the adoption of the vernacular should be made step by step and with the precautions demanded by prudence.

But I would propose first that some of the rigidity of the initial principle contained in clause No. 24 (lines 10–11), which reads: *linguae latinae usus in liturgia occidentali servetur,* should be softened to: *lingua Latina est lingua originalis et officialis ritus Romani.*

Secondly, I propose that it be left to episcopal councils in each region to decide if, and to what extent, it is convenient or not to adopt the vernacular in the liturgy. The text only leaves the episcopal conferences the responsibility of proposing the adoption to the Holy See—but there is no need to have an episcopal conference to put forward such a proposal. Any of the faithful could. Episcopal conferences should not be called just to propose, but to decide something, subject to the approval of the Holy See.

I propose, therefore, that clause No. 24 should end thus (lines 16–19): *sit vero conferentiae episcopalis in singulis regionibus . . . limites et modum linguae vernaculae in liturgiam admittendae statuere, actis sancta sede recognitis.* (Let the conference of bishops decide for each region what is to be the manner and the limits of the use of vernacular in the liturgy, the acts being approved by the Holy See.)*

In the next ten sessions the question of the use of Latin became a sort of shibboleth, separating into two camps those who were determined to bring to bear the whole vast depository of the Church's teaching and experience in dealing with the problems raised by the modern world; and those who were equally determined to restrain the Church's thinking and its liturgical practice within the narrow confines of a western juridically-oriented tradition. The latter group quickly rallied round Cardinal Ottaviani and the ultra-conservative faction including, not too surprisingly, most of the older Roman cardinals, with the Irish Dominican Cardinal Browne as their professional, scholastic theologian. The majority of these men had limited pastoral experience, and apparently lacked the breadth of vision that would have enabled them to rally to the papal plea for a renewal of the Church. Yet it was these very men, curiously, who were loudest in their protestations of loyalty toward the Holy See and in their often-expressed concern for safeguarding the rights of the Holy Father. It was unfortunate that this juridical concept was supported by so many Italian and Spanish bishops, men who had shown little sympathy for the need to modernize the apostolate of the Church in their own dioceses, as well as by certain American and Irish bishops, who seemed uninterested in the basic issues or were quite content with things as they were back home. This attitude was reflected, for example, in the remark of the Cardinal of Los Angeles to a fellow bishop who questioned his unbending opposition to all liturgical reform: "You must be a reader of *Worship!*" (This well edited monthly, published by the Benedictines of Collegeville, Minnesota, has

* Text in *La documentation catholique*, Nov. 18, 1962, and *The Tablet*, Nov. 10, 1962.

been influential in spreading knowledge of the liturgical movement and is widely read by the younger clergy.)

While the Council was in session the prelates from the United States held meetings every Monday at the North American College. They were at first dominated by blocs under Cardinals Spellman and McIntyre, but as Cardinals Ritter and Meyer gained in stature owing to their stand in the conciliar discussions, their leadership made itself felt among the bishops, first from the mid-west and then among a considerable group of the younger men from both the east and the west coasts. Those American bishops who had contact with the prelates and theologians of other lands quickly caught on to the immense educative value of the Council's doings. Unfortunately a number sat at home in their hotels or pensions, bemoaning the waste of time and the interminable longwindedness of the oratory. They left Rome, happily, at the close of the first session almost as uninformed as they were upon arrival. As one prelate was heard to remark, "The Holy Spirit came and departed at the Council and some of these people never even dreamed He had been there."

The 6th General Congregation on Wednesday, Oct. 24, was conducted under the presidency of Cardinal Pla y Deniel. It began with the celebration of mass according to the Byzantine rite by Archbishop Nabaa of the Melchite Patriarchate of Antioch, one of the Under-Secretaries of the Council, with the students of the Greek College supplying the choral parts. It was a moment of sadness, for on entering the Basilica that morning the 83 year-old, retired Archbishop Aston Chichester, S.J., of Salisbury, Southern Rhodesia, had suddenly dropped dead.

Cardinal Tisserant of the Vatican Library led off the debate by stating that Latin was not the only liturgical language, calling to the fathers' attention the fact that Hebrew and Greek had been used by the original Christians, as was indicated by the inscription on the cross in Hebrew, Greek and Latin. He said that the Slavic languages as well as Chinese had been recognized by the Congregation of Rites as permissible liturgical languages, noting, incidentally, that a unique copy of the only missal in the Chinese language could be seen in the Vatican Library.

On rising to talk, the tall graceful Indian Cardinal Gracias of Madras spoke of himself as a voice crying in the desert and said that since becoming a bishop he had incessantly striven for a readaptation of the liturgy. However, from his own background he recognized the difficulty caused by the great diversity of languages in the same cultural milieu and country. Still the vernacular languages were absolutely necessary for instructing the ordinary people as well as giving them a taste of a true Christian experience. He felt in the end that the question of languages should be left to the decision of conferences of bishops.

Cardinal Bea said that the development of thought on the liturgy seemed insufficiently mature to allow the Church to proceed with the founding of a totally new rite, but that the conciliar fathers should not close their eyes to the possibility of such a change.

Cardinal Bacci, on the other hand, was absolute in saying that the mass could not be celebrated in the national languages. He reminded the Council that in the middle of the last century Fr. Rosmini had been condemned for asserting that the use of Latin in the church's ceremonies served to erect a barrier between the people and the priest. He could see no difficulty in allowing the people to read their missals in the vernacular while the priest was celebrating in Latin at the altar. For him Latin was the bond of unity. Yet he could see that in the administration of some of the sacraments it might be necessary to use the popular languages, but this should not be done without Roman authorization for it was inconceivable that such a decision should be left to episcopal conferences. In that case, what would become of our unity?

The archbishop of Chicago, Cardinal Meyer rose to say that he was fully in accord with art. 24 of the schema, which legitimized the use of the vernacular languages in the liturgy, but he could see no reason why this matter had to be handed over to episcopal conferences for solution. What was wrong, he wanted to know, with the bishops individually making such decisions under the control of the Holy Father?

Archbishop Van Lierde, the pope's Sacristan, who was in charge of ceremonies in St. Peter's, spoke on the liturgy as a spiritual pedagogy and expressed himself in favor of a moderate use of popular languages in order that this function of the liturgy might be better emphasized.

Archbishop McQuaid of Dublin announced that he was not at all against the Latin language. He wanted it retained as now in the mass, but could see the utility of allowing the vernacular in the administration of the sacraments. He said that each bishop now had the power to determine what was proper in this matter for his own diocese and should not have to submit his judgment to national conferences of bishops.

Bishop Descuffi of Smyrna said that he could only express his joy at having heard so many speaking out on behalf of the need for having the mass said in the vernacular languages, for the liturgy was for the benefit of men and not men for the liturgy (*liturgia propter homines et non homines propter liturgiam*). Finally it was wrong to say that special arrangements should be made only for missionary countries, for today every country was a missionary country.

Bishop Gonçalves do Amaral (Brazil) reminded the fathers that the humanity of Christ was simply an instrumental cause of salvation and that the mystery of salvation, therefore, which is communicated through the liturgy, need not really be expressed in the vernacular languages. On the other hand, Bishop Ramantoamina (Madagascar) took the viewpoint that both liturgical custom and language should be adapted in accordance with the cultures foreign to the Latin milieu, such as one finds, for example, in the missionary areas of Africa and the South Pacific.

Archbishop Parente, Assessor of the Holy Office, expressed the irritation of the Curia with the implied criticism levelled against the arch-conservatives. "Many things have been said here," he declared, "which were neither prudent, just, nor consistent. The schema limps in its very preface; hence it ought to be turned over completely to the Theological Commission for reworking." He wound up by complaining about the continual attacks on the Holy Office and the disdain with which it was treated. "At the Holy Office we are all martyrs," he exclaimed. "We have already yielded on many points, yet this is the thanks we get! If any changes are to be sanctioned by the Council, they must be made with the greatest prudence (*maxima cum prudentia*)."

His colleague, Archbishop Dino Staffa, Secretary of the Roman Congregation of Seminaries and Studies, took much the same line. The maintenance of Latin in the liturgy was essential to preserving the Church's unity. Only the Holy See had the right to make decisions for the Church with regard to rites as well as doctrine. There could be no question of episcopal conferences having anything to do with such matters.

It was noted that while Archbishop Parente would speak one or two times more, these were the only interventions in the debate by Archbishops Vagnozzi, Staffa, and Dante.

The day's debate was brought to a close by the speeches of Archb. Gawlina (Poland), whose flow of oratory had to be interrupted by the President, and Archbishop Seper (Zagreb), who suggested that as Christians were so obviously in a minority in the modern world, every assistance should be extended to them to live the faith as well as possible, and this required that the whole treasury of the liturgy be open to them in a language that they could understand.

Cardinal Siri (Genoa) opened the proceedings on Oct. 26 by again stressing the theme that the schema should be referred to the Theological Commission because it touched on theological matters. It was dangerous to multiply rites. This left the door open to abuses and constituted a threat to unity. Episcopal conferences might *"proponere,"* but they could not *"statuere."* The Holy See must decide everything on its own authority. And the bishops were reminded of the great importance which the Church attached to the maintenance of Latin as evidenced by the publication earlier in the year of the papal constitution *Veterum sapientiae.**

Speaking in the name of the Dutch episcopate, Bishop Bekkers ('s-Hertogenbosch) said that while the schema was not perfect it embodied the substance of what was necessary for a revival, in the hearts of the faithful, of the mystery-laden life of grace in Christ through a meaningful attendance at mass and participation in the sacraments. On the prerogatives of bishops in these matters, it certainly was the Holy Father's right and duty to reserve certain powers to himself in dealing with individual dioceses or the whole Church. But as successors to the Apostles, the bishops possessed sufficient powers in these matters even though at present they were not exercising them out of deference and loyalty to the Holy See.

Bishop Ancel, auxiliary of Lyons, thought that the schema

* Feb. 22, 1962, on the study and use of Latin in the Latin Church. AAS, vol. 54 (1962) 129. Actually a forewarning of the attempt to keep theology in its hidebound forms was supplied in 1961 by the then Msgr. Staffa in a talk he gave for the inauguration of the Lateran University. He made three points: an undeviating scholastic approach in philosophy and theology; a vigorous pursuit of the dictates of Canon Law; and an unswerving use of Latin.

fully corresponded to the pastoral emphasis which the pope
desired the decisions of the Council to have. Unity did not
mean that there must be uniformity of rites. There was a
marvelous variety between the eastern and western liturgies
and this very variety was a mark of the beauty of the Church.*
Those bishops who had no pastoral charge were urged to try
to understand the plight of pastors who were faced with situa-
tions in which the Church was considered moribund, and
appreciate their longing for a liturgical renewal. Bishops who
still enjoyed the security of large, docile congregations were
asked not to close their hearts and eyes to the needs of those
living in dechristianized areas, where the mere pouring in of
money would be of little use. He could speak, he said, for a
large number of priests who were frequently seeking his counsel and encouragement in their attempt to revitalize the
Church and awaken a spiritual awareness in the lives of their
people. Two criteria ought to govern those who would adapt
the liturgy: they must have a profound knowledge of and
feeling for the liturgy; and they must understand the local
psychology. No adaptation would be worthwhile unless it
took these two things into account.

A large number, perhaps the majority, of western prelates
were inclined to agree with Bishop Calewaert of Gand, Belgium, who thought that it was best to retain Latin as the language of the principal parts of the mass in the Roman rite, at
least in those countries where the Church was long established
and people were used to it, reserving the vernacular for the

* Cf. the pope's remarks at the solemn papal chapel in St. Peter's, according to the Slavic Byzantine rite, in honor of St. John Chrysostom, on Nov.
13, 1960: "This association of various rites and languages and a different
approach to the mystery of the Trinity is a first and solemn manifestation
of respect for the unity of this divine institution which the Church is. No
beauty is comparable to the multiplicity of rites, languages, images and sym-
bols in which the liturgy is so rich, variously expressing the intimate union
of the faithful who constitute the Mystical Body of Christ." Also on many
other occasions. *Discorsi,* vol, 3, pp. 5–6.

catechetical or dialogue portion at the beginning of the mass, and for all other liturgical functions.

Yet Bishop Rau of Mar del Plata, Argentina, was for jettisoning Latin altogether in public or parish masses, as an obstacle to the prayer-life of the faithful. "The Church as such," he said, "has no proper culture of its own and therefore no proper language . . . The liturgy is employed *ratione signi,* after the fashion of a sign, actualizing what is signified; hence if its actions are not immediately understood by the participants, it is impeded in its effects . . . I will be faithful unto death to the Roman Church, but not to the Latin language!" were his final remarks.

Bishop Lokuang of Taiwan called attention to the very serious mistake made by the Roman Curia in the seventeenth and eighteenth centuries when it destroyed the work of the Chinese missions by condemning adaptations to Chinese customs.* He maintained that the Communists have made the problem a very live issue today. "If our people do not pray in their own language, they are accused of subservience to a foreign nationalism . . ." The latter theme was stressed on a later occasion by Bishop Spülbeck (Meissen, East Germany), speaking on behalf of the bishops of East Germany. Most of the Polish bishops likewise testified that the introduction of the Polish language in the mass, which had been in effect for the past fifteen years, was the salvation of the faith in their country.

The Japanese Bishop Kobayashi, speaking on the following day, Oct. 27, noted that the question of the use of national languages was most important to the Japanese. His people had an ancient cultural tradition of their own and Latin could only appear to them as something western and alien. It was a

* Cf. Benedict XIV's bull *Omnium sollicitudinum* of Sept. 12, 1744. The Jesuit missionaries, beginning with Matteo Ricci, were the principal exponents of the policy of adaptation.

mistake to tie Christianity to the Latin, and therefore, western tradition. The salvation of souls should not be sacrificed to a uniformity that was purely secondary. "Is our unity with the Holy See so feeble that it has to be maintained by a rigid uniformity?" he asked. His remarks were greeted with applause.

Later the same day, toward the end of the 7th General Congregation, Bishop Muldoon of Australia voiced the general feeling of the fathers when he suggested that sufficient discussion had now taken place on the preface and chapter I of the schema and that the matter should be put to a vote. This intervention was received with loud applause. But the President, Cardinal Ruffini, said that while many fathers had withdrawn their request to speak, it was impossible, under the existing rules, to curtail the right of anyone who wanted to speak. No rule of cloture had been devised by the committee responsible for drawing up the Rules of Procedure.

The following Monday, however, in the 9th General Congregation on Oct. 29, 1962, the Presidential board decided to bring the current discussion to an end and pass on to chapter II of the schema, dealing with the mass.

In the first speech on the new matter, Cardinal Spellman agreed with the need for active participation of the laity in the mass, but came out strongly against giving them communion with both bread and wine, as recommended in the schema, in keeping with the words of Christ: "Unless you eat the flesh of the Son of man and drink his blood . . ." (Jn. 6:53) and as had been the custom in the Roman Church down to at least the twelfth century. He was also against the concelebration of mass by a number of priests using one altar and going through the words and actions together. His priests, he remarked, frequently had to say three masses each on Sundays to accommodate all the people coming to church, and even on week days there were times when it was difficult to get a

priest to take care of the ordinary parish masses, funerals
and weddings. Hence he could see no need for such an innovation. He was on less solid ground in the judgment of
competent theologians, however, when he attempted to argue
that concelebration involved the Church in a loss of graces.
On the cardinal's behalf, it is only fair to add that a certain
theologian had told the American bishops that when 100
priests concelebrated, the Church was 99 masses short.

He was seconded by Cardinal Ruffini who cited hygienic
reasons against giving wine to the faithful, and the inconveniences for priests and churches in the matter of concelebration.
However he insisted it was the right of the Holy See alone to
make concessions in such matters.

The last speech of the day fell like a bombshell on the
assembly. It was made by Cardinal Léger of Montreal who
came out four-square both for concelebration by groups of
priests when possible, and for giving both bread and wine to
the people in the eucharist. He said that, as was demonstrated
in the Oriental rites where both these practices prevailed, it
was a sign of true unity and mutual charity to have a number
of priests around the same table imitating Christ and the
Apostles at the Last Supper. As for the inconveniences, he
could visualize none, other than the need for priests, in charity, to synchronize their prayers and actions at the altar. After
all, the mass was not a private devotion of the priest; it was
always a public function of the Church with the priest as
minister and the people as participants. He cited likewise the
daily practice of the Oriental rites in giving communion under both bread and wine; hence he could see no hygienic
problem. Finally he asked that the original text of the whole
liturgical schema as it left the Preparatory Commission be
brought into the discussions.

On October 30, in the 10th General Congregation, with
Cardinal Alfrink in the chair as President, the Cardinal of

England, Godfrey, attempted in a general fashion to reply to
the assertions of the Cardinal of Montreal. He was afraid that
the return to the practice of giving communion with both
bread and wine in a country such as his would lead people to
think that the Catholic Church was giving in to the Anglicans
and some of the other Protestant bodies who had retained this
practice. But he was even more concerned for hygienic reasons, because women with lipstick regularly approached the
altar for communion. Finally, he asked, what about reformed
alcoholics and abstentionists and prohibitionists? As for concelebration of mass, he could conceive of its propriety on
Holy Thursday, and in monasteries where a number of monks
might say mass together on private altars and for certain other
special gatherings of priests. But he felt generally that when
offering a stipend for a mass people would prefer to have it
said by one priest alone.

In his talk, Cardinal Gracias of Bombay, made reference to
the danger in which India stood at the moment with the Chinese penetrating its northern borders. He felt that much precious time was now being wasted in the Council for lack of a
proper order of business. On this matter of liturgical details,
for example, it should be left to the conferences of bishops in
each land to decide these things. He suggested that an accord
be reached, with the Holy Father's permission, giving the
bishops proper authority to decide, and that the Council
should then move on to the more important business relating
to other schemata. He spoke, he said, in the name of 72 Indian bishops, many of whom were seriously considering returning to their country in its hour of need. He requested the
prayers of the assembly for his native land and its leader,
Mr. Nehru.

Cardinal Bueno y Monreal of Seville discussed the question
of the eucharistic fast, with particular reference to evening
masses. Then Cardinal Alfrink rose to say that in the matter

of giving communion to the faithful, he was not bothered by matters of history, or theology, or hygiene. In refusing to give the chalice to the laity, the Church was depriving them of their right to conform to Christ's injunction. Since there were differences of opinion among the fathers with regard to this matter, he advocated that its solution be left to individual conferences of bishops in each land or area.

It was at this point that the famous speech of Cardinal Ottaviani occurred, after which he absented himself from the Council's public deliberations until Nov. 14. He rose to reply to Cardinal Alfrink in particular. What made the situation even more dramatic was that Cardinal Alfrink was the President of the day.

Seeing the way the wind had been blowing during the past few days, with determined expressions of opinion by such eminent figures as Cardinals Frings of Cologne, Doepfner of Munich, Doi of Tokyo, Léger of Montreal, Ritter of St. Louis and Meyer of Chicago, as well as the African bishops almost in a body, in favor of changes of all kinds, particularly regarding the use of the vernacular in the mass, the restoration of communion under both kinds on special occasions, and so on, Cardinal Ottaviani rose to ask, "Are these fathers planning a revolution?" He warned against scandalizing the faithful by introducing too many changes (an old Holy Office saw). He maintained that the proposal to have communion under both kinds had been turned down by a large majority in the Central Preparatory Commission, and it was only a small minority that was pressing for it now. He was against concelebration because it made the mass seem like something happening in a theater (an unintentional slap at the Oriental rites, where concelebration is normal). The liturgy should be regarded as sacred ground and approached with caution; had not God warned Moses to remove his sandals when approaching the burning bush? This last remark about Moses later caused an Austrian prelate to say that if the liturgy could be modernized merely by removing one's shoes, he would like to be the first to do so.

Unfortunately the cardinal ran on longer than his allotted ten minutes, refusing to be interrupted by the President, Cardinal Alfrink, who politely interposed: "Excuse me, Eminence, but you have already spoken more than fifteen minutes." The Secretary General, Archbishop Felici, thereupon conferred with Cardinal Alfrink, and Ottaviani was forced to stop; the microphone was then turned over to the next speaker. The Council fathers expressed their displeasure with the tenor of this speech by applauding Cardinal Alfrink's action. It was this unmistakable sign of the general feeling of the assembly, rather than the intervention of Alfrink, which seems to have caused Ottaviani to feel insulted and to remain away for almost two weeks.

When the applause had died down, Cardinal Bea noted that the mass was not only a "banquet" (*convivium*), but a "sacrifice" (*sacrificium*), and not merely a "sacrifice of praise," but a propitiatory sacrifice. He was in favor of having the sermon not only recommended but made obligatory at all masses, in order to stress the doctrinal import of the whole action and give greater meaning to the first part, or Liturgy of the Word, which the sermon brings to an end. Similarly the last part of the mass needed overhauling, with some kind of common prayer replacing the unsuitable Leonine prayers for the conversion of Russia, which usually follow the mass and are said in the vernacular.*

The Irish Dominican, Cardinal Browne, next treated the

---

* The Holy See has recently (1960) permitted these prayers to be omitted, under certain circumstances. Whether they are omitted or not has come to be regarded as something of a test of the conservativeness of parishes and of their receptiveness to the liturgical movement, in the U.S.A. at least.

fathers to a scholastic exposition of the thought of St. Thomas on these matters, as if that great thirteenth century savant and saint, who had avidly read and answered the Islamic philosophers in his own day and who was condemned at Paris and Oxford as an "innovator," would not have been in the avant-garde today, in adapting the Church's teachings to modern requirements. As the Cardinal droned on, many of the fathers retreated to Bar Jonah. This refuge from oratory was a little coffee shop set up off a corridor leading from a side entrance to St. Peter's. Because coffee shops are often known in Italy as "bars," one witty prelate with a taste for classical puns quickly nicknamed this one "Bar Jonah," since "Bar-Jonah," Hebrew for "son of John," is a reference to St. Peter in scripture. The fathers resorted to Bar Jonah in engulfing numbers for a morning coffee break. The pope himself is credited with originating the idea; he is said to have told the cardinal in charge of accommodations that if a place to smoke was not provided, "the bishops will be puffing under their mitres." One result of Bar Jonah was that in its narrow confines bishops rubbed shoulders with non-Catholic observers from all over the world, and consequently exchanged views. At times, certain bishops had to be routed out to vote on various amendments, as are dawdlers in the United States Senate cloakroom.

Bishop Alvim Pereira (aux. Lourenço Marques, Mozambique) and Archbishop Trinidade Salgueiro (Évora, Portugal) next spoke out strongly against innovation, but they were offset by the next group of speakers including Bishops Rusch (admin. Innsbruck, Austria), Zazinovic (Yugoslavia), Ddungu (Uganda), Stein (Trier, Germany), Sansierra (Argentina) and Abbot Kleiner (Cistercians), who were favorable to the schema generally but felt there was room for certain modifications and reservations. This was likewise the view of Bishop Dwyer of Leeds whereas, by contrast, Archbishop McQuaid of Dublin came out once more against any thought of change.

The next day (Oct. 31) Cardinals Lercaro of Bologna and Koening of Vienna led off the discussion, giving their full support to the innovations proposed in the schema. And Archbishop Hallinan, one of the few American bishops to be heard from throughout the Council, showed himself in full agreement. He called the liturgical prayer of the Church the proper corrective for the individualism so prevalent in the modern world; and asked that the liturgy be rendered simple and clear so that it could be understood and appreciated by all who had a part in it, priests, prelates and laity alike.

Surprisingly few American bishops spoke at the Council. Bishop Helmsing of Springfield gave up his turn saying he had submitted his paper to the Secretariat and did not wish to take up the bishops' time. It is known that the majority of younger and mid-western bishops were not always in agreement with the two American cardinals, Spellman and McIntyre, who seemed to speak for them. Hence Bishop Hallinan's talk was looked upon as a sort of declaration of independence. It was noted that Bishop Wright of Pittsburgh, considered one of the more forthright of the American bishops, took no part in the conciliar debates, nor was the accomplished speaker, Bishop Fulton Sheen, heard from. It was rumored that in the Monday meetings of the American hierarchy a new spirit was gradually manifesting itself. But the majority evidently felt that making an issue of their stand at an early stage in the game would not be either wise or fruitful.

As the discussion continued on Oct. 31, Bishop Elchinger (aux. Strasbourg, France) reminded the assembly that in his encyclical on the liturgy, *Mediator Dei*, so often quoted by the conservatives, Pope Pius XII had given ample theological justification for the custom of concelebration, as practiced particularly by the Oriental Church. Elchinger called for a simplification of the order of the mass and a return to the original text of the schema on this question. The Church was in the hands of the youth of today, he said. It was not possible to attract them by useless traditions or narrow conservativism; the mechanical repetition of prayers or ceremonies, no matter what historical importance might be attached to them, only bored the present generation. But they did comprehend us when we spoke of the Mysteries of the Church and the manifesting of Christ's incarnation through the liturgy. They wanted to comprehend the liturgy and have a direct part in it. Because the mass today had become in many places a series of almost meaningless ceremonies, we had lost the lower classes who were looking elsewhere for the spiritual sustenance which they craved. It was up to the Church to restore the spirit of community in Christ that was the birthright of every Christian through baptism. This talk was loudly applauded. It was followed by similar observations on the part of the Maronite Bishop Khoury, Archbishop Edelby (Edessa), and Archbishop Aramburu (Tucumán, Argentina).

Finally, Bishop Van Cauwelaert of the Congo, speaking in the name of 262 African bishops, welcomed the expression "Paschal Banquet" (*pascale convivium*) appearing in the schema. This must not be changed. He begged, further, that in the spirit of the early Church, great attention be paid to the "new churches of the Gentiles." As Saints Paul and Barnabas had not burdened the new Christians with circumcision and the old rites of the Jewish Law, so the new Churches in Africa and elsewhere ought not to be burdened with the unsuitable ceremonies and traditions of the Roman rite. The fathers again broke out into loud applause at this statement. But the speaker had to be stopped by the President because he had gone beyond his allotted time.

After a three days' recess provided by the feast of All Saints on Thursday, November 1, and the next day's commemoration of All Souls, on Sunday, Nov. 4, the whole Council took part in a solemn papal chapel in St. Peter's to commemorate the fourth anniversay of the pope's coronation. The solemn high mass was celebrated by Cardinal Montini, Archbishop of Milan, according to the Ambrosian rite, rarely if ever used in the Roman basilica before. This departure from custom was justified in the Holy Father's illuminating address. The concurrent feast of St. Charles Borromeo (Nov. 4), famous reforming archbishop of the period immediately following the close of the Council of Trent, whose acts the pope himself had edited while still a cardinal and on whom he is something of an authority, was seized upon by Pope John to impress upon the bishops a number of salient ideas which he wished to stress, midway through their labors.

After a salute to Latin as "the language in which the prelates of the universal Church communicate with the center of Catholicism, that is the Apostolic See, and which is the traditional language of Councils," he then abandoned this tongue and gave the rest of his talk in Italian, which is "better understood by the greater part of this assembly; better understood by the crowds of faithful who have come here to celebrate the anniversary of their Pastor and Father."

Like St. Charles, whom he called "the perfect model and most splendid light of bishops" (*episcoporum exemplar et splendidissimum lumen*), all bishops are bound to strive incessantly after holiness and devote themselves without stint to the ministry of souls, said Pope John. If they do this, their souls will be filled with peace, according to the opening words of today's liturgy: "Peace in heaven; peace on earth; peace for all peoples; peace for the priests of the Church of God."

The sight of the two thousand five hundred bishops before "the servant of the servants of God" (*servus servorum Dei*), united with the Apostolic Chair and representing nearly every see, reminded Pope John of the joy felt by his predecessor, Pope St. Leo the Great, in the fifth century at the sight of so many venerable brethren among the priests of Rome (in Leo's phrase, a "splendidissimam frequentiam") likewise gathered to do that Saint honor on his anniversary, who seemed "like an assembly of angels and saints joined together in a heavenly exultation," to use the words of Leo himself.

The enthronement of the Gospel every morning meant that "the sacred book and law of Christ" was shining in the Council's midst during the discussions, while the morning mass was not only a symbol of the Church's unity and catholicity, but, in the variety of rites used, was also a witness to the "fullness of its mystical splendor," according to the often quoted words: *"The queen stood on thy right hand in gilded clothing, surrounded with variety"* (Ps. 44:10). Hence the pope's pleasure that the mass today should be in the Ambrosian rite of Milan, one of the oldest of western rites and "closest" in origin to the Roman rite, and his joy that it was celebrated by the Cardinal Archbishop of Milan, the first cardinal to be created by him, and the one who, according to tradition, had the right to celebrate in papal chapels on the pope's anniversary.

Pope John was reminded, of course, of a great predecessor of St. Charles in the See of Milan, St. Ambrose, in the fourth century, who was among the first to enunciate the wise principle that devotion to the see of Peter was perfectly compatible with nonconformity in liturgical and administrative matters; the important thing was to be in harmony with the "type and form" of the Roman way, not a slavish uniformity: "We are not ignorant that the Roman Church has not this custom. Her type and form we follow in all things," said St. Ambrose, (*De Sacramentis,* III, 5). Pope John likewise recalled the honor which Pope Martin V did to the church of

Milan by going there personally in 1418 to consecrate the high altar of the cathedral, according to the Ambrosian, not the Roman rite.

Finally, speaking of St. Charles also reminded Pope John of the effort that youthful cardinal had made to renew the Church at the Council of Trent, and of his efficient intervention to bring the latter to a successful close.

The pope concluded by reminding the fathers:

It is perfectly natural that new times and new circumstances should suggest different forms and methods for transmitting externally the one and same doctrine, and of clothing it in a new dress. Yet the living substance is always the purity of the evangelical and apostolic truth, in perfect conformity with the teaching of holy Church, who often applies to herself the maxim: "Only one art, but a thousand forms."

This message was clearly one of hope and optimism, so typical of Pope John, but it also contained the semblance of a gentle rebuke to those who, as the debates so far had amply disclosed, were intent upon steering the Council in a direction not desired by the pope, and at variance with his declared wishes.

When the Council resumed with its 12th General Congregation on Monday, Nov. 5, the topic of debate was still Chapter II of the liturgy schema.

The Archbishop of Los Angeles, in a commentary on the words *"actuosa participatio"*—active participation, with reference to the part to be played by the faithful at mass—gave utterance to the following remark: "Active participation of the faithful in the mass is nothing but a distraction" (*Actuosa participatio fidelium non est nisi distractio*). These words caused considerable amazement. The theologian who supplied him with this phrase apparently did not know that it came from an article by Jacques Maritain in which that

philosopher had said that religion was a kind of contemplation, and not an action. But it was precisely this notion of
religion that had been combatted by the early fathers of the
Church, and in particular by St. Ambrose and St. Augustine,
who demonstrated that the Platonic notion of contemplation
of the good as the final end of man, even when supplemented
by the Stoic and Ciceronian modification in favor of participation in the common welfare of one's fellowmen, was not
the Christian idea of religion. Maritain later repudiated the
article, but evidently the Cardinal's theological mentor had
never caught up with this fact. In any case, what further dis-
mayed a large number of the bishops was the fact that since
the statement was made so late in the debate, it seemed to
indicate that the Cardinal of Los Angeles had paid little attention to the heart of the discussion which turned around
the mysteries of the faith as they were to be made actual in
the lives of both priests and faithful through the liturgy.
For his intervention had come after the magnificent avowals
of the African and Asian bishops, who had amply demonstrated that, as in the early Church, it was now necessary to
adapt the liturgy to the social, intellectual and natural milieu
of their people, whose culture, though perhaps primitive and
pagan, was not therefore necessarily evil or diabolic. It had
come, likewise, after the devastating speech of the Melchite
patriarch, Maximos IV Saigh, who proved, along with a number of other Oriental prelates, the absurdity of maintaining
that the use of Latin in the mass was necessary so far as the
Church Universal was concerned. It is reported that the Cardinal of Los Angeles arrived in Rome with a number of prejudices on his mind which he did not hesitate to ventilate,
wounding the sensibilities of both the German and Dutch
episcopates by referring to them as "disobedient" long before the Council opened, and expressing a horror for what

he is said to have termed the "noisiness" of the German dialogue and sung masses.

Cardinal Spellman appeared also to have been poorly advised. When these two American prelates who, while vigorous in defense of the retention of Latin* in the mass, came out, contrary to all expectations, in favor of the clergy being allowed to read their breviaries in English, an Italian archbishop was compelled to exclaim: *"Ah! Questi Americani!* Now they want the priest to pray in English, and the people to pray in Latin!"

Among the Italian bishops, a number seemed to feel that the honor of the Italian Church and its presumed theological pre-eminence demanded that they take an active part in all the discussions. Hence their return to the microphone three or four times in the course of the earlier debates. Fares (Catanzaro and Squillace), D'Avack (Camerino), Costantini (Sessa Aurunca), Carli (Segni), and Battaglia (Faenza) were among the names occurring most frequently in this group. All took the same line. The inviolability of Latin must be maintained, the Holy See must continue to control all liturgical matters, the introduction of changes posed a threat to the Church's unity and the integrity of its doctrine. Battaglia, in the role of a sort of *enfant terrible,* gave vent to the extravagant statement that to say that Latin was a dead language was to commit a crime against Holy Mother the Church whose language it was. Bishop D'Agostino (Vallo di Lucania) ended his peroration with the ringing cry: *"Civis Romanus sum, civis Christianus sum, lingua Latina servetur!"* The Italians generally labored under a common rhetorical failing, in that they required ten minutes to warm up to the theme on which they wished to discourse.

---

* Continental bishops had great difficulty in understanding the Latin enunciation of the American bishops.

On Nov. 6 the Holy Father at length intervened and ruled that when, in the opinion of the Cardinal Presidents, the debate had exhausted a subject, they had the right to propose a vote to close the discussion and order the Council to pass on to a consideration of the next item. Those fathers who were thus prevented from speaking could submit their speeches in writing to the Secretary General. The announcement was made at 10 A.M. Cardinal Tisserant, who was presiding, immediately proposed that the debate on Chapter II of the liturgy schema be ended. All those in favor were asked to rise. Only a solitary Franciscan bishop remained seated! The move was greeted with general applause.

Accordingly, the same day, in its 13th General Congregation, the Council was able to pass on to Chapter III dealing with the sacraments and the sacramentals. The following day, an announcement was made that after a discussion of Chapter IV on the divine office, which was to begin on Nov. 7 and would be debated separately like the previous chapters, the Council would then discuss the remaining Chapters V–VIII en bloc, in the interests of shortening the time spent on the first schema. The next schema to be taken up would be that on the "Sources of Revelation," one of the schemata submitted to the bishops during the summer before the Council opened.*

As things turned out, it appears to have been a stroke of genius on the pope's part not to have given the Council a fixed agenda. It was an act of prescience on his part, and requires little hindsight now, to realize how extremely important this point was if he was to be successful in guiding

---

* Seven only of the 70 schemata approved by the Central Commission were submitted to the bishops in July, 1962, for their study: namely, those on the sources of revelation, the moral order, the deposit of faith, the family and chastity, the liturgy, communications media, and unity. *Informations Catholiques Internationales,* Nov. 1, 1962, p. 12.

the Council's destinies. His experience with the various Preparatory Commissions and with the Central Preparatory Commission, in particular, had revealed both how strong the urge for reform in the Church really was, and also to what lengths the arch-conservatives were prepared to go to "put over" their own ideas. Had an agenda been fixed in advance, the conservatives would certainly have tried, and perhaps succeeded, in imposing an order of business that suited their purposes. The debates would have led off with a discussion of some relatively noncontroversial theme like the treatise on the Blessed Virgin Mary or the communications media, during which they would have tried to establish their ascendancy. Later if there had been a serious clash on some fundamental subject, such as the nature of the Church or the role of bishops, they would then have tried to appear as the "martyrs" of truth and so win sympathy for their cause. But they were deprived of the opportunity to put these plans to the test. The choice of the liturgy schema as the first item of business (officially announced in the 2nd General Congregation on Oct. 16) meant that a topic sufficiently important in itself, both from a theological and practical point of view, but not one that would be likely to disrupt the proceedings, was to serve as a kind of catalyst, drawing out both sides but allowing the advocates of reform to set the tone of the assembly, in accordance with the principles enunciated in the pope's opening speech.* While at this point victory was not yet assured, as the debate on the liturgy came to a close and the pace of the Council quickened, the hand of a master strategist on the grand scale began to become apparent, slowly guiding the proceedings—and educating public opinion along with them.

Still another week was consumed on what might be called

* Cf. *La Croix*, Nov. 24, 1962.

liturgical details. Chapter IV of the schema on the divine office occupied the fathers for two and a half sessions, and through most of the 16th General Congregation on Saturday, Nov. 10. The 17th and 18th General Congregations, Nov. 12–13, were sufficient to wind up affairs with a blanket consideration of the liturgical year, sacred ornaments and vestments, church music and church art. No new principles were laid down, the main lines of cleavage already being apparent, but several interesting things were said.

Cardinal Gilroy of Sydney, Australia, won the nickname of "the telegraphic cardinal," or "the inflexible guardian of the ten-minutes," because of his strictness in applying the rule which limited speakers to ten minutes. The name was appropriate, because before entering the seminary as a youth, he had served for a time as a telegrapher (Cf. *La Croix,* Nov. 7, 1962).

Cardinal Ruffini, who was presiding on Saturday, Nov. 10, introduced the proceedings by announcing that applause must cease, especially in the far corners of the hall, because this method of expression was being used by some of the fathers to give vent to their displeasure as well as their approbation. All speakers ought to be treated with equal respect, especially members of the Roman Curia, "men who know much and live holy lives." He was referring in particular to the case of Cardinal Ottaviani who had been mortified by the treatment accorded his remarks and, as we have seen, absented himself from the assembly. This advice was not well received by the Fathers.*

Cardinal Spellman surprised everybody by speaking for only two minutes and coming out in favor of the proposal that the liturgical calendar ought to be synchronized with the civil calendar.

* Cf. *New York Herald Tribune* story, "Of Brevity and Boycott," Nov. 12, 1962.

Speaking the same day (Nov. 10), the aged Bishop Petar Čule (Mostar, Yugoslavia) put in a long plea for the inclusion of the name of St. Joseph in the canon of the mass, but as he talked on, nervously repeating himself, murmurs began to be heard and Cardinal Ruffini was prompted to interject: "Complete your holy and eloquent speech. We all love St. Joseph and we hope there are many saints in Yugoslavia." The next speaker launched into a long and tedious sermon on the Blessed Virgin Mary, which also brought forth murmurs. He too had to be cut off by Ruffini, who remarked: "One does not preach to preachers" (*Praedicatoribus non praedicatur*). Winding up the day's proceedings at 12:45 with the customary *Angelus* and *Gloria Patri,* the Cardinal President brought down the house with a loud invocation of the name of St. Joseph.

It was this cutting off of Bishop Čule that prompted Pope John to order the insertion of the name of St. Joseph in the canon on his own authority (decree announced Nov. 13, effective Dec. 8, 1962), without waiting for any conciliar recommendation in the matter. This caused great astonishment, but few were aware that the Pope, following the debates on closed circuit television in his apartments, knew Bishop Čule personally and also knew that his nervous manner of speaking had a tragic source: he had suffered through one of those long trials made famous by the Communists and was sentenced to four years in a concentration camp in Yugoslavia. He and other prisoners were then put on a train which was deliberately wrecked in an attempt to kill all aboard. The bishop survived, but both his hips were broken. In poor health, he had nevertheless made great effort to attend the Council and speak up for St. Joseph. Thus his wish was granted.*

* New York *Times,* Nov. 19, 1962; Bishop Fulton Sheen, *The Catholic Reporter,* Kansas City, Feb. 22, 1963.

SUMMARY

*October 22, 1962, Monday—*4TH GENERAL CONGREGATION
PRESIDENT: Card. *Gilroy* (Sydney, Australia). MASS: Celebrated
by Arch. *Jaeger* (Paderborn, Germany). PRESENT: 2,351 fathers.
SUBJECT: Discussion of schema on liturgy begun.

SPEAKERS: Card. *Larraona* (President of Liturgical Commission)
and Fr. F. *Antonelli,* O.F.M. (Secretary of Liturgical Commission). Cards. *Frings* (Cologne), *Ruffini* (Palermo), *Lercaro* (Bologna), *Montini* (Milan), *Spellman* (New York), *Doepfner* (Munich), *Doi* (Tokyo), *Silva Henríquez* (Santiago, Chile), *Rugambwa* (Bukoba, Tanganyika); Patr. *Paul II Cheikho* (Babylon of the Chaldeans, Iraq); Archbps. and Bps. *Vagnozzi* (ap. delegate, U.S.); *Hurley* (Durban, South Africa), *Young* (Hobart, Australia), *Del Rosario* (Zamboanga, Philippines), *Scapinelli di Léguigno* (Curia), *Dante* (Curia), *García Martínez* (Spain), *Kempf* (Limburg, Germany), *Saboia Bandeira de Mello* (Palmas, Brazil), *Ungarelli* (Brazil), and *Hervás y Benet* (Ciudad Real, Spain).

Papal rescript, dated Oct. 19, 1962, granting Secretariat for Promoting Christian Unity status equivalent to that of a conciliar Commission, read by Secretary General.

Results of elections to Commissions on Sacraments, Religious, and Seminaries announced by SG (Secretary General).

*October 23, 1962, Tuesday—*5TH GENERAL CONGREGATION
PRESIDENT: Card. *Spellman* (New York). MASS: Celebrated by Archbp. *Krol* (Philadelphia). PRESENT: 2,363 fathers. SUBJECT: General discussion on the liturgy.

SPEAKERS: Cards. *Ottaviani* (Holy Office), *Ritter* (St. Louis); Archbps. and Bps. *Fares* (Catanzaro, Italy), *Argaya Goicoechea* (Mondoñedo-Ferrol, Spain), *Volk* (Mainz, Germany), *Méndez-Arceo* (Cuernavaca, Mexico), *D'Avack* (Camerino, Italy), *Amadouni* (exarch for Armenians, France).

SUBJECT: Discussion of the Preface and Chapter I. SPEAKERS: Cards. *Ruffini* (Palermo), *De Barros Câmara* (Rio de Janeiro, Brazil), *Feltin* (Paris), *McIntyre* (Los Angeles), *Léger* (Montreal), *Godfrey* (Westminster), *Landázuri Ricketts* (Lima), *Browne* (Curia); Patr. *Maximos IV Saigh* (Antioch, Syria).

Announcement by the SG regarding the rules of debate, the submission of amendments, and voting on the latter.

Announcement by the SG that the Holy Father would allow the Fathers to return to their sees for "grave pastoral reasons" and that it was merely necessary to inform the SG of their intention, despite the provisions of Canon 225 of the C.I.C. and art. 41 of the Rules of Procedure.

October 24, 1962, Wednesday—6TH GENERAL CONGREGATION
PRESIDENT: Card. *Pla y Deniel* (Toledo, Spain). MASS: In Greek Melchite rite, celebrated by Archbp. *Nabaa.* PRESENT: 2,337 fathers. SUBJECT: Preface and Chapter I of liturgy schema.

SPEAKERS: Cards. *Tisserant* (Curia), *Gracias* (Bombay), *Bea* (Curia), *Bacci* (Curia), and *Meyer* (Chicago); Archbps. and Bps. *Van Lierde* (Vatican City), *McQuaid* (Dublin) on behalf of Card. *D'Alton, Descuffi* (Smyrna, Turkey), *Gonçalves do Amaral* (Uberaba, Brazil), *Ramantoamina* (Fianarantsoa, Madagascar) on behalf of the entire African episcopate, *Kozlowiecki* (Lusaka, Northern Rhodesia), *Zanini* (nuncio), *Parente* (Curia), *Staffa* (Curia), *Cooray* (Colombo, Ceylon), *Gawlina* (Curia), *Seper* (Zagreb, Yugoslavia).

Fathers recite *De Profundis* for Archbishop *Aston Chichester,* S.J., of Salisbury, Southern Rhodesia, who collapsed this morning in the portico of St. Peter's and died on his way to this congregation.

Calendar of congregations for the month of November distributed to the fathers.

Pope receives pilgrims in weekly general audience.

General assembly of French bishops.

Conferences by Fr. *Jean Daniélou* (on the episcopate) and Bp. *Jenny,* aux. of Cambrai (on the liturgy).

October 25, 1962, Thursday—*No congregation.*

Press conference by Fr. *Hermann Schmidt,* S.J., professor at Gregorian University, on the liturgy.

Establishment of Secretariat General for the African Episcopate, president Card. *Rugambwa.*

Annual conference of the American bishops.

Second plenary conference of the Italian bishops.

October 26, 1962, Friday—7TH GENERAL CONGREGATION
PRESIDENT: Card. *Frings* (Cologne). MASS: Celebrated by Bp. *Yougbare* (Koupela, Upper Volta). PRESENT: 2,323 fathers. SUBJECT: Schema on Liturgy in general and Chapter I.

SPEAKERS: Card. *Siri* (Genoa); Archbps. and Bps. *Bekkers* ('s-Hertogenbosch, Holland), *Flores* (Barbastro, Spain), *Ancel* (aux. Lyons, France), *Hervás y Benet* (Ciudad Real, Spain), *Carli* (Segni, Italy), *Hoa Hguyen-van-Hien* (Dalat, Vietnam), *Mansilla Reoyo* (aux. Burgos, Spain), *Costantini* (Sessa Aurunca, Italy), *La Ravoire Morrow* (Krishnagar, India), *Añoveros Ataún* (coadj. Cadix and Ceuta, Spain), *Calewaert* (Gand, Belgium), *Le Cordier* (aux. Paris), *Enciso Viana* (Mallorca, Spain), *Rau* (Mar del Plata, Argentina), *Del Campo de la Bárcena* (Calahorra, Spain), *Lokuang* (Tainan, Formosa), *Isnard* (Nova Friburgo, Brazil), *Borromeo* (Pesaro, Italy); Abbots (O.S.B.) *Butler* (England), *Reetz* (Beuron, Germany), *Prou* (France).

Meetings of Cardinal Presidents and Secretariat for Extraordinary Affairs.

October 27, 1962, Saturday—8TH GENERAL CONGREGATION

PRESIDENT: Card. *Ruffini* (Palermo). MASS: Celebrated by Archb. *Miranda y Gómez* (Mexico City). PRESENT: 2,302 fathers. SUBJECT: Chapter I of liturgy schema.

SPEAKERS: Archbps. and Bps. *Olaechea* (Valencia, Spain), *da Cunha Marelim* (Caxias do Maranhão, Brazil), *D'Souza* (Nagpur, India), *García de Sierra* (coadj. Oviedo, Spain), *Marty* (Reims, France), *Zohrabian* (Armenia), *Jenny* (aux. Cambrai), *McGrath* (aux. Panama), *Rolim de Moura* (Cajazeiras, Brazil), *Kémérer* (Posadas, Argentina) on behalf of 25 Argentinian bishops, *Devoto* (Goya, Argentina), *Kobayashi* (Sendai, Japan) on behalf of all Japanese bishops, *Thiandoum* (Dakar, Senegal) on behalf of all African bishops, *Pildáin y Zapiáin* (Canary Islands, Spain), *Melas* (Nuoro, Italy), *de Vito* (Lucknow, India), *Schoiswal* (Seckau, Austria), *C. Weber* (Ichon, China), *Saboia Bandeira de Mello* (Palmas, Brazil), *Muldoon* (aux. Sydney, Australia), *Carraro* (Verona, Italy), *Ferrero di Cavallerleone* (Italy), *Vielmo* (vic. ap. Aysén, Chile); Father *Fernandez* (Master General of the Dominicans).

Fathers approve message (telegram) to Holy Father on 4th anniversary of his coronation.

Plenary assembly of the Italian episcopate.

Conference of Fr. *De Lubac.*

October 28, 1962, Sunday—Feast of Christ the King.

Pope replies (telegram) to message of Council.

Pope comments, at *Angelus,* on peace of Christ's kingdom.

October 29, 1962, Monday—9TH GENERAL CONGREGATION

PRESIDENT: Card. *Caggiano* (Buenos Aires). MASS: Celebrated by Archb. *Yamaguchi* (Nagasaki, Japan). PRESENT: 2,227 fathers. SUBJECT: Discussion of Chapter I of Liturgy schema completed.

SPEAKERS: Archbps. and Bps. *Santin* (Trieste, Italy), *Battaglia* (Faenza, Italy), *Melendro* (Anking, China), *Franic* (Split, Yugoslavia), *Nicodemo* (Bari, Italy), *Spülbeck* (Meissen, East Germany), *Benitez* (aux. Asunción, Paraguay), *Garcia Martinez* (tit. bp., Spain), *Scandar* (Assiut, Egypt), *Ferraz* (Brazil), *Barranchina Estevan* (Orihuela-Alicante, Spain), *Simons* (Indore, India), *Kandela* (aux. Antioch of the Syrians, Lebanon), *D'Agostino* (Vallo di Lucania, Italy), *Benedetti* (Lodi, Italy), *Peruzzo* (Agrigento, Italy).

SUBJECT: Discussion of Chapter II of the schema begun. SPEAKERS: Cards. *Spellman* (New York), *Ruffini* (Palermo), and *Léger* (Montreal).

SG reads reply of Holy Father to the Council.

SG announces appointment by pope of 9 members to each of 10 Commissions, instead of 8 provided for in Rules of Procedure.

Conference of Fr. *Gustave Thils* on the theology of the episcopate.

October 30, 1962, Tuesday—10TH GENERAL CONGREGATION

PRESIDENT: Card. *Alfrink* (Utrecht). MASS: Celebrated by Bishop *Mangers* (Oslo, Norway). PRESENT: 2,257 fathers. SUBJECT: Chapter II of liturgy schema.

SPEAKERS: Cards. *Godfrey* (Westminster), *Gracias* (Bombay), *Bueno y Monreal* (Seville), *Alfrink* (Utrecht), *Ottaviani* (Curia), *Bea* (Curia), *Browne* (Curia); Archbps. and Bps. *Florit* (Florence, Italy), *Melendro* (Anking, China), *Alvim Pereira* (Laurenço Marques, Mozambique), *Lokuang* (Tainan, Formosa), *Rusch* (ap. adm. Innsbruck, Austria), *Dwyer* (Leeds, England), *Trinidade Salgueiro* (Evora, Portugal), *Zazinovic* (Krk, Yugoslavia), *Arattukulam* (Alleppey, India), *McQuaid* (Dublin), *Fernandes* (coadj. Delhi, India), *Helmsing* (Kansas City), *Ddungu* (Masaka, Uganda); Fr. *Kleiner* (Abbot General of the Cistercians); Bps.

Stein (aux. Trier, Germany), and *Sansierra* (aux. San Juan de Cuyo, Argentina).

Reception for fathers of the Council by President *Segni* of Italy, in the Quirinal.

October 31, 1962, Wednesday—11TH GENERAL CONGREGATION

PRESIDENT: Card. *Tisserant* (Curia). MASS: According to Dominican rite, celebrated by Archb. *Lemieux,* O.P. (Ottawa, Canada). PRESENT: 2,230 fathers. SUBJECT: Chapter II of liturgy schema.

SPEAKERS: Cards. *Lercaro* (Bologna), and *König* (Vienna); Archbps. and Bps. *Cambiaghi* (Crema, Italy), *Jop* (Poland), *Iglesias Navarri* (Urgel, Spain), *Nuer* (aux. Tebe-Luqsor, Egypt), *Jubany* (aux. Barcelona, Spain), *Przyklenk* (Januaria, Brazil), *Devoto* (Goya, Argentina), *Satoshi Nagae* (Urawa, Japan), *Hallinan* (Atlanta) on behalf of various bishops, *Jäger* (Paderborn), *da Cunha Marelim* (Caxias do Maranhão, Brazil), *Weber* (Strasbourg, France), *Elchinger* (aux. Strasbourg, France), *Koury* (Tyre of the Maronites, Lebanon), *Edelby* (tit. abp. of Edessa), *Aramburu* (Tucumán, Argentina), *Pao-Zin-Tou* (Hsinchou, Formosa), *Himmer* (Tournai, Belgium), *Van Cauwelaert* (Inongo, Congo [Leopoldville]) speaking for 260 African bishops, *Zohrabian* (tit. bp., Armenian), *Boillon* (coadj. Verdun, France), *De Voto* (Lucknow, India), *Melas* (Nuoro, Italy).

Announcement by SG that it was forbidden to distribute private documents during the congregation, without the consent of the Council.

Pope receives pilgrims in weekly general audience.

November 1, 1962, Thursday—Feast of All Saints

November 2, 1962, Friday—Commemoration of All Souls

November 3, 1962, Saturday—Conference of Fr. *Marsigli,* O.S.B., of Sant' Anselmo, Rome, on liturgical reforms.

Oriental patriarchs and bishops appoint a working committee.

November 4, 1962, Sunday—Papal Chapel in St. Peter's in honor of 4th anniversary of pope's coronation, mass according to the Ambrosian rite, homily by pope.

Visit by pope to S. Carlo al Corso in afternoon.

Reception for Fathers of Council by City Government of Rome, on the Capitoline.

November 5, 1962, Monday—12TH GENERAL CONGREGATION

PRESIDENT: Card. *Liénart* (Lille). MASS: According to the Maronite rite, celebrated by Archb. *Khoury.* PRESENT: 2,196 fathers. SUBJECT: Chapter II of liturgy schema.

SPEAKERS: Cards. *Confalonieri* (Curia), and *McIntyre* (Los Angeles); Archbps. and Bps. *Duschak* (vic. ap. Calapan, Philippines), *László* (Eisenstadt, Austria), *Ferrari* (Monopoli, Italy), *Fares* (Catanzaro and Squillace, Italy), *Saboia Bandeira de Mello* (Palmas, Brazil), *Cousineau* (Cap Haitien, Haiti), *Jenny* (aux. Cambrai, France), *André Perraudin* (Kabgayi, Ruanda), *Barrachina Estevan* (Orihuela-Alicante, Spain), *Lopes de Moura* (Portalegre-Castelo Branco, Portugal); Abbot B. *Gut* (O.S.B.); Archbps. and Bps. *Yü Pin* (Nanking, China), *Bekkers* ('s-Hertogenbosch, Holland), *Vicuña Aránguiz* (Chillán, Chile), *Seitz* (Kontum, Vietnam), *Pont y Gol* (Segorbe-Castellón de la Plana, Spain), *Muldoon* (aux. Sydney, Australia), *Xenopulos* (Sira, Greece), *Théas* (Tarbes et Lourdes, France), *Mosquera Corral* (Guayaquil, Ecuador), *Modrego y Casáus* (Barcelona, Spain), *D'Avack* (Camerino, Italy).

Announcement by SG of appointments by pope to Administrative Tribunal.

Conference of Bishop *Duschak* (Philippines) on liturgical reforms.

November 6, 1962, Tuesday—13TH GENERAL CONGREGATION

PRESIDENT: Card. *Tappouni* (Antioch of the Syrians). MASS: Celebrated by Archb. *Hamvas* (Casanád, Hungary). PRESENT: 2,211 fathers. SUBJECT: Chapter II of liturgy schema.

SPEAKERS: Bps. *Zak* (Sankt Pölten, Austria), *Zauner* (Linz, Austria), *Kandela* (aux. Antioch of the Syrians), *Pildain y Zapiain* (Canary Islands, Spain).

Announcement by SG (10 A.M.) that Holy Father had granted permission to Council of Cardinal Presidents to end debate when in their opinion the subject had been sufficiently exhausted.

Announcement by SG regarding submission of résumé and 2 copies of speech by each speaker to the Secretariat General (one copy for the archives and one for the interested conciliar Commission).

SUBJECT: Chapter III of the liturgy schema. SPEAKERS: Cards. *Ruffini* (Palermo), *Cento* (Curia), *Browne* (Curia); Archbps. and Bps. *Hengsbach* (Essen, Germany), *Arnerić* (Sibenik, Yugoslavia),

Capozi (Taiyüan, China), *Kozlowiecki* (Lusaka, Northern Rhodesia), *Pham-ngoc-Chi* (Quinhon, Vietnam), *Maziers* (aux. Lyons, France), *Plaza* (La Plata, Argentina), *Lebrum Moratinos* (Valencia, Venezuela), *Botero Salazar* (Medellín, Colombia) on behalf of all the bishops of Colombia, *De Carvalho* (Angra, Portugal [Azores]), *Cabrera Cruz* (San Luis Potosí, Mexico), *Tomizawa* (Sapporo, Japan), *Ruotolo* (Ugento, Italy), *Garković* (Zara, Yugoslavia); Abbot *Reetz* (Beuron, Germany); Bps. *Barbero* (Vigevano, Italy), and *Pailloux* (Fort Rosebery, Northern Rhodesia.

Announcement by SG that first session of Council will end on Dec. 8.

November 7, 1962, Wednesday—14TH GENERAL CONGREGATION

PRESIDENT: Card. *Gilroy* (Australia). MASS: Celebrated by Archb. *Nguyen Van Binh* (Saigon, Vietnam). PRESENT: 2,214 fathers. SUBJECT: Chapter III of liturgy schema.

SPEAKERS: Archbps. and Bps. *Rougé* (coadj. Nimes, France), *Angelini* (Italy), *Kempf* (Limburg, Germany), *Isnard* (Nova Friburgo, Brazil), *Sansierra* (aux. San Juan de Cuyo, Argentina), *Faveri* (Tivoli, Italy), *Mistrorigo* (Treviso, Italy), *Del Pino Gómez* (Lerida, Spain), *Sibomana* (Ruhengeri, Ruanda), *Peralta y Ballabriga* (Vitoria, Spain), *Djajasepoetra* (Djakarta, Indonesia), *Bekkers* (s'-Hertogenbosch, Holland) on behalf of Dutch bishops, *Wojtyla* (aux. Kraków, Poland), *Van Bekkum* (Ruteng, Indonesia), *D'Souza* (Nagpur, India), *Mendoza Castro* (Abancay, Peru), *Wronka* (aux. Gniezno, Poland), *Malula* (aux. Leopoldville, Congo) on behalf of African episcopate, *Romo Gutiérrez* (Torreón, Mexico) on behalf of Mexican bishops, *García Martinez* (tit. bp., Spain), *Tagle Covarrubias* (Valparaiso, Chile). The following gave up their right to speak: *Arnerić* (Sibenik, Yugoslavia), *McQuaid* (Dublin), *Connare* (Greensburg, USA), *Méndez Arceo* (Cuernavaca, Mexico), *J. Weber* (Strasbourg, France), *González y Robleto* (Managua, Nicaragua).

SUBJECT: Chapter IV of liturgy schema. SPEAKERS: Cards. *Frings*, on behalf of German language episcopate, *Ruffini, Valeri* (Curia), *Quiroga y Palacios* (Santiago de Compostela, Spain), and *Léger* (Montreal).

Announcement by SG that Chapters V, VI, VII and VIII of the liturgy schema would be discussed simultaneously, not separately, and that the next schema to be taken up would be on the "Sources of Revelation."

Weekly general audience of the pope.

November 8, 1962, Thursday—Requiem Chapel in St. Peter's for all deceased cardinals and bishops.

Press conference of Cardinal *Bea.*

November 9, 1962, Friday—15TH GENERAL CONGREGATION

PRESIDENT: Card. *Frings* (Cologne). MASS: Celebrated by Archb. *Cunial* (Vicegerent of Rome). PRESENT: 2,216 fathers. SUBJECT: Chapter IV of liturgy schema.

SPEAKERS: Cards. *Gonçalves Cerejeira* (Lisbon), *Spellman, Wyszynski* (Warsaw) on behalf of the Polish bishops, *Godfrey* (Westminster), *Lefebvre* (Bourges, France), *Doepfner* (Munich), *Meyer* (Chicago), *Santos* (Manila), *Landázuri Ricketts* (Lima) *Bacci* (Curia), *Bea* (Curia), *Albareda* (Curia); Archbps. and Bps. *Connare* (Greensburg, USA) speaking on behalf of large number of American bishops, *Méndez Arceo* (Cuernavaca, Mexico), *J. Weber* (Strasbourg, France), *Franič* (Split, Yugoslavia), *Corboy* (Monze, Northern Rhodesia), *Reh* (Charleston, USA), and *Aguirre* (San Isidro, Argentina).

SG reads telegram sent by Council to Bishop *Alfonso Carinci,* secretary emeritus of Congr. of Rites, on his 100th birthday.

Observer-delegates visit Subiaco.

November 10, 1962, Saturday—16TH GENERAL CONGREGATION

PRESIDENT: Card. *Ruffini* (Palermo). MASS: According to rite of Braga, celebrated by Bp. *da Silva* (aux. Braga, Portugal). PRESENT: 2,172 fathers. SUBJECT: Chapter IV of liturgy schema.

SPEAKERS: Archbps. and Bps. *Flores* (Barbastro, Spain), *Garcia Martinez* (Spain), *Vielmo* (vic. ap. Aysén, Chile); Abbot *Prou* (Solesmes, France) on behalf of various monastic orders; Archbps. and Bps. *Reuss* (Germany), *Piérard* (Chalons, France), *García y García de Castro* (Granada, Spain), *Gonzi* (Malta), *Leven* (aux. San Antonio, USA), *Garrone* (Toulouse, France), *Marling* (Jefferson City, USA), *Guano* (Livorno, Italy); Fr. *Fernandez* (Master General of the Dominicans); Archbps. and Bps. *Carli* (Segni, Italy), *Yago* (Abidjan, Ivory Coast) on behalf of bishops of West Africa and also certain others, *Souto Vizoso* (Palencia, Spain); Fr. *Van Hees* (General of Order of Holy Cross, Holland); Bp. *Costantini* (Sessa Aurunca, Italy).

SUBJECT: Last four Chapters of liturgy schema. SPEAKERS: Card. *Spellman;* Archbps. and Bps. *Nabaa* (Beirut, Lebanon), *Plaza* (La Plata, Argentina), *Čule* (Mostar, Yugoslavia), *Tedde* (Ales, Italy), *González Moralejo* (aux. Valencia, Spain).

Announcement of Cardinal President about avoidance of applause and treatment of all speakers with equal respect, especially members of the Roman Curia.

Press conference of Msgr. *Igino Cardinale,* Chef de Protocol of the Secretariat of State.

*November 11, 1962, Sunday—*Pope visits Aristide Gabelli Reformatory in Rome.

*November 12, 1962, Monday—*17TH GENERAL CONGREGATION

PRESIDENT: Card. *Caggiano* (Buenos Aires). MASS: Roman rite, but in the Paleoslavic or Glagolitic language, celebrated by Bp. *Arnerič* (Sibenik, Yugoslavia). PRESENT: 2,185 fathers.

SUBJECT: Last four Chapters of liturgy schema.

SPEAKERS: Cards. *De Barros Câmara* (Rio de Janeiro, Brazil), *Feltin* (Paris), *Rugambwa* (Bukoba, Tanganyika); Archbps. and Bps. *Bafile* (nuncio, Germany), *Melendro* (Anking, China), *Marling* (Jefferson City, USA), *Baraniak* (Poznan, Poland), *Soares de Resende* (Beira, Mozambique), *Khoury* (Tyre of the Maronites, Lebanon, *Reed* (Oklahoma City, USA), *Zohrabian* (tit. bp., Armenian), *Jannucci* (Penne-Pescara, Italy), *McVinney* (Providence, USA), *Bereciartua Balerdi* (Siguenza-Guadalajara, Spain), *Hoa Nguyen-van Hien* (Dalat, Vietnam), *Raymond* (Allahabad, India), *Castellano* (Siena, Italy), *Ngo-dinh-Thuc* (Hué, Vietnam), *Larrain Errázuriz* (Talca, Chile), *Gasbarri* (aux. Velletri, Italy), and *Gouyon* (Bayonne, France).

Announcement by SG that first session would end Dec. 8 with solemn ceremony presided over by the pope, and that the latter would canonize three new saints the following day, Dec. 9. The Second Session would begin May 12, 1963 and end June 29, 1963. Meanwhile, the conciliar Commissions would remain in session.

Press conference of Bp. *Nagae* (Japan).

*November 13, 1962, Tuesday—*18TH GENERAL CONGREGATION

PRESIDENT: Card. *Alfrink* (Utrecht). MASS: Celebrated by Archb. *Serrano Abad* (Cuenca, Ecuador). PRESENT: 2,209 fathers.

SUBJECT: Discussion of last four Chapters of liturgy schema concluded.

SPEAKERS: Archbps. and Bps. *Urtasun* (Avignon, France), *Alonso Muñoyerro* (Spain), *Fustella* (Todi, Italy); Abbot *D'Amato,* O.S.B. (San Paolo fuori le Mura, Rome); Bp. *Almarcha Hernández* (León, Spain); Abbot *Zilianti,* O.S.B. (Monte Oliveto Maggiore, Italy); Fr. *Soetemans* (Abbot General of the Lateran Canons, Belgium); Archbps. and Bps. *Golland Trinidade* (Botucatú, Brazil), *Kowalski* (Chelmno, Poland), *Yoshigoro Taguchi* (Osaka, Japan), *Jop* (Poland), *Van Lierde* (Vatican City), *Kempf* (Limburg, Germany), *Sapelak* (vic. ap. for Ukrainians in Argentina, Poland), *Seitz* (Kontum, Vietnam), *Volk* (Mainz, Germany), *Nowicki* (coadj. Gdańsk, Poland), *Baudoux* (St. Boniface, Canada), *Cheng Tien-Siang* (Kaohsiung, China [Formosa]), *Miranda y Gómez* (Mexico), *López Ortiz* (Tuy-Vigo, Spain), and *Pohlschneider* (Aachen, Germany).

Announcement by Card. *Cicognani,* Secretary of State, that Holy Father had decided to insert name of St. Joseph in the canon of the mass, the decree effective Dec. 8, 1962.

Pope visits church of S. Andrea al Quirinale.

V

The Debate on the "Sources of Revelation"

THE COUNCIL now embarked on the discussion of the fateful schema, *De Revelatione,* prepared by the Preparatory Theological Commission under Cardinal Ottaviani and personally presented by him as head of the corresponding conciliar Commission. The schema consisted of 5 Chapters, divided into 29 numbered Articles.*

* SCHEMA DE FONTIBUS REVELATIONIS: *Chap. I, The two sources of revelation—*Art. 1, the revelation of the Old and New Testaments; 2, The first propagation of the revelation of the New Testament; 3, The transmission of the revelation of the New Testament; 4, The two sources of revelation; 5, The relationship between the two sources; 6, The relationship of each of the two sources to doctrine. *Chap. II, The inspiration, inerrancy, and literary genres of Scripture—*Art. 7, The inspiration and canon of Holy Scripture; 8, The nature and definition of inspiration; 9, The different human authors; 10, The personal inspiration of the author and the community; 11, The extent of in-

From the very first the opposite sides in the Church were locked in heated debate, for this was one of the most important issues before the Council—basic, in a sense, to all else. Recent years have witnessed a swing by many Catholic theologians away from the view largely favored since the Council of Trent that the Bible and tradition are two separate, virtually independent sources of divine revelation. They have returned to the older position wherein scripture and tradition must not be thought of as completely independent of each other but as constituting a whole—two modes, the written and unwritten, by which the Word of God comes down to us within the framework of the Church. As Father Yves Congar, O.P., a spokesman for the new outlook, puts it: "There is not a single dogma which the Church holds by Scripture *alone,* not a single dogma which it holds by tradition *alone.** Obviously this view is also much closer to the traditional Protestant thesis of "the Bible and the Bible alone." The new tendency was ignored by the Theological Commission when working on its draft.

The debate was opened on Wednesday, November 14, with some admonitory remarks by Cardinal Ottaviani. "There are," he said, "a number of schemata in circulation which op-

---

spiration; 12, Inerrancy, a consequence of inspiration; 13, Judgement with regard to inerrancy; 14, The divine condescension. *Chap. III, The Old Testament*—Art. 15, The authority of the Old Testament in the Church; 16, The relationship of the Old and New Testaments; 17, The true character of the Old Testament; 18, The human authors of the Old Testament. *Chap. IV, The New Testament*—Art. 19, The Gospels and their authors; 20, The historical value of the Gospels; 21, The truth of the acts of Christ in the Gospels; 22, The truth of the words of Christ in the Gospels; 23, The truth of the teaching of the Apostles in the canonical writings. *Chap. V. Holy Scripture in the Church*—Art. 24, The care of the Church for Holy Scripture; 25, The Latin translation of the Vulgate; 26, The reading of Scripture by priests; 27, The reading of Scripture by the faithful; 28, Catholic exegetes; 29, The relationship of theology and Holy Scripture. (*La Documentation Catholique,* Dec. 16, 1962, pp. 1578–79, quoting KIPA, Nov. 11, 1962).

* *Informations Catholiques Internationales,* Dec. 1, 1962, p. 2.

pose that which I am about to introduce.* But this procedure violates the regulations . . . The presentation of a schema belongs solely to the Holy Father; hence this way of doing things is hardly respectful of his prerogatives." The cardinal was referring to at least three different proposals prepared by committees of French, German and Dutch theologians, of which the last was the most radical. These schemata had been in circulation for well over two weeks, and had evidently displeased the opposing faction. The cardinal continued: "Here in Council we have the right to propose amendments, and then only on the schema proposed, not on any other.

"As regards the 'pastoral tone,' " he went on, "might I remind you that the foundation of all pastoral theology is provided by safe doctrine. The fact that this schema deals primarily with doctrine renders it likewise pastoral. These proposals have been edited for a Council, hence they have nothing in common with an encyclical or a homily or a pastoral letter. Regarding the complaint that it has not been inspired by the so-called New Theology, might I remark that our teaching is traditional and will and must ever remain the same." In an appeal to the theologians and scholars among the bishops at the Council, he concluded by stating that all those who had worked in the Theological Commission and in the Central Committee on this material were scholarly and experienced men, and respect was due the work of such people.

His Eminence was then replaced on the rostrum by Msgr. Garofalo, who gave the fathers a summary of the matter contained in the schema. He announced as the primary end of

---

* Cf. art. "Synthèse des derniers travaux," *La Croix*, Nov. 24, 1962, which mentions Fr. Karl Rahner, S.J. as the author of one; Fr. Wenger says that the German schema had the approbation of the Austrian, Belgian, French, German and Dutch episcopates, *La Croix*, Nov. 16, 1962.

the Council the defense and promulgation of Catholic doctrine in its most exact form. Doctrine does not change, although it can and does develop. Repeating the words of his predecessor, he explained that in style and format the schema was meant to be a decree or formula, hence it had not been elaborated as a literary document. Its objective, he confessed, was to demonstrate once more that, by its condemnation of error, the Church was ever prompt to purify the world of its errors and evils. This presentation, as far as the majority of prelates were concerned, could not have been more unfortunate coming in the wake of Cardinal Ottaviani's complaints. The immediate result was not hard to predict.

Cardinal Liénart rose at once to lead the opposition. "This schema," he said, "does not please me. It is not adequate to the matter it purports to deal with, namely Scripture and tradition. There are not and never have been two *sources* of revelation. There is only one fount of revelation—the Word of God, the good news announced by the prophets and revealed by Christ. The Word of God is the unique *source* of revelation. This schema is a cold and scholastic formula, while revelation is a supreme gift of God—God speaking directly to us. We should be thinking more along the lines of our separated brothers who have such a love and veneration for the Word of God. Our duty now is to cultivate the faith of our people and cease to condemn. Hence I propose this schema be entirely refashioned."

As at the opening session, the French Cardinal was replaced by Cardinal Frings of Cologne, like his colleague a scripture scholar. In a milder tone he announced his *non placet,* and then tackled the Ottaviani proposition head on. "The primary purpose of a Council is to provide for the pastoral needs of the day," he said, "to teach the truth, to stimulate its preaching in such wise that it will be received. At the first

Vatican Council complaints were raised against the professional tone of the schemata, particularly those proposed by Cardinal Franzelin.* Here that approach is even further exaggerated. But what is even worse than the manner of presentation is the doctrine itself. Why speak of two sources of revelation? This is not traditional. Neither the fathers, nor the scholastic theologians, nor St. Thomas himself, nor the previous Councils knew anything about this way of explaining our teaching. It is not traditional and only in recent centuries, as a result of a false historicism, have certain theologians tried to explain the matter thus."

This statement touched a sore spot, for a primary characteristic of the ultra-conservative theologian is his fear of and disdain for a positive or history-oriented approach to theology. The Cardinal of Cologne continued inexorably: "What is said here of inspiration and inerrancy is at once offensive to our separated brothers in Christ and harmful to the proper liberty required in any scientific procedure. We are facing a conflict of schools given to diverse procedures, as was realized at Trent four hundred years ago. It is not the business of a Council to enter into discussions between Catholic theologians. Its task is to react against heresy, but not to interfere when there is no danger of such errors."

Hardly had the German cardinal concluded when his presidential colleague, Cardinal Ruffini of Sicily, took the microphone in hand. "We are now faced with a question of extreme importance," he announced. "It is the heart and center of the Council. I am not of the opinion of the cardinals who preceded me. This schema pleases me completely. It has

* During Vatican Council I the dogmatic schema prepared by the then Professor Franzelin was finally rejected as too obscure, a fact that gave his students at the Gregorian University no little glee, enabling them to announce: "We always maintained that Professor Franzelin's lectures were confusing. Now we have it confirmed by a Council."

been prepared by men who are both eminent and wise. It has been reviewed by men not less eminent on the Central Committee. How then can it be rejected in its totality? Further it is the Holy Father who has given us this matter for discussion. With what right then can we dismiss it without discussion? Granted that it is not perfect I myself have certain reservations and recommendations I would like to make about it. It will at least give us a basis for our work. Should we consider another schema, we will never finish."

In a more conciliatory tone Cardinal Ruffini was supported by the Archbishop of Genoa, Cardinal Siri. He admitted the justice of many of the criticisms levelled at the schema. However, he pointed out the connection between the condemnations proposed and the consequences of the heresy of Modernism, condemned in 1908 by Pope Pius X. He felt it still necessary to justify that condemnatory action, as did a majority of Italian bishops. "By discussing the interpretation of the Scriptures," he said, "there is hope of arriving at a clearer expression of the faith. Hence let us discuss the schema before us." Of similar advice was Cardinal Quiroga y Palacios of Compostela, Spain.

By now the heavy artillery was ready. In quick succession, the Cardinals of Montreal, Vienna, Utrecht and Malines rose to demolish the Ottaviani thesis. The Canadian cardinal, Paul Emile Léger, not only proposed the scrapping of the document, but went on to make a plea for freedom and tolerance within the world of Catholic scholarship, defending biblical scholars in particular who are opening up new paths of investigation. Though he began his career as a Sulpician, under the tutelage of the old-guard French Canadian hierarchy, and served his Roman apprenticeship as Rector of the Canadian College in the Eternal City, Léger has undergone an interior revolution. He is now a staunch advocate of that

IN PRIMA SESSIONE
SACRI CONCILII OECUMENICI VATICANI II
DIE 11 OCTOBRIS 1962

Die undecima Octobris, festo Maternitatis B. Mariæ Virginis, mane hora indicenda E.mi et Rev.mi Domini Cardinales, ac Exc.mi Domini Patriarchæ, Primates, Archiepiscopi, Episcopi, Abbates, ceterique locum in Concilio habentes convenient in aulas designatas, et assumptis sacris vestibus cuique Ordini propriis albi coloris et mitris, sollicite se disponent pro supplicatione inchoanda.

E.mi Cardinales in aula Paramentorum Summi Pontificis adventum expectabunt. Eum postea comitaturi ad Paulinum sacellum ubi sanctissimum Sacramentum expositum erit.

Facta adoratione, et intonato a Pontifice hymno: *Ave, maris stella* quem Schola Cantorum prosequetur, ordinabitur Supplicatio, servato ordine in « Methodo » præscripto.

Cum perventum fuerit in Basilicam Vaticanam, Summus Pontifex e sella gestatoria descendet et genuflexus ante altare intonabit, Schola Cantorum prosequente:

VIII

V e-ni, Cre- à-tor Spí- ri-tus, Mentes tu-ó-rum ví- si- ta: Imple superna grá-ti- a Quæ tu cre- á-sti pécto-ra.

Qui díceris Paráclitus,
Altíssimi donum Dei,
Fons vivus, ignis, cáritas,
Et spiritális únctio.

Tu septifórmis múnere
Dígitus patérnæ déxteræ,
Tu rite promíssum Patris
Sermóne ditans gúttura.

Page from official Ceremonial for Vatican Council II

interior reform of the Church that aims at getting back to the fundamental roots, and would restore Catholicism today as a mystery-conscious, apostolic-minded, yet tolerant institution, along the lines of the primitive Church.

Cardinal Koenig, the fifty-seven-year-old Cardinal of Vienna spoke next. A theologian in his own right who has taught moral theology and published books on the study of comparative religion, he rejected the schema as having almost nothing to do with the program called for by the Holy Father. This was the theme, likewise, of Cardinal Alfrink, a pupil of Cardinal Ruffini when doing his theological studies in Rome, and now archbishop of Utrecht. He had long outgrown his teacher's ideas. Before leaving Holland for the Council he had warned his people not to expect miracles or sensations from the Council; and because of well-founded rumors in ecclesiastical circles crediting him with being a principal opponent of the Ottaviani thesis, he disclaimed all desire to prove a hero at the council. With a bow of deference to Cardinal Ruffini, he regretted he had to contradict his venerable teacher, but he found the schema on revelation nothing more than a re-elaboration of a chapter in any good theology text-book. It certainly was not capable of clarifying the mind of the Church now; nor would it promote in the least the aim of the Council, by renewing the face of the Church so that it could invite all Christians to share with it the treasures of divine Truth.

Striking a practical note, the recently created Cardinal of Belgium, Leo Joseph Suenens, expressed his fears that in view of all the talking, Vatican Council II threatened to outlast the eighteen years of the Council of Trent. He announced that he was against the schema because it was a botched-up job which had no relevance to the problems of the hour. He proposed a new method of procedure, in the hopes of getting the Council to act in a more parliamentary way. His suggestion was interesting in view of subsequent developments and seemed to prove to those benefiting from second-sight that he was perhaps closer to the throne than had formerly been suspected. Trained at Louvain, long a professor of moral theology there, and since 1945 Archbishop of Malines, he had written a book on conjugal love which had caused a mild sensation in Catholic theological circles. His intervention marked a kind of turning-point in the debate.

Cardinal Ritter, the cheerful, dynamic Archbishop of St. Louis, for all the apparent simplicity of his approach, turned out to be the outstanding American prelate at the Council. He next took the microphone to announce bluntly that the schema must be rejected: *"Rejiciendum est!"* Warming to the effect of this bombshell, he went on to condemn the draft as pessimistic, negative and full of unjust suspicions and fears. "What a tedious and unrealistic attitude it betrays toward the Word of God which we call the Scriptures!" he said, adding that the schema was calculated to inspire not love for the Bible, but rather servile fear.

It was Cardinal Bea, eighty-two years old, feeble-looking, but patently rejuvenated in mind and heart who, with beguiling candor, laid the facts straight on the line. He began by graciously praising the work put into the schema, but informed its authors that they had evidently been marching in the wrong direction. Their end result "did not agree with the purpose set down by the Holy Father in summoning the Council." What then did the pope have in mind?" he asked. If ever there was a moment when someone should have shouted *"Attenzione!"* to the opposition, this was it. The pope, said Cardinal Bea, had in mind "that the faith of the Church be presented in all its integrity and purity, but in such manner that it will be received today with benevolence. For we are shepherds."

There was no need now for patristic or theological argument, he continued. "What our times demand is a pastoral approach, demonstrating the love and kindness that flow from our religion." This schema was totally lacking in the pastoral spirit. If a schema like this were to be called pastoral, then the same thing could be said of every theological textbook. "It represents the work of a theological school," he said, "not what the better theologians today think." He pointed out the many references in the schema to the scripture scholars; yet there was only one favorable mention—all the rest were held suspect. It was not the Council's business, he said, to do the work of exegetes; to solve problems of inspiration, authorship, or inerrancy. "We must do an ecumenical job." The schema must be radically redone, he concluded, to render it shorter, clearer, and more pastoral. The voice was indeed that of Augustin Bea, but the sentiments were those of the Patriarch of the West, Angelo Roncalli, now Pope John XXIII.

The Melchite Patriarch of Antioch, Maximos IV Saigh, concluded the arguments by making a fairly long statement in French: "What we expect is a peaceful and positive message, worthy of the attention of our separated brethren. The spirit of this schema is once again the spirit of the Counter-reformation . . . Since Vatican Council I only a partial and incomplete picture of the Church has been presented. The prerogatives of the Visible Head have been put in evidence in such an isolated way that the rest of the body of the Church seems dwarfish in comparison. We must reestablish the true proportions between the body and its head and thus give a truer and more complete picture. I ask once again that the schema on the Church and the hierarchy be submitted as soon as possible. Everything depends on that schema, because then we can take up pastoral and social questions. All of us await that moment."

At the conclusion of the patriarch's speech, as if in fulfillment of his wish, an official announcement was made that the
very schema he was pleading for, *"De Ecclesia,"* would be distributed to the fathers at the end of the week or the beginning of the next.*

The day's proceedings were wound up with two forceful
speeches by the Indonesian Archbishops Manek and Soegijapranata, who came out strongly against the schema, and a
final plea by the Archbishop of Saragossa in Spain, Morcillo
Gonzalez, who argued that though it was perfectible, it
"breathed a true ecumenical spirit."

Shortly before the end, however, the results were announced of the voting on the liturgy schema as a whole,
which took place before the discussions began. The ballots
had been handed out by the Secretariat General, marked by
each father with an electronic pencil, and then handed in to
be tabulated by the electronic computer specially installed
for this purpose. An overwhelming majority was registered
in favor of the advocates of reform, who had been behind the
schema; 2,162 votes for, 46 votes against, and 7 abstentions.
It was also a victory for the Liturgical Movement itself, which
had inspired its authors throughout. The voting was interpreted by many as a clear sign of the way in which the wind
was blowing.†

That afternoon and evening the "little councils" of theologians were in a ferment of excitement and optimism.
Things seemed to be going in the right direction at last.
Rumor had it that at one of the last meetings of the Central
Preparatory Commission, in May or June, Cardinal Léger
had spoken out equally sharply in favor of biblical scholars,
denouncing the attacks made on the Biblical Institute and

* Actually distributed on Friday, Nov. 23, 1962.
† Cf. *Informations Catholiques Internationales,* Dec. 1, 1962, pp. 5–6.

deploring the obscurantist attitude toward scriptural studies manifested by the Lateran University.* The African bishops had met on Tuesday to coordinate their efforts with a view to the rejection of the schema. What transpired on Thursday (no congregation) in the Ottaviani camp, after the first day's rebuff, was not generally known. However, it soon became evident that they too had been reviewing their resources.

The next or 20th General Congregation was held on Friday, Nov. 16, and was introduced by a word of caution from the President, Cardinal Liénart, who called for an amicable expression and the fraternal consideration of opposing viewpoints. The first speaker was Cardinal Tisserant who, in a rapid flow of Latin that proved too much for the majority of the Fathers, reviewed the policy laid down by Pius XII on the investigation of scriptural questions, beginning with the letter of Fr. Vosté to Cardinal Suhard in 1943. He insisted that the Council leave the field of scripture open to the free discussion of the exegetes and theologians.

Cardinal Gonçalves Cerejeira of Lisbon, the Primate of Portugal, then took the microphone to begin the defense of the schema. But his main efforts were directed against the leakage of information to the press which he had observed in recent days. How was it possible for the press to know about what was going to be said before it was actually said in the hall of the Council? He pleaded with all present, therefore—fathers, experts and observers—to guard the secret of the Council. Then, in short order, Cardinals De Barros Câmara, McIntyre, and Caggiano launched into a repetition of the plea by Ruffini for a just examination of the existing schema, while Cardinal Lefebvre, conscious of his debt to the men on the other side, merely cited his objections to it and then handed his paper to the Secretariat.

* See p. 48.

Cardinal Santos was for retention, but suggested that more thought be given to making precise what was meant by "pastoral." Referring to the question raised by the Cardinal-Patriarch of Lisbon, Cardinal Urbani of Venice complained that not only were the newspapers, journals and *conférenciers* of Rome and elsewhere discussing freely what was going on in the Council and airing the disputes, but that seminarians in various parts of the world were being spiritually disturbed by the apparent confusion among those who were supposed to be the teachers of the Church. Hence he was for retaining the schema as a working basis in order not to give substance to these fears.

Speaking for the South American Bishops, Cardinal Silva Henriquez of Chile stated that the pastoral aims of the Council should be directed particularly toward the sheep separated from the fold and hence, as the pope indicated, the Council ought to display an ecumenical spirit. As to the schema, not only did it offend against possible reunion with non-Catholics, but it could not even bring about agreement among Catholics, as was evident in the seminaries and faculties of theology. Its primary error was to set the Church up as a judge who condemns. The pope wants rather pastors who counsel and demonstrate love for those to whom they are trying to bring the truth. In a theological sense, he insisted that truth was born of the charity of Almighty God, hence, in all charity, the Council should come out with a doctrine that would be clear, amicable, positive, timely and adaptable to modern needs. His conclusion was: re-do the draft in a much briefer form, and omit all questions of a purely exegetical nature only. "We are pastors, not theologians. We have no time for the disputes of the schools."

The Irish Dominican Cardinal Browne next rose to demonstrate that not all the prelates were pastors, as had been asserted. In true scholastic form, he went through eleven points attempting to prove that since the doctrine of "two sources" [scripture and tradition] formed part of the Church's doctrinal patrimony, it was therefore to be retained, regardless of whether the expression was ancient. St. Thomas, Trent, Vatican Council I, the encyclicals of Leo XIII, Pius XII, etc. were all in agreement, he maintained.

The following two speakers were at opposite poles. The conservative Bishop Fares of Catanzaro, Italy, said that he was afraid of a resurgence of Modernism. The Council of Trent had warned against those who "twist the Scriptures" and Vatican Council I had asserted that dangerous innovators must be "coerced" and errors driven out, as St. Pius X had done when he condemned this heresy. For Bishop Bengsch of divided Berlin, on the other hand, the schema was bad and could not be improved even by amendments. It contradicted the wishes of the Holy Father by reflecting a spirit of condemnation, rather than one of mercy. It was full of anathemas, censures and suspicions. The Church was made to appear not as our *Mater et Magister,* but solely as our *Magistra* (mistress). Some of the errors castigated in it were so obscure as to be hardly known even by theologians. It was a museum-piece, not something alive.

Bishop Reuss, the auxiliary of Mainz, Germany, called for a decision, by the Council or the pope, on certain fundamental questions such as the "two sources," the nature of the Church, the place of the episcopate, and the like, otherwise they would merely be floundering about without getting anywhere. Bishop Gargitter of Bressanone, Italy, was in favor of a completely new, positive and pastoral schema. The Church owed a great debt of gratitude to Catholic exegetes and scholars generally, and should do nothing to put obstacles in their path. Bishop Hoa Nguyen-van Hien, of Dalat,

Vietnam, likewise stressed the pastoral theme, but somehow lost himself in a sermon on the Trinity and had to be called to order by the President.

Some spirit was introduced into the debate by the Bishop of Faenza, Msgr. Battaglia, who labelled the arguments against the schema "fallacies and inanities." He attacked the Biblical Institute and the whole development of modern theology. Then in a rapid fire of irony and sarcasm, he acknowledged that the schema would probably be rejected, while announcing himself as a new Daniel in a den of lions, retaining his integrity withal.

Archb. Guerry of Cambrai next rose to speak in the name of the French episcopate. He desired to remove a certain equivocation that seemed to overshadow the debate. In speaking of a pastoral approach, there was no room for a loose or inexact statement of doctrine. The word of God must be set before the world in its purity and entirety. What was wanted actually was a deepening and enlarging of our doctrinal perspective, to include all the advances made by science and discovery in our world of today. This was not asking for a diminution, but an extension, of our doctrinal tenets. But this should be done with charity, which means choosing the hard way of working selflessly to approach modern man in his needs and anxieties, and not the easy way out by condemning and negating and rejecting.

After a plea for the scholastic approach contained in the schema by the Archbishop of Florence, Msgr. Florit, and a contrary one in favor of rejection by the Bishop of Tehuantepec in Mexico, Dom Butler, Abbot of Downside in England, closed the day's discussion by aligning himself squarely with the rejectors. Although it had been said that the schema could be corrected, two days of debate had revealed that agreement was virtually impossible of attainment on the present text. There must be unanimity, or virtual unanimity, when decisions are reached by the Church on doctrinal matters. Experience had shown that there would always be some *non placet,* even if the present schema were corrected. Therefore, it was better to scrap it and prepare another that would have some prospect of achieving this unanimity.

The debate on Saturday, Nov. 17 (21st General Congregation), further accentuated the differences of opinion in the assembly and proved the justice of Dom Butler's contention; it was also highlighted by a certain number of personal exchanges and insinuations which, while not transgressing the outward decorum and courtesy expected of the conciliar fathers, nevertheless testified to the increasing tension on both sides and the conviction that a crisis was at hand.

Cardinals De la Torre of Quito and Garibi y Rivera of Guadalajara (Mexico) first took the floor to argue for retention, at least as a basis for discussion. But they were immediately followed by the youthful-looking and intense Cardinal Doepfner of Munich, who had evidently determined to bring matters to a head. He began by challenging the introductory remarks of Cardinal Ottaviani. "The President of the Theological Commission," he said, "has informed us that in the preparation of this schema, which took two years, there was a general accord on the part of the participating theologians and prelates. Cardinals Frings and Léger, however, have indicated just the opposite. Hence there is at least some doubt as to this accord and alleged unanimity. The regulations under which we operate specify that we can either accept, amend, or reject the schema. My impression is that the Theological Commission was too much under the influence of one school, represented by Lateran University. There was no concern for any other tendencies. As an in-

stance of this intransigence, I cite the fact that a proposal
made by the Secretariat for Promoting Unity with a view to
collaborating with the Theological Commission, was turned
down. It was therefore easy to foresee that dissensions would
arise in the Council, because in the Council one can speak
freely and openly. This is no sign of any irreverence toward
the Holy Father, for he is the one who has given us permission to discuss, amend, or reject. Our right to judge is complete and we must finally vote. The schema which we would
like to propose has been drawn up by theologians of various
tendencies and is quite different in spirit from the one before
us."*

This speech was greeted with considerable applause, and
caused consternation in the opposing camp. In quick succession, Cardinals Concha and Bacci each put in a plea for
the schema, the latter saying that it had been given to the
Council by the pope and Central Commission to be discussed, not rejected.

Bishop Schmitt of Metz, France, a scriptural scholar in
his own right, led off episcopal comment by referring to the
question of "two sources" brought up by Cardinal Browne.
Trent had deliberately rejected the use of the terms *"partim
. . . partim"* with reference to scripture and tradition, because this would have implied the sanctioning of a school of
thought which was not traditional or in accord with the best
tradition: "All revelation consists in the person of Christ,"
he asserted, "for He is its author, the Word of God. His
whole life, death and resurrection reveal Him to us. Let us
not reduce Christian revelation and Christianity itself to a
kind of ideology. It is the whole means (economy) of salvation, and not something purely intellectual."

* For Card. Doepfner's speech, see G. Zizola, *L'Italia* (Milan), Nov. 18, 1962.
See above, p. 142.

In apparent good humor Cardinal Ottaviani next took the floor. He proposed, he said, to answer the observations made by Cardinal Doepfner which, though obviously not intended maliciously, nevertheless sprang from misinformation. "It is not true that this schema was made in my name," he said. "In the Commission those matters in the schema that were the subject of discussion or disagreement were put to a vote. It was normal for the opinion of the minority then to be excluded. The members of this Commission came from various countries, from different universities. It is not true that only one opinion or one school of thought was represented." After claiming that members of the Biblical Institute had been invited to sit on the Commission, he concluded by repeating that the rules did not provide for the rejection, but merely the discussion of the schema.

This last assertion was immediately and successfully challenged from the floor. An appeal was made to the President to read the Regulations; it was thereupon settled once and for all that schemata could be discussed, amended or *rejected.* Meanwhile, a member of the Theological Commission whose opinions had not been received by the cardinal disagreed with him about the presence of a member of the Biblical Institute on the Commission, and one of the cardinals said openly: "It's hardly worth repeating that His Eminence is not telling the truth. All the world knows it." Even in the preparatory stages of the Council, it became generally known, opponents were skillfully maneuvered out of their places at Commission meetings, threatened with reprisals, and votes taken when they were absent.

---

* Art. 33.1 of the Rules of Procedure states specifically: "Each Father may express his opinion with regard to each schema presented and ask either for its adoption, rejection, or amendment." *Motu Proprio Appropinquante Concilio,* Aug. 6, 1962. (The Rules are an appendix to this document; text in *La Documentation Catholique,* Oct. 7, 1962, p. 1231.)

Archbishop Parente next made a feeble attempt to defend the schema which contained a *"sana doctrina,"* as everyone knew, reiterating in particular its main theory about the "two sources" of revelation, but as he droned on beyond the allotted time he had to be cut off by the President. With his customary disregard for the proprieties, he then demanded time to conclude and stressed once again the soundness of the document before the fathers, "worthy of being recommended for your discussion." His successor Bishop Butorac had hardly finished his remarks in the same sense, when Cardinal Frings took the floor.

"One word is all I desire," he said, "to answer Msgr. Parente. No one denies that revelation comes to us through both scripture and tradition. What we are arguing about is the *source* of revelation, which is one and unique, namely the Word of God."

Bishop Charue of Namur, Belgium, put his finger on the real difficulty with the Ottaviani approach. Calling attention to the fact that all the Belgians and French bishops were against the schema, he attacked the necessity of going over the condemnation of Modernism. There are other errors, he insisted, that are just as dangerous. "It is not up to the Council to do the work of the Holy Office, or of theologians," he said, "but it is up to the Council not to set the stage for another Galileo incident! Our Council should imitate that of Jerusalem, and not put unbearable burdens on those outside the Church or the faith. The fact that the Church can house men of diverse opinions and attitudes gives us hope for the future."*

After Bishop Temiño Saiz of Spain had voiced once again what may be regarded as the Italian-Spanish view of the matter, a bishop from Central Africa, Msgr. Zoa, speaking in

* See H. Fesquet, *Le Monde,* Nov. 21, 1962.

the name of all African bishops, said that they rallied to the opinions expressed by Cardinals Alfrink, Bea, Léger, and Liénart. The schema "was not satisfactory at all" (*omnino non placet*) and ought to be rejected. He also agreed with what Abbot Butler had said the previous day with regard to moral unanimity.

This was the sense also of the two following speakers, Bishop Pourchet of France and Bishop Hakim (Israel). The latter's discourse was interesting for the light it threw on the Eastern approach to the question of tradition. He said that oriental theology was completely at a loss to understand a tradition of "two sources," as presented by the schema. The Eastern Churches remained faithful to what St. Cyril of Jerusalem and St. Maximos the Confessor, a fourth and a seventh century Father of the Church, respectively, had to say on the matter, which was surely much closer to the primitive tradition.

"The authors of this schema have monopolized the universal faith for the benefit of their own personal theologizing," he said. "With us the liturgy is the chief means of instruction in the faith through its symbolism. Instruction is never separated from scripture or the fathers. The schema does violence to our conception of the faith, by separating things which ought not to be separated. It is perhaps a good example of what the scholastic approach leads to, but it certainly cannot be considered as exhausting the Gospel message, which cannot be confined within any one conceptual system. It should speak of man as the image of God, of the mystery of redemption, of Christ's death and resurrection. Instead of all this, it speaks only of satisfaction for sin, as if this were the main consideration behind the mystery of man's redemption."

The hopelessness of being able to arrive at any kind of

compromise on the schema was borne in on the fathers as they assembled for their 22nd General Congregation on Monday morning, Nov. 19, with Cardinal Spellman in the chair. Most of the speeches touched upon the theme that was uppermost in their minds, namely how to find a way of escape out of the present impasse. It was apparent that the majority of the fathers were not in favor of the schema as it stood, but there was uncertainty about the wisdom of rejecting it outright. Many felt that to remand it to the Commission that had originally submitted it (the Preparatory and Conciliar Theological Commissions were both headed by Cardinal Ottaviani and staffed by many of the same people) would only complicate matters, hardening Ottaviani and his supporters in their advocacy of it.

Various suggestions were put forth. Returning from India where he had gone when his country was invaded by China, expressly in order to take part in the important debate, Cardinal Gracias revealed that he was wholly in favor of rejection. It was not possible to say that the Holy Father had approved it, as the opposition were maintaining. What he had approved was the submission of it to the Council, as desired by the Theological Commission—quite a different thing. When a house was falling into ruin it was better to demolish it and build another, rather than to attempt repairs. "The Preparatory Commission had no monopoly of the Holy Spirit and wisdom." The Council was assisted by the Holy Ghost in a way that theologians were not. The schema ought to be re-done, but he had no concrete suggestions about method.*

Neither had Cardinals De Arriba y Castro or Gilroy, the first speakers of the day, who inclined to making the best of a bad situation. The following two speakers, Cardinals Meyer

* See Fesquet, *Le Monde*, Nov. 21, 1962.

of Chicago and Landázuri Ricketts of Lima, were congratulated by Cardinals Léger and Ottaviani, respectively, when each had finished, but they too had nothing concrete to offer in the way of an expedient. Both sides, however, still welcomed support. Bishop Griffiths, one of the auxiliaries of New York, was of the opinion that the schema would have to be rejected *"radicaliter"* and a new one prepared, one, that is, that the whole assembly could accept.

The speech of the morning, however, was admittedly that delivered by Bishop De Smedt, of Bruges, Belgium, a member of the Secretariat for Promoting Unity, who rose to say that he was speaking for the Secretariat. As on an earlier occasion when Cardinal Bea spoke, so on this one, the fathers had the unmistakable impression that they were listening to the words of the pope himself.

He began by remarking that there had been much discussion of ecumenism or the ecumenical spirit with reference to the subject under debate, some arguing that the schema reflected a proper ecumenical concern, others that it did not. What then was an authentic ecumenical outlook? Speaking as a member of the Secretariat for Promoting Christian Unity, which had been created by the Holy Father expressly for the purpose of aiding the fathers in the ecumenical aspect of their work, he would attempt to define what an ecumenically-oriented document ought to be. It was one, in short, which favored and promoted a conversation (dialogue) between Catholics and non-Catholics.

"For centuries, we Catholics have thought that it was sufficient to explain our doctrine clearly. Non-Catholics thought the same. Both sides explained their own point of view using their own terminology and from their own point of view only; but what Catholics said was not well received by non-Catholics, and vice versa. According to this method, no progress was made on the road toward unity, quite the reverse. . . . But for several decades now another method has been tried: the ecumenical dialogue. What does it involve? It means not being concerned by a preoccupation for truth alone, but also with the way in which it is presented, so that it can be made comprehensible to others. . . . Both sides must strive to explain their faith clearly, objectively, and in a way that is psychologically acceptable and without engaging in controversy. It is this new method which should be applied by the Council, according to the wishes of the Holy Father. If we wish the documents issued by the Council to be intelligible to non-Catholics, a certain number of rules must be observed:

"1. We must understand the doctrines of the Orthodox and Protestants.
"2. We must know what they think (rightly or wrongly) about Catholic teaching.
"3. We must know what they regard as unclear or lacking in Catholic teaching.
"4. Scholastic terminology is not well understood by non-Catholics; on the other hand, by using Biblical or patristic terms we can prevent many errors and prejudices.
"5. Expressions must be carefully chosen with regard to their effect on non-Catholics.
"6. Judgments must be carefully weighed and account must be taken of the context in which they appear to non-Catholics.
"7. Documents must be worded in such in such a way as to appear convincing to non-Catholics also.
"8. All useless controversy must be avoided.
"9. Errors should be clearly rejected, but without wounding sensibilities."

Msgr. De Smedt then went on to note that, although the Secretariat for Promoting Unity had been created to help with the preparations for the Council and had offered to collaborate with the Theological Commission, "for reasons which I do not care to judge," the Theological Commission "never wished to do so." The Secretariat also proposed the creation of a mixed subcommission, but this offer too was turned down.

In the judgment of the Secretariat, the present schema had "grave faults from an ecumenical point of view: It would not encourage a dialogue with non-Catholics, or represent progress, but a retreat. . . . Today a new method has been discovered, thanks to which a precious dialogue has been begun. The fruits of this method are apparent to all in the presence of observer-delegates in this council hall. The hour is one of pardon, but also one of great seriousness. If the schema prepared by the Theological Commission is not modified, we shall be responsible for causing Vatican Council II to destroy a great, an immense hope. I speak of the hope of those who, like Pope John XXIII, are waiting in prayer and fasting for an important and significant step finally to be made in the direction of fraternal unity, the unity of those for whom Christ Our Lord offered this prayer: *Ut unum sint."** There was loud and continuous applause when the bishop finished.

The search for some kind of a solution now seemed more imperative than ever. Earlier, Cardinal Rugambwa had suggested asking the Holy Father to stop the discussion now, since they could reach no agreement, and proposed taking it up again at the next session on the basis of a new document. Bishop Henríquez felt that any new document must reflect the influence of the Biblical Commission.

* The complete German text of Bishop De Smedt's speech, translated from the Latin, was made available by the Swiss news agency KIPA, Nov. 23, 1962, and was widely commented on in the European press. Henri Fesquet, writing in *Le Monde,* Nov. 21, 1962, said: "This was one of the great moments of the Council." Cf. *La Documentation Catholique,* Dec. 16, 1962.

It was Archbishop Garrone of Toulouse who made the concrete proposal about setting up a mixed commission to prepare a new draft. Since the schema could not be returned to the commission that had originated it, "it is necessary that the Theological Commission should work in unison with the Secretariat for Unity and with the *periti* (experts)." This would bring about that unanimity which the whole Council desired.

"The original sin of the Council lay in the defective work of the Preparatory Commissions," observed Archbishop Hurley of South Africa. The proper solution in this case was for the schema to be re-done by a new commission which would be careful to put back in the draft all that was left out by the Theological Commission.

Finally, Bishop Ancel of Lyons noted that a two-thirds majority being clearly impossible either for or against any proposal, there was no alternative but to appeal to the Holy Father to appoint new experts to prepare a new schema. The last speaker, Bishop Seitz (Vietnam), proposed that the Council vote on one or another of the suggestions put forth.

Accordingly, on the next day, Nov. 20 (23rd General Congregation), at 10:30 in the morning, the debate was dramatically halted by Secretary General Felici, who announced that a proposal by the Council of Presidents would be put to a vote.* Those in favor of halting the discussion of the schema were to vote *Placet* (Yes); those favoring a continuation of the discussion *Non placet* (No). The announcement was then repeated in all six languages by the subsecretaries. Cardinal Frings, the President of the day, explained: "Although this proposal does not please us completely, it seems to me the best solution, the most harmonious, and the one

---

* Although there was no statement to this effect, the pope no doubt had permitted this move.

that will best serve the common good." After a moment, Secretary General Felici again said: *"Audiant omnes,* there have been queries about the voting. I repeat: *Placet* means interrupting the debate, *Non placet* continuing with the discussion. Those who have made a mistake can ask for new ballots." At 10:55 he was forced to repeat what he had said.

Apparently there was widespread confusion among the fathers as to what they were being asked to vote on, owing to the illogical way in which the question had been framed.* While they were deliberating what to do or filling out their ballots, Cardinal Ruffini, sitting at the table of Council Presidents, gratuitously announced: "Interrupting the debate means that this schema will be completely overhauled and changed. Therefore if you vote *Placet,* it means the last of this schema." This attempt to influence votes was not at all well received by the Council. There were many protests and much talking. Nevertheless Ruffini repeated his remarks two more times until he was finally drowned out.

The debate was then resumed at 11 A.M., but at 11:23 it was again halted by the Secretary General, who announced the results of the voting: "Present: 2,209 fathers; 1,368 *Placets;* 19 invalid votes; and 822 *Non placets.* Since a majority of 1,473 votes is required, we shall therefore now take up Chapter I of the schema."

Thus the supporters had won a technical victory, but the fruits were to be denied them. It was the conviction of many that the total of the majority would have been even greater but for the confusion surrounding the voting, and the total of the minority correspondingly less—some fathers on both

* Was this done deliberately, a desperate last-minute move on the part of the supporters of the schema in the hope of winning an overwhelming victory by confusing the voters, or was it merely accidental? The words of Cardinal Ruffini would seem to lend weight to the former supposition, but those of Cardinal Frings appear to rule this possibility out.

sides were known to have voted unwittingly against their principles.

The next morning, while Cardinal Ruffini was presiding, another dramatic announcement was made. Despite the vote, the pope had ordered the schema withdrawn. He had decided that the whole matter should be reconsidered by a special commission, on which Cardinals Bea and Ottaviani would serve as joint presidents, with Cardinals Frings, Liénart, and Meyer representing the liberals, Cardinals Browne of Ireland and Ruffini the traditionalists, and Cardinal Lefebvre, of Bourges, the center. They were to be assisted by the bishops belonging to the Secretariat for Promoting Christian Unity and the bishops elected to the Theological Commission by the Council, as well as by a number of *periti,* or official theologians. The new decree to be drafted in accordance with the aims of the Council was to be short, irenic in tone, and pastoral in approach.

Though there was nothing more to say, this meeting was prolonged until noon, so that an early breakup would not give rise to rumors. Nevertheless, the essential facts were soon in the newspapers. On this occasion, the Vatican newspaper *L'Osservatore Romano,* which consistently reflected the curial line, departed from its usual terseness. Although it disclosed some of the details about the impasse, it failed to mention the all-important outcome of the vote, thus veiling the discomfiture of the conservative bloc as long as possible.

It is bewildering how a man of Cardinal Ottaviani's intelligence could have miscalculated so badly. It seems strange that he did not anticipate that the majority would be for the reforms, which had been advocated in respectable circles for many years now, and were looked upon with favor by the pope. One supposition was that Ottaviani's closest advisers and informants—Monsignor Parente and the Franciscan

Father Ermenegildo Lio, of the Holy Office, and such Americans as Monsignor Joseph Fenton, of Catholic University, and Monsignor Rudolph Bandas, of St. Paul, Minnesota—had convinced him that only a handful of extremist German and French prelates really wanted drastic changes in the Church. Apparently, they and the others who assisted in the preparation of the schema (like the Jesuit Fathers Sebastian Tromp and Franz Huerth, the Dominican Luigi Ciappi, and the Franciscan Carl Balič) could conceive of no other way of presenting Catholic truths than by repeating the tried-and-true formulas of the past and condemning all innovation.

Undoubtedly, the most important single disclosure of this first session was the great strength shown by the advocates of renewal and reform. It had not previously been known just how influential this tendency in the Church really was.* The chief spokesman in the Curia for the new approach was unquestionably Cardinal Bea, whose efforts over the past two years had been and continue to be nothing short of phenomenal. "My whole life has been a preparation for this," he has said.

The new Secretariat for Promoting Christian Unity, over which he presides, was the first Roman office to have achieved the miracle—Bea's own word—of being completely outside the domination of the Holy Office. Since Bea has been directed by papal decree to collaborate with Ottaviani in drafting a new schema on the sources of revelation, this means that he has now been given the right to be heard on strictly theological matters, which, up to the present, Ottaviani has successfully retained within the exclusive control of the Holy Office. The consequences of this decision could be far-reach-

---

* Cf. the statement of Card. Frings: "The majority of bishops shares a moderate progressive tendency, and it appears that they will have the two-thirds majority against the more conservative minority." *The Catholic Transcript,* Mar. 21, 1963.

ing. In effect, it warned the old guard that they were not the
sole guardians of orthodoxy, and that henceforth they must
heed the advice of authentic biblical scholarship and manifest
a more ecumenical spirit. A familiar sight in Rome is the
poster for British European Airways, or BEA, and Italian wits
now claim that a new sign has been posted over the door of
the Holy Office: "Travel with BEA."

Another fruitful result of the Council was the interchange
of ideas made possible by the concentration of so many
learned priests in one place at one time. Most of the bishops
rejoiced at this development, and took advantage of free
hours between meetings to brush up on issues by inviting
periti to lecture before their episcopal conferences. The Holy
Office, unaccustomed to so much uncontrolled theologizing,
found this distasteful and alarming. Toward the middle of
November, Cardinal Ottaviani asked the pope to request the
Jesuit fathers of the Biblical Institute not to give any more
lectures before individual groups of bishops, and to order the
famous Innsbruck theologian Father Karl Rahner, S.J., to
leave Rome. When the pope inquired who had asked the
Jesuit fathers to lecture, and was told that it had been the
bishops themselves, he said he could not be expected to interfere with the legitimate right of bishops to inform themselves regarding the issues before the Council. At the same
time, he is said to have shown Ottaviani a testimonial, signed
by three cardinals, that praised Father Rahner as an outstanding theologian. This incident reminded old Roman
hands of the disgraceful treatment meted out to Professor
Altaner, the famous authority on the fathers of the Church,
in 1950, when he was told to leave Rome because of his opposition to the project for defining the Assumption of the
Blessed Virgin. They likewise recalled the shabby treatment
recently accorded the Dominican theologian Father Rai-

mondo Spiazzi, who, during the preparatory phase of the Council, was bold enough to publish a pamphlet discussing possible changes in the attitude toward clerical celibacy. The mere suggestion of any revision in this regard being frowned upon by the Holy Office as a sure sign of heresy, Father Spiazzi was immediately relieved of his job in the Roman Chancery, transferred from his teaching post, barred from Rome, and sent to Tuscany as provincial. Eventually, this came to the attention of Pope John, who at once ended Father Spiazzi's exile and appointed him a member of the Council's Preparatory Commission on the Laity.

In any attempt to reconstruct the strategy behind the Council, one basic question arises: Who are the pope's principal counsellors and advisers? It is now obvious that the pope has nurtured for a long time most of the ideas he expressed at the opening of the Council about simplifying and modernizing the Church. He is a fairly good historian, being very much at home in the works of the Church Fathers, and particularly familiar with the reform movement that followed the Council of Trent. Besides this, he has gathered a wealth of information about men and ideas from his experience abroad as papal representative in the Near East and France. The influence of his private secretary, the able Monsignor Loris Capovilla, whom the pope brought with him from Venice, is evidently great. This still fairly young man is capable of turning his attention to almost any topic, mastering it in short order, and putting it before the pope in readily graspable form. Among the cardinals, the key figure is undoubtedly Cardinal Bea, whose stature as a leader in the ecumenical movement has bounded sky-high. It seems certain also that Cardinals Montini, Suenens, and Léger have been consulted not infrequently by the pope. What direct influence such people as Cardinals Alfrink, Frings, Doepfner, and

Liénart wield is anyone's guess. This does not mean that the pope's old friends among the conservatives, such as Cardinals Ruffini, Pizzardo, and Bacci, cannot have access to his ear any time they wish. After all, as he made clear in the inaugural address, the prophets of doom still see him regularly.

SUMMARY

November 14, 1962, Wednesday—19TH GENERAL CONGREGATION
PRESIDENT: Card. *Tisserant* (Curia). MASS: Celebrated by Bp. *Cheng* (aux. Taipeh [Formosa]). PRESENT: 2,215 fathers. SUBJECT: General discussion of the schema on the two sources of revelation begun.

SPEAKERS: Card. *Ottaviani* (President of Theological Commission), and Msgr. *Garofalo,* member of Theological Commission), Cards. *Lienart* (Lille), *Frings* (Cologne), *Ruffini* (Palermo), *Siri* (Genoa), *Quiroga y Palacios* (Santiago de Compostela, Spain), *Léger* (Montreal), *König* (Vienna), *Alfrink* (Utrecht), *Suenens* (Malines-Brussels), *Ritter* (St. Louis, USA), *Bea* (Curia); Patr. *Maximos IV Saigh* (Antioch of the Melchites, Lebanon); Archbps. *Manek* (Endeh, Indonesia), *Soegijapranata* (Semarang, Indonesia), both in the name of Indonesian bishops, *Morcillo* (Zaragoza, Spain), also on behalf of certain Spanish bishops.

Fathers are requested by SG to vote, by ballot, on 1) whether liturgy schema is approved in principle; 2) whether proposed amendments, after being acted upon by Liturgy Commission, shall be submitted later to a vote in the general congregation.

The results were : 2,162 votes in favor, 46 against, and 7 abstentions.
Weekly general audience of the pope.
Conference of Archb. *Morcillo Gonzales* on the functioning of the Council.
Conference of Fr. *P. M. Gy,* O.P. on a pastoral liturgy.
November 15, 1962, Thursday—Consistory in the Vatican
Journalists visit Castel Gandolfo.
*November 16, 1962, Friday—20*TH GENERAL CONGREGATION
PRESIDENT: Card. *Lienart* (Lille). MASS: According to Armenian rite, celebrated by Archb. *Layek* (Aleppo of the Armenians). PRESENT: 2,212 fathers. SUBJECT: General discussion of schema on sources of revelation.
SPEAKERS: Cards. *Tisserant, Gonçalves Cerejeira* (Lisbon), *de Barros Câmara* (Rio de Janeiro, Brazil), *McIntyre* (Los Angeles), *Caggiano* (Buenos Aires), *Lefebvre* (Bourges, France), *Santos* (Manila), *Urbani,* (Venice), *Silva Henriquez* (Santiago de Chile), *Browne* (Curia); Archbps. and Bps. *Fares* (Catanzaro and Squillace, Italy), *Bengsch* (Berlin), *Tabera* (Albacete, Spain), *Reuss* (aux. Mainz, Germany), *Gargitter* (Bessanone, Italy), *Hoa Nguyen-van Hien* (Dalat, Vietnam), *Battaglia* (Faenza, Italy), *Guerry* (Cambrai, France) on behalf of the French episcopate, *Florit* (Florence, Italy), *Alba Palacios* (Teuantepec, Mexico); Abbot *Butler,* O.S.B. (Downside, England).
Conference by Dr. Hans Küng.
*November 17, 1962, Saturday—21*ST GENERAL CONGREGATION
PRESIDENT: Card. *Gilroy* (Australia). MASS: Celebrated by Archb. *Baraniak* (Poznan, Poland). PRESENT: 2,206 fathers. SUBJECT: General discussion of schema on sources of revelation.
SPEAKERS: Cards. *De la Torre* (Quito, Ecuador), *Garibi y Rivera* (Guadalajara, Mexico), *Döpfner* (Munich), *Concha* (Bogotá, Colombia), *Bacci* (Curia), *Ottaviani* (Curia), *Frings* (Cologne); Archbps. and Bps. *Schmitt* (Metz, France), *Parente* (Curia), *Butorac* (Dubrovnik, Yugoslavia), *Simons* (Indore, India), *Charue* (Namur, Belgium), *Temiño Saiz* (Orense, Spain), *Zoa* (Yaoundé, Camerun) also on behalf of many African bishops, *Pourchet* (Saint-Flour, France), *Hakim* (Akka of the Melchites, Israel), *Argaya Goicoechea* (Mondoñedo-Ferrol, Spain), *Rosales* (Cebù, Philippines) speaking for the majority of Philippine bishops.

Before today's discussion, the SG requests the fathers to vote on four amended paragraphs of the Introduction or Preface to the schema on the liturgy.

Bishops of the United States received in special audience by the pope.

November 19, 1962, Monday—22ND GENERAL CONGREGATION

PRESIDENT: Card. *Spellman*. MASS: Celebrated by Archb. *Beovich* (Adelaide, Australia). PRESENT: 2,197 fathers. SUBJECT: General discussion of schema on sources of revelation.

SPEAKERS: Cards. *De Arriba y Castro* (Tarragona, Spain), *Gilroy* (Sydney, Australia), *Gracias* (Bombay), *Meyer* (Chicago), *Landázuri Ricketts* (Lima, Peru), *Rugambwa* (Bukoba, Tanganyika); Archbps. and Bps. *Martin* (vic. apo. New Caledonia, Oceania), *Henriquez* (aux. Caracas, Venezuela), *Griffiths* (aux. New York), *De Smedt* (Bruges, Belgium), *de Sousa* (Funchal, Portugal), *Garrone* (Toulouse, France), *D'Avack* (Camerino, Italy), *Del Pino Gómez* (Lerida, Spain), *Hurley* (Durban, South Africa), *Ruotolo* (Ugento, Italy), *Ancel* (aux. Lyons, France), and *Seitz* (Kontum, Vietnam).

The Council of Cardinal Presidents met immediately after this congregation in the conciliar hall.

French bishops received in special audience by the pope.

Conference of Fr. *Jean Daniélou*.

November 20, 1962, Tuesday—23RD GENERAL CONGREGATION

PRESIDENT: Card. *Frings* (Cologne). MASS: Celebrated by Archb. *Rodríguez-Quirós* (San José de Costa Rica). PRESENT: 2,211 fathers. SUBJECT: General discussion of schema on sources of revelation.

SPEAKERS: Archbps. and Bps. *Cabana* (Sherbrooke, Canada), *Echeverria Ruiz* (Ambato, Ecuador), *García Martínez* (Spain), *Klepacz* (Lodz, Poland), *Nicodemo* (Bari, Italy), *de Proença Sigaud* (Diamantina, Brazil), *Quarracino* (Nueve de Julio, Argentina), *Carli* (Segni, Italy), *Costantini* (Sessa Aurunca, Italy); Fr. *Fernández* (Master General of the Dominicans, Spain); Archbps. and Bps. *Barbetta* (Italy), *Ferro* (Reggio Calabria, Italy), and *Franic* (Split, Yugoslavia).

SG announces that Council of Cardinal Presidents has decided to ask Council to vote on schema as a whole, in view of sharp differences of opinion about its merits, before undertaking discussion of various chapters. Those in favor of interrupting debate and considering another schema were to vote *Placet;* those in favor of continuing with debate on present schema, were to vote *Non placet*. Results: 1,368 *Placets;* 822 *Non placets*.

SUBJECT: Chapter I of the schema on sources of revelation.
SPEAKERS: Cards. *Tisserant* and *Ruffini;* Bp. *Jacono* (Italy).
Conference of Card. *Bea* in Venice.

November 21, 1962, Wednesday—24TH GENERAL CONGREGATION

PRESIDENT: Card. *Ruffini*. MASS: In the Ukrainian rite, celebrated by Bp. *Bukatko* (coadj. Belgrade). PRESENT: 2,185 fathers.

Before the day's proceedings got under way, the SG, on behalf of the Secretary of State, announced that the Holy Father had decided that the schema on sources of revelation should be withdrawn in accordance with the wishes of the majority, in spite of the fact that the vote on it yesterday had not reached the two-thirds majority required by the Rules, and be entrusted to a mixed Commission consisting of the members of the Theological Commission and the Secretariat for Promoting Christian Unity, to be redrafted, shortened, and have greater emphasis placed on "the general principles of Catholic doctrine already treated by the Council of Trent and Vatican Council I."

The SG announced that on Friday the Council would take up the schema on the Communications Media as its next item.

SUBJECT: Chapter I of the schema on sources of revelation.
SPEAKERS: Bps. *Guana* (Livorno, Italy), *Martínez* (Zamora, Spain); Abbot *Butler,* O.S.B. (Downside); Archbps. and Bps. *Chang Tso-huan* (China), *Hermaniuk* (Winnipeg), *Rupp* (Monaco), *Marty* (Rheims, France), *Henriquez* (aux. Caracas, Venezuela), *Cantero Cuadrado* (Huelva, Spain), *Seper* (Zagreb, Yugoslavia), *Veuillot* (coadj. Paris), *Jaeger* (Paderborn, Germany), *Barneschi* (Manzini, South Africa), *Wojtyla* (aux. Kraków, Poland), and *Cibrián Fernández* (vic. ap. Corocoro, Brazil).

Weekly general audience of the pope.

November 22, 1962, Thursday

Press conference of Fr. *Baragli,* S.J. on communications media and the Church.

Important defense of thesis by Fr. *Lohfing* at Biblicum, attended by 12 cardinals, 100 bishops, hundreds of clergy, Dr. *Cullmann,* Msgr. *Cassian,* and others.

VI

The Debate on the "Communications Media"

✠

THE MOOD of the Council fluctuated considerably during the two weeks that had just gone by, from one of discouragement and dejection at the slow pace of the deliberations, to relief at the termination of the debate on the liturgy, then from varying shades of determination, excitement, dejection and frustration over the schema *De Revelatione,* to one of final elation and optimism over the success achieved. Pope John himself appears to have been the only person capable of maintaining a serene air throughout in keeping with his habitual optimism. There was some resentment among the fathers over the way in which the voting had been handled on Tuesday. Yet curiously, the following day, when word of the pope's intervention was announced, there was no applause,

174

merely stunned amazement. The number of smiles as the fathers emerged from their Wednesday session clearly betokened the change of mood. The euphoria engendered that day continued to sustain the Council till the end, despite a renewed controversy over the schema *De Ecclesia*.

On Friday, November 23, the Council took up the schema on Modern Means of Communication, including the press, radio, motion pictures and television, in its 25th General Congregation presided over by Cardinal Caggiano, Archbishop of Buenos Aires. The mass was said by Archbishop Giacinto Tredici of Brescia, who, that very day, was celebrating the sixtieth anniversary of his ordination to the priesthood. For the occasion a number of priests and lay people from Brescia were allowed to attend the opening ceremonies. The Gospel was enthroned by Bishop Albert Scola of Norcia.

Immediately that the meeting proper came to order, the Secretary General arose to announce that the next subject for discussion would be the schema on the Unity of the Church, prepared by the Commission for the Oriental Churches. It was to be followed by that dealing with the Blessed Virgin Mary, and finally that on the Church. The latter two schemata were contained in a separate booklet that was distributed during this session, causing considerable distraction to a large number of fathers who had been anxiously awaiting the treatise on the Church, for it was feared that as this was the work of the Theological Commission, it was bound to reflect the scholastic and juridical approach manifested in the schema on revelation. It was rumored, likewise, that there had been no attempt to co-ordinate the various schemata dealing with aspects of the Church prepared by different Commissions. In the event, both these suspicions proved well grounded.

Cardinal Cento, chairman of the Commission for the Laity

and Communications Media, in his preliminary remarks, stated that the project now being presented had been prepared by a special Secretariat presided over by Archbishop Martin J. O'Connor, Rector of the American College in Rome, and for the past fourteen years president of the Pontifical Commission for Motion Pictures, Radio and Television. In turning the rostrum over to Archbishop René Stourm of Sens, who was to give the fathers a general outline of the schema, Cardinal Cento asked for the good will of the audience in dealing with a matter which though not strictly theological in substance, was still a most important element in the pastoral work of the Church, for "these instruments of communication could prove to be either a great blessing or a terrible curse both for the Church and the faithful." In turn, Bishop Stourm remarked that while the substance of this schema should prove to be theologically less strenuous than its immediate predecessor, it was precisely here that the Church was called upon to function as a Mother, well aware of the needs of her children. She was naturally concerned about these communications media, which are a source of entertainment for the modern world; and her interest was to see that this entertainment should not be harmful, either to the mind, or the conscience, or the dignity of man. Citing a statistical abstract as to the number of people, and particularly the youth, reached by the press, radio, motion pictures and television, every day, he demonstrated the importance of using these means in preaching the Gospel to every creature, and the equally imperative need for the Church to lay down both positive and negative norms for their use. Finally he outlined the schema itself, which was divided into a preface and four parts: the first dealt with the doctrine of the Church; the second provided a commentary on the apostolic function of the means of communication; the third dealt with the disciplinary aspects of these means; and the fourth laid down special considerations for the press, radio and television, and motion pictures.

Cardinal Spellman took the floor immediately after the exposition of the schema. While praising its usefulness, he called for a considerable abbreviation of the material, asking that it be reduced to propositional formulas. This was likewise the gist of Cardinal Ruffini's remarks, though he also stressed the pastoral spirit of the document. Archbishop Enriquez y Taracón of Solsona in Spain, while agreeing wholeheartedly with the importance of the schema, pointed out the necessity for technical competence in properly employing modern means of communication, and asked if priests were really competent to direct work in this field; or if it should not be stated, definitely, that this was an area where the layman's special training and experience were to be utilized to the full.

Bishop Sanschagrin, of Amos in Canada, departing somewhat from the theme under discussion, registered a complaint that bishops were frequently among the last to receive authentic information regarding the decisions and documents of the Holy See. He requested that air-mail and other quick, international means of communication be employed by the Vatican, and that the bishops be informed of major moves or decisions before the latter were given to the press. He cited for example, the considerable stir about socialism that followed the publication of *Mater et Magister,* and the confusion that reigned several years earlier when the changes in the regulations governing the eucharistic fast were first announced in the newspapers. He requested the Council to go on record as insisting on the bishops' right to be informed about official acts of the Holy See before these were released to the press.

Bishop Beck of Salford, England, suggested that it was rather useless for so large and important an assembly as the Council to attempt to discuss at length the employment of particular communication media. In order to save time, he felt the schema should be reduced to a series of propositions outlining the principles involved and laying down guidelines for a dynamic utilization of these indispensable instruments of the gospel in modern times. Bishop Llopis of Coria-Cáceres in Spain was of a similar mind; but Bishop Bednorz, of Katowice in Poland, said that it was absolutely essential for all pastors to recognize the fact that today "we are living in a civilization of the image, and no longer in a civilization of abstract thought." As a consequence, churchmen could not adopt a passive and aloof attitude toward the communications revolution going on about them. Incidentally, he stated his annoyance with photographers who were allowed to pursue their trade in the very midst of liturgical functions in church.

Bishop Charrière, of Lausanne and Fribourg, Switzerland, stated that as counsellor of UNDA for fourteen years he felt that it was the Council's duty to insist unconditionally on the importance of this subject for the work of the Church today. Agreeing that modern civilization was devoted to the cult of images, he outlined the concomitant danger of a depersonalization of the individual; and the consequent necessity of keeping in mind that from the very beginning the "Word of God" was communicated "by hearing." Hence, he said, these means of communication were much more important for us as preachers, than they were for secular moralists and philosophers. Bishop Fernández-Conde of Cordova, Spain, criticized the failure of the schema to condemn more precisely the evils connected with modern entertainment; but Bishop D'Avack of Camerino, Italy, congratulated the authors for the generally optimistic tone adopted, then suggested that along with the positive measures for the effective employment of these means in preaching the Gospel, stress should be laid particularly, on their use in seminaries and religious houses, and on their non-use as works of mortification and self-denial. He likewise called for the establishment, on a worldwide basis, of Legions of Decency similar to those existing in the United States, and a reminder to fathers of families of their duty to control what their children see and read.

Bishop d'Souza of Nagpur in India said that he regretted the insistence on the rights of the Church expressed in the document. He believed that such declarations were easily misunderstood by modern governments. Rather he felt that the emphasis should be placed on the rights and duties of bishops within the Church to utilize these media, and to entrust their employment to competent laymen rather than to priests whose primary tasks were preaching and the administration of the sacraments. Bishop Cantero of Huelva, Spain, complained about the length of the document, but then launched into such an extended consideration of particular points that he had to be stopped by the Cardinal President for going over the allotted time. Bishop de Castro of Campos, Brazil, condemned the evils accompanying secular use of the media, while Bishop Heuschen called for the utilization of international press agencies also. Three speakers brought the morning's discussions to a close. In general, they dealt with the conditions of the press in their own countries: the controlled press in Lithuania; the possibilities of an effective apostolate even where the Church is only a small minority, as in Indonesia; and the problems that must be faced in a modern nation like France.

The discussion was continued Saturday in the 26th General

Congregation under the presidency of Cardinal Alfrink, with Cardinal Wyszynski as the first speaker. But first the attention of the conciliar fathers was directed to a telegram of congratulation sent to the Holy Father, in the name of the Council, on the occasion of his eighty-first birthday on the morrow. The text was read by Secretary General Felici:

The fathers of this Ecumenical Council, which is being celebrated according to your wishes, raise their eyes, minds and hearts to you, our most beloved Pastor, on the happy recurrence of your birthday. At the same time, they express their hope that you may govern the Church happily for many years more, and may see it bear abundant fruit in unity and peace for the glory of her who is the Spouse of God. We pray you, Holy Father, to strengthen us in our labors with your Apostolic Blessing.

Cardinal Wyszynski spoke of the effectiveness of radio and television in reaching those indifferent to religious values—people who though they never enter a church were tempted, out of curiosity at least, to watch something religious on the radio or television. Hence he asked that Vatican radio and others under ecclesiastical control give much more time to the reading of the Gospel and the explanation of the faith. Cardinal Godfrey of Westminster, expressed his doubts as to the suitability of this schema as an integral part of the Council's acts. He felt it would be better to transform it into a pontifical document for the guidance of clergy and laity; and have the Council confine its attention to the elaboration of a number of principles. He praised the value of television and cinema, but said that churchmen needed to interest themselves in curbing the excesses and evils to which these propaganda and entertainment media gave rise. In praising the diocesan press, he called attention, however, to the necessity for encouraging the laity generally to follow the issues of the day in the secular journals under the guidance of their pastors, in order that the Church be kept fully abreast of the world's doings and problems.

The question of church rights was stressed by Cardinal Léger of Montreal. He warned against too great an insistence on them, calling rather for a statement that would make clear the Church's maternal solicitude for the rights of all men to have the truth placed before them. "The power of modern means of communication is so great," said the cardinal, "that it is ridiculous to try to insulate people against it; rather we must adopt it fearlessly, putting an end to the negative type of criticism characteristic of so many churchmen in the past." It was Cardinal Suenens of Malines-Brussels who brought up the important, practical problems presented by modern journalism, with its disregard for a man's right to privacy. He said great injustice was involved in interference with the mails, eavesdropping, wire- and telephone-tapping, and the invasion of a man's home. He proposed that the Council lay down principles for a code of ethics that would be the equivalent of the rules governing legal and medical practice, and that some organizations, similar to that employed by lawyers and doctors in their fair-practice commissions, be set up to discipline the communications media. He suggested finally that Catholic reaction to radio and television presentations should be educated and then utilized to influence the producers. In so doing, great effort should be made to avoid the banal and trite when calling for time in the interest of things religious.

Calling attention to the fact that there are some nine hundred million Christians in the world, Cardinal Bea stated that if they were to co-operate with all men of good will in safeguarding human and divine values in a positive fashion, it would not be too difficult to solve most of the problems connected with the means of communication. Picking up the suggestion made the previous day, in favor of a world-wide press agency run from the Vatican, he said such a project was urgent, and should be encouraged by the fathers of the Council.

The Bishop of Meaux, Msgr. Ménager, complained that the schema did not put the part played by the laity in the Church in proper perspective. Here, certainly, was the field in which the layman was not only competent but required by the very nature of things to give testimony to the world of a Christian and therefore dignified way of life, by making his presence felt in the use of every type of communications media. Bishop Perraudin of Kabgayi, Ruanda, speaking in the name of the African bishops, thanked the Preparatory Commission for the schema, which they felt was a great encouragement in facing the problems of a land in turmoil and thirsting for the solid truth of the Catholic faith. Then he made an appeal to the conciliar fathers generally to aid in the establishment of radios for the people of all Africa, saying that the necessity of getting the Word of God to his people was so pressing now, that in five years' time it would be too late.

The Bishop of Versailles appealed to the Council to carry out Christ's commandment to preach the Gospel to all creatures, by insisting that priests and laity leave the security of their ancient way of doing things and throw themselves whole-heartedly into the business of educating public opinion, by means of the press, radio and television. This was likewise the view of Bishop Bernacki of Gniezno, Poland, and Archbishop Morcillo of Saragossa, Spain. Archbishop Baldassarri of Ravenna agreed with his immediate predecessors, while Cardinal Bea suggested that episcopal conferences should be entrusted with the implementation of this apostolate, since for the most part, it had to be dealt with on a regional or national plane. The African Bishop Nwedo (Nigeria) returned to the theme of his fellow Africans to insist that the Church in their continent could possibly be saved, if they had sufficient radio stations and receivers to reach the tiny villages and settlements where a priest or catechist could only penetrate occasionally.

Concern for the way in which the Catholic journalists reported events in countries which they either did not know well, or whose peculiar traditions and history they were unable to understand, was voiced by Bishop Gonzalez of Astorga, Spain. This statement was of course a reflection of the sensitiveness of the Spanish bishops to the widespread criticism of the way in which their government handled religious minorities, in the Catholic press of France, the Netherlands, Germany and the United States, in particular.

The next speaker, Ismaele Mario Castellano, Archbishop of Siena, brought up the subject of the *Index of Forbidden Books* and suggested that it be abolished. This was something of a surprise, coming from an Italian prelate. Contrary to reports in the press, however there was little discussion of this topic on the floor of the assembly. The fathers were wholly concerned with principles, or tried to be; there was a general feeling that all details relating to the practical application of these principles should be left in the hands of experts. Thus, the *Index* did not become an issue.

When Bishop Ruotolo (Ugento, Italy) launched on a tirade against positivism and idealism in modern art, he was asked by the President to return to the text of the schema. Then, while turning his attention to the question of church music, he quickly got off once more on a philosophical bias and again had to be interrupted by Cardinal Alfrink. The importance of radio sermons was stressed by Bishop Ona of Lugo, Spain, who suggested that episcopal conferences should lay down norms for training the clergy in the proper tech-

niques. Bishop De Uriarte (Peru) had to be called to order
several times for his vigorous denunciations of priests and
religious who wasted time going to the moving pictures instead of attending to their duties in the confessional and in
church, but the aged prelate who is hard of hearing appeared
not to understand.

The timeliness and importance of the material in the
schema were praised by Bishop Nezič (Yugoslavia). He suggested, however, that it would perhaps be better to incorporate it in a separate document published with the Council's
approval. In its present state it was too unwieldy for a conciliar decree. He proposed likewise, that since the schema had
been sufficiently exhausted, the Council should move on to a
new topic.

Resuming discussion of the Communications schema on
Monday, Nov. 26, in its 27th General Congregation, the
Council began its labors that day with a reading to the fathers
of the pope's reply to their telegram of congratulation on his
birthday. It was then announced that because of the short-
ness of the remaining time, the Council would meet in session
every day except Sunday during December, until the 8th,
when it was due to adjourn with a solemn ceremony presided
over by the pope. After consideration of the schema on the
Unity of the Church, which was to come next, it would take
up the schema on the Church.

The distribution of this long-awaited document, prepared
by the Theological Commission and touching upon some of
the most crucial theological problems in which there was
widespread interest, had proved to be a distracting influence
on the previous Friday. Many of the prelates plunged at once
into a study of its pages, thus allowing their attention to be
diverted from the subject under consideration, and contributing to the belief that the Council was wasting its time discussing Communications.

Hence there was no appreciable opposition when the President proposed, at 11:10, that a standing vote be taken on ending the debate on Communications Media. The following day this schema too was voted on in principle, the proposal specifying that it be sent back to committee to be shortened and reworked with principles separated from the more practical matters, and the latter incorporated in a pastoral instruction prepared by the Pontifical Commission for Radio, Cinema and Television. The results were overwhelmingly in favor: 2,138 to 15, with 7 invalid ballots.

SUMMARY

November 23, 1962, Friday—25TH GENERAL CONGREGATION

PRESIDENT: Card. *Caggiano* (Buenos Aires). MASS: Celebrated by Bp. *Tredici* (Brescia, Italy). PRESENT: 2,153 fathers. SUBJECT: Schema on Means of Social Communication.

SPEAKERS: Card. *Cento* (Commission for Apostolate of Laity, Press and Communications Media), and Archb. *René Stourm* (Secretariat for Press and Communications Media); Cards. *Spellman* and *Ruffini;* Archbps. and Bps. *Enrique y Tarancón* (Solsona, Spain), *Sanschagrin* (coadj. Amos, Canada), *Beck* (Salford, England), *Llopis Ivorra* (Coria-Cáceres, Spain), *Bednorz* (coadj. Katowice, Poland), *Charrière* (Lausanne, Freiburg and Geneva, Switzerland), *Fernández-Conde* (Córdoba, Spain), *D'Avack* (Camerino, Italy), *D'Souza* (Nagpur) and *Cantero Cuadrado* (Huelva), *de Castro Mayer* (Campos, Brazil), *Heuschen* (aux. Liège, Belgium),

Brizgys (aux. Kaunas, Lithuania), *Soegijapranata* (Semerang, Indonesia), and *Boudon* (Mende, France).

Announcement by SG that following schema on Communications Media, the Council would take up schema *Ut unum sint* on reunion with Orthodox (distributed summer 1962), and then the schema on the Blessed Virgin Mary. Booklet containing latter together with schema on the Church distributed to the fathers today.

Msgr. *Willebrands,* of Secretariat for Promoting Christian Unity, disavows in press conference criticism of presence of Russian Orthodox Observers contained in protest of Ukrainian Catholic bishops, unofficially published in Italian press (cf. *Il Giornale d'Italia,* Nov. 24, 1962), and affirms their welcome.

Press conference of Prof. Oscar *Cullmann* on behalf of the observer-delegates.

November 24, 1962, Saturday—26TH GENERAL CONGREGATION

PRESIDENT: Card. *Alfrink* (Utrecht). MASS: Celebrated by Bp. *Charrière* (Switzerland). PRESENT: 2,136 fathers. SUBJECT: Schema on communications media.

SPEAKERS: Cards. *Wyszynski* (Warsaw), *Godfrey* (Westminster), *Léger* (Montreal), *Suenens* (Malines-Brussels), *Bea* (Curia); Archbps. and Bps. *Ménager* (Meaux, France), *Perraudin* (Kabgayi, Ruanda) on behalf of African episcopate, *Renard* (Versailles, France), *Bernacki* (aux. Gniezno, Poland), *Morcillo* (Zaragoza, Spain), *Baldassarri* (Ravenna, Italy), *Chang* (China), *Nwedo* (Umuahia, Nigeria) speaking for bishops of Africa, *González Martín* (Astorga, Spain), *Castellano* (Siena, Italy), *Gouyon* (Bayonne, France), *Ruotolo* (Ugento, Italy), *Ona de Echave* (Lugo, Spain), *De Uriarte Bengoa* (ap. pref. San Ramón, Peru), *Zazpe* (Rafaela, Argentina), *Nežić* (Poreč i Pula, Yugoslavia); Abbot *Reetz,* O.S.B. (Beuron, Germany); Bps. *László* (Eisenstadt, Austria), and *Lommel* (Luxembourg).

SG reads telegram of Council to Holy Father on his birthday, Nov. 25, 1962.

Announcement of composition of Mixed Commission to redraft schema on Sources of Revelation (published in OR Nov. 25, 1962).

November 25, 1962, Sunday

Pope replies to telegram of Council on his birthday.

Pope celebrates mass at Propaganda University.
Mass celebrated for journalists by Archb. *Pessôa Câmara* (aux.
Rio de Janeiro) in church of Sant'Ivo alla Sapienza.
November 26, 1962, Monday—27TH GENERAL CONGREGATION
PRESIDENT: Card. *Tisserant* (Curia). MASS: Celebrated by Archb.
Rosales (Cebù, Philippines). PRESENT: 2,133 fathers.

SG reads pope's reply to telegram of Council on his birthday.

SG announces calendar of congregations for December: meetings to be held every day except Sunday with solemn closing ceremony on Dec. 8 presided over by pope; schema *Ut unum sint*, to be taken up next, will be followed by schema on the Church, at the request of many fathers. Schema on the Blessed Virgin Mary to be considered along with latter.

SUBJECT: Schema on communications media. SPEAKERS: Archbps. and Bps. *Civardi* (Italy), *Höffner* (Münster, Germany), *Duval* (Algiers, Algeria), *Moro Briz* (Avila, Spain), *Kempf* (Limburg, Germany), *Kozlowiecki* (Lusaka, Northern Rhodesia), *Tagle* (Valparaiso, Chile) on behalf of Chilean episcopate, *Soares de Resende* (Beira, Mozambique), *Del Pino Gómez* (Lerida, Spain), *Sana* (Akra, Irak), *Fernández Feo-Tinoco* (San Cristobal, Venezuela) on behalf of Venezuelan bishops, *Simons* (Indore, India), and *Zarranz y Pueyo* (Plasencia, Spain).

VII

The Debate on "Unity"

THE TRAGIC DISUNITY of Christians of which contemporaries are so acutely aware is almost as old as Christianity itself. There have always been groups separated from the main body of Christians, going back to Apostolic times. The scandal in our time is that, in a world in which Christianity itself is under such heavy fire, the three major segments of Christendom —including some 540,000,000 Roman Catholics, 215,000,000 Protestants, and 130,000,000 Orthodox—are not in communion with one another. Clearly the injunction of Christ, contained in his priestly prayer, "May they all be one (*ut unum sint*): as thou, Father, art in me, and I in thee, so also may they be in us, that the world may believe that thou didst send me" (John 17:21), has not yet been realized.

Ignoring the details, it may be said that the sundering of Christendom was effected in three main stages:

1. First, in the 5th century, the separation of the Nestorian and Monophysite Churches of the East—in Persia (Nestorians or Chaldeans), in Egypt (Copts), and in Syria (Jacobites)—from the Byzantine (Melchite) Church of Rome and Constantinople.

2. The separation, which became effective in the 11th century, between Rome and Constantinople (involving also all the other Eastern Melchite churches in communion with Constantinople, including the newer churches of Russia, Bulgaria, Serbia, etc.) causing a definite split between Catholics and Orthodox Christians.

3. In the 16th century, the schism between the Roman Catholic Church and the various Protestant bodies which separated from it.

These separations are still current, while the picture has been further confused by the fact that various groups have shifted their ecclesiastical allegiance back and forth from time to time. Those Oriental Churches which have re-established communion with Rome are known widely as "Uniats," originally a derogative term (Polish) first used in the 16th century by the Orthodox with reference to the Ukrainians who had returned to the Roman communion following the union of Brest (1595–96), and then, after acquiring a kind of respectability, applied also to other bodies having similar ties with Rome. The "Unia," or status of the Uniats, has been a burning question with the Orthodox for the past four hundred years and is regarded by them as one of the main obstacles to Catholic reunion, for they see these bodies in communion with Rome while enjoying the same rites and traditions as other Orthodox Churches, as a challenge to their own position. It is generally agreed that, were reunion with Rome to

be effected, the Uniats would disappear as separate bodies
and the sundered Oriental Churches would once again be
reunited.

The schema on the Unity of the Church, appropriately
entitled *"Ut unum sint,"* which was taken up during the
remaining hour of the 27th General Congregation, on Monday, Nov. 26, and debated on the following four days, had
been prepared by the Preparatory Commission for the Oriental Churches. It was concerned exclusively with the principles,
ways and means of achieving reunion with the Eastern Orthodox.* Two other schemata had also been prepared dealing
with the general theme of unity, that by the Theological
Commission, which had in mind particularly the Protestants,
and another by the Secretariat for Promoting Christian Unity,
which was concerned with general ecumenical principles. The
question naturally arises, why, in view of the obvious similar-
ity of these schemata, and particularly when it was remembered that the Secretariat had been created expressly for the
purpose of coordinating all activity in this field,† it had not

* The schema was not divided into chapters but consisted of 52 consecu-
tively-numbered paragraphs or titles. However, the latter formed three distinct parts or sections, as follows: 1–10 were concerned with theological principles; 11–47 with the means by which unity could be achieved; 48–52 with a
more specific description or definition of unity. In more detail: 1: the work
of redemption; 2–4: the Church on earth and the Church in heaven; 5: the
hierarchical Church; 6: the visible unity of the Church under the authority
of Peter; 7: the indivisible unity of the Church; 8: unity in diversity; 9: the
causes of separation; 10: the traces or *vestigia* of unity; 11–12: the task of
the Church to re-establish unity; 13–17: the supernatural means; 18–22: the
theological means; 23–26: the liturgical means; 27–28: the canonical and disciplinary means; 29–37: the psychological means; 38–47: the practical means;
48–52: the conditions and modalities of unity. (Cf. *La Documentation Catholique,* Jan. 6, 1963, p. 26.)

† When the Secretariat was first formed (1960) it was thought that it would
concern itself only with Protestants within the framework of its larger responsibility, but this soon proved to be impractical. Its members have been
in contact both with Orthodox and Protestant Churches, individuals as well
as corporate bodies, without any discrimination whatsoever. Cf. Cardinal
Bea's press conference in New York (where he was at the time of the pope's
appointment, to receive an honorary degree from Fordham University)

been decided to present a single schema to the Council, or at least three coordinated drafts that could later be fused into one? One factor seems to have been the total unwillingness of the Theological Commission to cooperate with any other organ than itself by monopolizing all theological discussion.* Another was the fact that the Commission for the Oriental Churches, dominated like all the commissions by the corresponding Congregation of the Roman Curia, in this case the Congregation for the Oriental Churches, regarded all the Eastern Churches as its particular sphere, although in fact its activities were traditionally confined almost entirely to contacts with the various Oriental Churches in communion with Rome. The separated Orthodox, by and large, would have nothing to do with either Congregation or Commission, looking upon both as mere "tools" designed to undermine their position and Latinize the East. A certain amount of internecine, rivalry, therefore, was undoubtedly responsible for the present situation, which the Central Preparatory Commission either would not, or could not, resolve. It must be acknowledged, likewise, that Cardinal Bea's Secretariat did not at first enjoy, within the confines of the Church, the tremendous prestige which it has since acquired, and the advantages of having it coordinate *all* aspects of the problem of reunion, theological as well as practical, were not fully seen at first, although laid down in theory.

At 11:10 Cardinal Cicognani took the microphone to introduce the schema, which, as we have said, dealt only with the prospects for reunion with the Orthodox Churches. He

---

printed in the collection of the cardinal's speeches and articles entitled *L'Unione dei Cristiani,* Ed. La Civiltà Cattolica, Roma, 1962, p. 190. It will be remembered also that the Secretariat was given a status equivalent to that of the other Conciliar Commissions by the pope on Oct. 19, 1962. See above p. 94.

* See p. 163.

pointed to the fact that never before in history had such an
effort been made to find ways of drawing all Christians back
into the true fold of Christ and asked that all prejudice, fear
and distrust connected with the historical causes of the separation now be laid aside. The schema itself was then outlined
by Fr. Athanasius Welykyj of the Order of St. Basil of St.
Josaphat, who had served as secretary of the Preparatory
Commission. Noting that problems having to do with rites
and ceremonies were being covered by other commissions,
he said that the purpose of the present schema was to study
the best way of achieving reconciliation with the separated
Eastern brethren. The first part explained the theological
unity of the Church, based on a unity of government, with
the successor of St. Peter as the Church's head. The difficulties felt by the Orthodox on this score were next considered; but emphasis was placed on the notion that true
unity could only be achieved by agreement on the essential
truths contained in the Church's deposit of faith.

The second part outlined the theological, liturgical, juridical, psychological and practical means that must be applied to achieve reunion with the Orthodox. Particular
stress was laid on the need for all Christians to unite, in
order to defend God's truth against the ravages of atheism
and materialism. In the third part, the road to reconciliation
was envisaged as involving a complete respect for the special
religious, historical and psychological heritage of the Eastern Churches. The schema closed with a reference to the
Prayer of Jesus for unity.

Cardinal Liénart led off this discussion. While admitting
that the schema contained useful principles, he felt that its
general tenor was too authoritative; and that by its insistence
upon a "return to the true fold" it was placing a hopeless
obstacle in the way of reunion. He suggested that a truly

pastoral approach should admit faults on both sides that had contributed in the past to the split between the Churches. Besides, he said, attention should be paid to the fact that the Orthodox Churches were many, each with its own traditions; hence they could not be approached *en bloc*. What should be brought out, however, was that as the Orthodox Christians were marked with the same baptismal character and shared the same faith and sacraments as Catholics, whatever was holding the various groups apart was accidental and could be removed by a vigorous effort at mutual understanding. For this purpose a special commission should be created that would follow up the Council's recommendations.

Cardinal Ruffini spoke next, suggesting that the schema should be coordinated with those prepared by the Theological Commission and the Secretariat for Promoting Unity. He then listed various corrections that ought to be made in the text, but insisted that while Catholics may not have been exempt from fault in occasioning the split, one should not say that both sides were equally to blame. The Catholic Church "has ever remained firm in the midst of the storms" and was "without spot or wrinkle" in its possession of the truth. Hence it was not proper to speak of others as "parts of the Church," but rather as "parts of Christendom."

Cardinal Bacci quibbled with the title "On the unity of the Church," remarking that as the Church was already one, the schema should be called *De omnium christianorum unitate procuranda,* at once satisfying theological precision and a penchant for elegant Latinity. He was against creating a new commission, however, since "one has the Roman Curia" and use should be made of what already existed.*

* It was, and remains, one of the constant complaints of the Oriental Churches in communion with Rome that the Roman Curia is constantly attempting to override their special privileges and subject them to its own regulations, at variance with Eastern tradition and reflecting a western or

The day's debate was concluded by Cardinal Browne who maintained that, in his opinion, the schema was excellent. While in a matter of this kind one must proceed with extreme charity, still equal care must be taken to safeguard the truth, both from a theological and social point of view. Hence before being discussed in earnest, the schema ought to be completed with a clear statement of theological principles.

The 28th General Congregation convened on Tuesday, Nov. 27, under the presidency of Cardinal Liénart. The Secretary General read a statement announcing that in view of the recommendations of so many prelates, the Holy Father had decided to postpone the second session from May 12, 1963 to Sept. 8, 1963, in order to give those from great distances more time at home.

He then read a declaration, in the name of the Commission for the Oriental Churches, intended to clear up objections and confusion regarding the purpose of the schema under consideration. It related only to the Orthodox, not Protestants. In the first part, the intention was to outline the actual situation of those Churches separated from the Catholic Church, and not to give a complete theological explanation of the constitution of the Church. The proposals made in the second part regarding the principles to be applied in working for reunion were without prejudice to what the Theological Commission proposed in its schema on the Church. Finally, the schema was designed to help Catholics adopt a right attitude toward the problem of reunion with the Orthodox.

Latin mentality. This is one of the main themes aired by the Melchite Patriarch Maximos IV Saigh and his co-bishops. (See the recent collected edition of their statements, *Voix de l'Eglise en Orient: Voix de l'Eglise Melchite,* Herder, Basle, 1962.)

Cardinal de Barros Câmara of Rio de Janeiro spoke first. He declared himself to be against any false irenicism, but suggested that in the Litany of the Saints where both those in error and infidels were prayed for, the two categories should be separated, for the *errantes* were not outside the faith.

The patriarch Maximos IV Saigh of Antioch, speaking in French, said that as the schema dealt with the Orthodox it did not concern Oriental Catholics directly. However, as it was of such great importance, he desired to point out that certain sections, particularly in the first part, would only serve to enrage rather than attract those among the Orthodox who were benevolently disposed toward Catholicism, for they were evidence of the old Roman absolutism, and gave an unbalanced picture of both the history and the responsibility for the earlier split in Christendom. It must be realized, he insisted, that the Oriental Churches were completely distinct from the Latin Church. They owed their origins directly to Christ and the Apostles, and received their traditions and rites from the Greek and Oriental Fathers. Hence, even in their organization, they were not dependent on the See of Rome. Since this was the case, he asked, were Fathers such as Basil, the Gregories, Cyril and Chrysostom to be considered as Catholics of a lower rank than the Latin Fathers? The schema should speak a truly Catholic language. First it should mention the collegial character of the Church's pastorate, the bishops being the successors of the college of Apostles, and then only come to the Primacy as the basis, foundation and center of that collegiality.

Next he recommended that the three separate schemata prepared by the Theological and Oriental Commissions and the Secretariat for Unity should be combined. "When many hands prepare the cooking, the meat is sure to be burnt," said an old Arab proverb. The schema has been entitled "The unity of the Church," but it only dealt with the approach to the Orthodox. By rights it should only form a chapter in a more general decree on the subject. In actual fact, said the patriarch, we Catholics were much closer to the Orthodox than to the Protestants. The question of the Roman Primacy was all that now held us apart. With the Protestants, on the other hand, the outlook was totally different: "For us oriental Catholics this separation from our Eastern brethren is a terrible agony that touches the very core of our hearts. Reunion is our greatest desire; and for this purpose we are willing to make great sacrifices. We form one family with them, hence we want to forget past quarrels and human considerations and join them in Christ to realize His wish 'That they may be one.' "

Archbishop Principi, of the Congregation in charge of St. Peter's basilica, one of the few non-cardinal members of the Curia to speak in the latter sessions of the Council, expressed ideas somewhat similar to those of Patriarch Maximos and gave the fathers a long discourse on the efforts of Pope Leo XIII to promote reunion with the Orthodox.

Bishop Pawlowski of Poland warned against any precipitate action that might be interpreted as a false irenicism, while Bishop Nabaa, one of the Under-Secretaries General of the Council (Melchite, Beirut), suggested that while the schema laid down various principles for reunion, the actual work would have to be done on a social level by cooperating with the Orthodox in projects for peace and justice, by observing together special feasts and occasions for joint prayer, and finally by abrogating the recent marriage legislation contained in the new Code of Canon Law for the Oriental Church.

Archbishop Parecattil of Ernakulam, India, objected to a

PRECES

IN CONCILIO OECUMENICO VATICANO II

AB ORIENTALIBUS HIERARCHIS

SOLEMNITER RECITANDAE

IUSSU

SANCTISSIMI DOMINI NOSTRI

IOANNIS PP. XXIII

CATHOLICAE ECCLESIAE EPISCOPI

ROMAE
CURA SECRETARIAE GEN. CONCILII
MCMLXII

الابتهالات
التي يتلوها باحتفال الاحبار الشرقيون
في المجمع المسكوني الفاتيكاني الثاني

بأمر

سيدنا الحبر الاعظم

يوحنا الثالث والعشرين

اسقف الكنيسة الكاثوليكية

روبـــة
بعناية امانة سر المجمع العامة
١٩٦٢

ΔΕΗΣΙΣ

ΤΕΛΕΣΤΕΑ ΥΠΟ ΤΩΝ ΠΑΤΕΡΩΝ ΑΝΑΤΟΛΗΣ
ΕΠΙ ΤΗ ΕΝΑΡΞΕΙ ΤΗΣ ΟΙΚΟΥΜΕΝΙΚΗΣ ΣΥΝΟΔΟΥ
ΒΑΤΙΚΑΝΟΥ Βʹ

ΕΝΤΟΛΗ
ΤΗΣ Α. ΑΓΙΟΤΗΤΟΣ

ΙΩΑΝΝΟΥ ΠΑΠΑ ΚΓʹ

ΕΠΙΣΚΟΠΟΥ ΤΗΣ ΚΑΘΟΛΙΚΗΣ ΕΚΚΛΗΣΙΑΣ

ΕΝ ΡΩΜΗ
Φροντίδι τῆς Γενικῆς Γραμματείας τῆς Συνόδου
Ἐν ἔτει ͵αϡξβʹ

МОЛЕ́БНОЕ ПѢ́НІЕ

ВЪ НАЧА́ЛѢ.

ВТОРА́ГѠ ВАТИКА́НСКАГѠ СОБО́РА
ѿ ВОСТО́ЧНЫХЪ АРХІЕРЕ́Й СОВЕРША́ЕМОЕ

по велѣ́нїю

СВАТѢ́ЙШАГѠ ГОСПОДИ́НА НА́ШЕГѠ ІѠА́ННА ПА́ПЫ КГ
ЕПІСКОПА КАТОЛІ́ЧЕСКІЯ ЦЕ́РКВЕ

РИМЪ, ͵аѰѯв
Попеченіемъ Гла́внагѡ Секрета́ря Собо́ра

Title pages of Oriental Litanies recited on October 11, 1962, in
Latin, Arabic, Greek, and Old Slavonic

number of expressions in the schema and particularly to a reference to the orientals as "the ornaments of the Church." While he was thankful for the honor, he said that he felt it would be better to be considered an integral part of the Church.

Archbishop Senyshyn, Ukrainian Metropolitan of Philadelphia, asked that the first eight paragraphs of the schema be eliminated, as they dealt with a subject which belonged within the province of the Theological Commission; by the same token, everything relating to the problem of ecumenism should be taken out of the schema on the Church. It was a defect of the present schema that it said nothing about communion *in sacris* with the Orthodox and that it likened them, rather tactlessly, to the Protestants, although there was all the difference in the world between them, for the Orthodox had the same hierarchy, sacraments, mass and priesthood as Catholics, whereas the Protestants did not.

Archbishop Vuccino (auxiliary bishop of Paris for eastern-rite Catholics) expressed his astonishment that this "decree" could be considered as a suitable basis for reunion, when its whole attitude was geared rather to repelling those outside Catholic communion. The pope was referred to as a "shepherd of sheep"; this meant a *diakonia* or service, not a power. The primacy was given to Peter so that he might serve the Church, not dominate it. The schema should bring out the fact that charity rules all in the Church, especially our relations with our brethren.

Bishop Fernández of Badajoz, Spain, followed with words of praise for the schema and a long diatribe on the importance of distinguishing carefully between theological principles and practice in the matter of reunion. For Archb. Edelby (auxiliary to Patriarch Maximos IV), on the other hand, the first section misrepresented the history of the sepa-

ration and ought to be entirely rewritten. There was too
much of a theological flavor about it. Whereas the presentation
of the facts ought to be inspired by a spirit of truth in charity
and clarity, it gave the impression of a certain animosity
toward the East. The statement that "the Catholic Church
had always used every means possible to bring about reunion"
was simply not true. Everyone knew that both the Catholic
Church and the other side had at times striven to prevent
reunion. Finally, the absence of any reference to the collegiality of the bishops put the Primacy in a false light.

Msgr. Zoghby, Melchite patriarchal vicar for Egypt, speaking in French, was particularly outspoken in his analysis of
the differences between the Eastern and Western attitudes
toward theology and in condemning the evils of Latinization.
With regard to the first point, he noted that the Eastern
Church has had an entirely different dogmatic and disciplinary development from the West, quite as legitimate as the
Western counterpart, and therefore had every right to be considered as a "Source-Church." Dogma was the same in substance, of course, but theology differed. Rome had always
recognized the validity of Eastern rites, but it was necessary
to go a step further and recognize the legitimacy of the differences in discipline and theology as well. The doctrine of the
Trinity was a case in point. The Eastern Church was faithful
to the explanation favored by the fathers at Nicaea and Constantinople, and was not influenced by the Augustinian theology. Likewise, as regards the redemption, the East insisted
upon the divinization of man in Christ, whereas the West
stressed the satisfaction that Christ made for the sins of mankind. On the feast of the Annunciation the Oriental Church
meditated on the incarnation, while the West chanted the
glories of Mary. These two currents were not in opposition,
nor did they obstruct the unity of the Church, but they were

complementary and had a legitimate place in the catholicity of the Church.

Whereas the Latin Church, responding to historical circumstances that were peculiar to it, evolved toward an ever greater centralization, the East, by contrast, had evolved toward an ever greater autonomy. Just as in God there was one sole and same nature, yet there were three distinct Persons, so the same thing was true analogously of the Church: there were distinct Churches, but the Church was nevertheless one. The Catholic Church today was unfortunately crushingly Latin, in that the majority of the faithful belonged to the Latin Church or rite. The 130 bishops belonging to the various Eastern-rite Churches present at the Council were drowned in the midst of the more than 2,000 Latin-rite bishops. The patriarchs, who formerly held synods to which the popes sent legates, were accorded an inferior rank in the present assembly, after the array of cardinals. While the latter might be the glory of the modern Church, they did not exist in those days. The East, he concluded, would never deny its nature and accept Latinization. Hence as long as Christendom remained divided, no Council such as the great assembly now meeting could possibly afford to neglect the problem of reunion. Let the East be the East and the West the West, each Church going its own separate way but collaborating in unity, a unity in diversity, not uniformity. Only when the Roman Church was decentralized and began to respect the traditions of its sister Churches, would there be true hope for the Church universal.*

Bishop Méndez of Cuernavaca, Mexico, next rose to make some interesting observations about the work of the Council. He began by registering a complaint about the lack of collaboration between the various Preparatory Commissions and the

---

* Quoted at length in *La Croix,* Nov. 29, 1962.

lack of the pastoral spirit displayed by many of the schemata which the Council had so far considered. He criticized the fact that when the Rules of Procedure were drawn up, no provision was made for allowing a true dialogue or exchange of views on the floor. *"Proh dolor!"* he said, "we are the victims of an interminable flood of monologues." He then observed that it was necessary to decentralize the functions of the Curia, and finally made the suggestion that the work of the Council could be effectively entrusted or delegated to a special commission of some 250 bishops, who would have the assistance of the *periti*, but would not be encumbered by the prejudices of the Theological Commission. The day's debate was brought to a close by Bishop Romero Menjibar of Jaén, Spain, who pleaded for unity in diversity, and Fr. Hage, Superior General of the Basilian Order, who summed up the various points made in criticism of the schema.

Discussion of the schema was continued in the 29th General Congregation on Nov. 28, presided over by Cardinal Tappouni. The morning's mass was probably the most impressive—certainly the strangest to many of the fathers—of all those inaugurating the day's proceedings and was celebrated in the Ethiopian rite by the tall, bearded Archbishop Yemmeru of Addis Ababa. The rite itself was extremely ancient, going back in outline at least to the fourth century, but with many later additions and ceremonies of a distinctly African flavor. It was characterized by a constant dialogue between the celebrant and the faithful, and by a moving simplicity and solemnity. The language was classical Ethiopian or Gheez. As the book of Gospels was being enthroned, the spirited chanting of the seminarians and priests belonging to the Ethiopian College on Vatican Hill behind St. Peter's—they also chanted the mass—was accompanied by the deep rhythms of African drums, the ringing of bells, and the clapping of tambourines, causing the New York *Journal American* to headline its story: "African drums boom in Vatican rite" (Nov. 28, 1962).

Against this background, Cardinal Tappouni began the discussions by asking the assembly to show greater regard for the separated brethren of the East. He insisted in particular on their closeness to the Catholic Church by reason of their devotion to the eucharist and the Blessed Virgin Mary. It was obvious, he said, that the title of the schema had to be changed, but he also believed that it was proper to speak of only "one Catholic Church," while recognizing that the unity of the Church was a patrimony common to all those who shared the same faith and sacraments and was something communicable. The schema pleased him, on the whole, and he wished it to be retained.

Cardinal Spellman also spoke in favor of retention. He was followed immediately by Cardinal Ottaviani, who was of the same mind. The speech of Ottaviani, however, was interesting from another angle. Evidently without prior consultation with the Council of Presidents, he stated that "after this schema (*Ut unum sint*) it has been announced that we are to take up the one on the Church. But in the treatise on the Church there is again question of unity and ecumenicity, and there are still ten months before the next session. Accordingly I propose that we should not take up the schema *De ecclesia* now, but should take up the one on the Blessed Virgin Mary. I am astonished that after being informed that the latter subject would be dealt with next, we now find that it has been postponed. As a matter of fact, we have many points in common with our separated brethren. We are united in our love for her. After discussing various points of difference, it is well for us to remember that she can serve to unite us. Hence I wish and ask that we start with this schema on Friday . . ."

The cardinal then launched into a peroration in which he

mentioned the glories of Lourdes, Fatima, and other Marian apparitions with a view to winning acceptance for his proposal. He concluded with the axiom: "Those who explain my [Mary's] prerogatives, will have eternal life" (*qui elucidant me vitam aeternam habebunt*). This attempt to deflect the Council from its course proved to be unsuccessful.*

Paul II Cheikho, Patriarch of Babylonia of the Chaldees, spoke next. He was satisfied with the schema as such, but said it proved conclusively that reunion with the Orthodox required more than mere human reconciliation. What was needed was the aid of the Holy Spirit. Consequently, he desired the Council to compile a prayer for unity to be recited frequently, so that God would see fit, in our day, to grant the reunion so earnestly desired by all sincere Christians. Meanwhile, he hoped that a spirit of charity, demonstrated by the fathers, would spread throughout the world.

Archbishop Tawil, patriarchal vicar for the Syrian Melchites asked that all the human elements in the schema which might give offense should be removed. For example, he said that the schema referred to the Orthodox bodies as *"coetus"* or assemblies, whereas in fact they were true Churches. It would perhaps be better to refer to them simply as the "Orthodox," as was done in common parlance. At no time was the Eastern Church ever considered as a part of the Roman Church or under its immediate jurisdiction, as parts of the West or the West as a whole were. It always had its own leadership. Finally, the schema noted that everything should be preserved in Orthodox ceremonies which was not against faith or morals. But this was also unnecessarily brusque. "I have personally searched through our liturgy, but can find nothing against either faith or morals!" The great difficulty to be overcome before the Orthodox would ever consider

* See p. 207.

reunion was to remove from their minds any fear of being reduced to the status of those Eastern Catholics already in communion with Rome. They believed that the latter were kept in an inferior position and that they themselves would suffer the same fate if reunion took place. Unfortunately, the historical record was not good in this respect. Since the schema did nothing to remove this impression, it should be completely rewritten.

Bishop Velasco of Hsiamen, China (expelled), expressed himself in complete agreement with Cardinals Ruffini and Browne and was for the schema as it stood. To say that the Latin Church had been guilty of the same crimes and excesses in bringing about the rupture between the two parts of Christendom was absolutely false. It was all very well to adopt an irenic approach, but truth and principles must come first. Archbishop Olaechea of Valencia, Spain, who followed, was of the opposite view. There were many things in the schema, he said, which were not in harmony with the Holy Father's injunction for a pastoral approach. The statement, noted above, that the Latin Church had always sought to bring about reunion, must be taken with a grain of salt.

The Maronite Bishop Khoury, on the other hand, took exception to what he regarded as extreme statements made in the course of the debate. He could not associate himself, for example, with the sentiment that "the East is the East and the West is the West" and that it was merely a question of parallel developments. Unity in Peter meant that there was no longer any East or West but a "new creature," as St. Paul said. The Church must be on guard against becoming too enslaved to any one culture or age. It was not always Rome that was required to say *mea culpa*.

The theme of charity was again stressed by Bishop Darmancier, Vicar Apostolic for the Wallis Islands in the South

Seas. However, while Mother Church wept over the dissensions in its ranks that led to schism, it should realize also that not infrequently acts by its own priests and prelates had caused, and were still causing, difficulties. A case in point was the current dissatisfaction of orientals in union with Rome with the new Code of Canon Law mentioned above. The excessively Latin spirit of the latter betrayed a lack of comprehension of the problems and different traditions of Eastern Catholics on the part of the officials who compiled it. There were many other instances of the kind that could be cited.

Archbishop Addazi of Trani, Italy, then treated the Council to a scholastic disquisition on the nature of the Church, in which he said that it was improper to suggest that the Roman pontiffs had in any way been responsible for beginning or continuing the schism. The Orthodox must be invited to "return" to the house of their father, along the path laid down for them by Rome, and that was that.

Bishop Ancel (auxiliary of Lyons) took up the matter of the truth of the faith that had been raised in three or four of the recent talks. He said there was need for a true humility on the part of Catholics, who should realize that they were not "the masters, but the servants of truth." Whereas Catholics could rejoice that the truth had always been held in the Church, it should be a matter of sadness that they had not always given a good account of that truth. "It is not our right to condemn those who have gone wrong, particularly when Catholics have frequently, to say the least, occasioned misunderstandings and difficulties. Now is the time to do proper penance for such wrongs. By acknowledging before God and man the fact that our ignorance and faults have helped bring about these divisions—and not merely those of our forebears—we can begin to cope with the continuing misapprehensions and faults that remain as obstacles to reunion today. Just as in

St. Paul's day the Apostle had to object to imposing the obligations of circumcision and the use of special foods on his
pagan converts, so today, the Catholic Church should not
force issues where the truths of faith are not really involved.
In any case, we should not judge our brethren, but ourselves."

Archbishop Assaf, of Petra, Jordan, spoke in French. He
said that the schema was one of the most important to come
before the assembly, since it bore directly on the desire of
Pope John for the reunion of Christendom. He was willing to
accept it in outline, in accordance with the observation of
Patriarch Maximos IV. However, he deplored the oblique
references to the liturgies of the Orthodox, which said that
they could be retained "as long as they contained nothing
offensive to faith or morals." This was an insult to the Orthodox. Of all the matters which were causing friction between
the Churches, however, the question of rites was the least of
their worries. Their main worry, he said, was the fear of Latinization, in view of the instinctive desires of certain Latin
prelates.

Bishop Dwyer of Leeds, England, was the last to speak on
Wednesday, remarking that the schema as presently drafted
could not possibly make any impression on the Orthodox because it failed to enter into their mentality. Then, broadening
his perspective, he noted that unless the decrees of the Council reflected a true spirit of charity and truth, the millions
outside the Church would be tempted to feel that "these
prelates are not truly serious" about their desire to convert
the world.

Just before the Angelus, the Secretary General asked the
fathers to join in a novena of prayers to the Blessed Virgin in
preparation for the feast of the Immaculate Conception (Dec.
8), when the Council's first session was scheduled to end, for
the spiritual welfare of all the Church's bishops, both those

at the Council and those prevented from attending for various reasons. The proposal was inspired by Pope John's inaugural address of Oct. 11, in which he had made special mention of all bishops who could not be present and asked prayers for them. It was greeted by considerable applause.

On Thursday evening, *L'Osservatore Romano* took note in a special editorial of the rumors which had been circulating regarding the pope's health. It stated that, on his doctor's insistence, the pope had cancelled all audiences since last Tuesday. It was further disclosed that the medical and dietetical treatment which he had been undergoing for some time had produced a rather severe anemia. The anxiety caused by this announcement toward the end of the session paralleled to a certain extent the fear of thermonuclear warfare which had weighed heavily on the minds of the fathers in mid-October.

The 30th General Congregation on Friday, Nov. 30, presided over by Cardinal Spellman, saw the end of the discussion relative to the unity schema. First, however, the decision of the Council of Presidents to turn down the proposal of Cardinal Ottaviani that the Council should next take up the schema on the Blessed Virgin Mary was announced in these words: "We are all agreed about the great importance of this devotion. But for special reasons, particularly in order to prepare for the coming session next September, we have decided to observe the announced order and will take up the schema *De ecclesia* as the next order of business." With this terse communiqué, the hope of the cardinal of being able to avert another defeat like that suffered by the schema on revelation, vanished.

The debate was led off by Cardinal Wyszynski who said that in his opinion the schema was good. It was important at the present time, when the Church was threatened by atheism and materialism, to insist upon the need for unity. Pius XII had stressed this in *Mediator Dei* and the thought constantly recurs in the works of the Church Fathers. It was not necessary to re-do the schema: certain parts needed correction, it should be abbreviated, and too much insistence should not be placed on the means. The episcopate of each country should be free to adopt whatever means seemed best under the circumstances, because conditions differed greatly from one country to another.

The speech of Cardinal Bea, which came next, began with the remark that the schema, prepared by the Commission for the Oriental Churches, was intended above all to be a homage to the Eastern Churches and could be explained, historically, by what had taken place in the 15th and 16th centuries. It was natural that there should be a separate schema in the light of all that had gone before. But today we were living in a new age, with different requirements. Many points touched upon in the schema belonged to the province of the Secretariat for Unity. For a complete presentation of the problem of reunion it would be necessary to bring together the three schemata now touching on various aspects and make them into one. He revealed that his Secretariat had prepared a special prayer for unity, but that it had not yet been printed. He said, moreover, that the inspiration for the Secretariat had come to Pope John XXIII from plans which Pope Leo XIII had for establishing a "Concilium" along this line, but which had to be abandoned when that pope died.

After Bishop Trinidade of Evora, Portugal, expressed his agreement with the sentiments of Cardinal Bacci reported earlier in the debate, Ukrainian Archbishop Hermaniuk of Winnipeg, Canada, noted that the reunion of Christians would amount to the inauguration of a "new era" in world history. Hence it was important for the Council to work out a constitution that would be truly efficacious in bringing about this end. It should be based on an explanation of the collegiality of the bishops under the authority of the pope. He proposed the creation of two mixed commissions: one composed of Catholics and Orthodox, the other of Catholics and Protestants, to work on theological problems connected with reunion. The present schema seemed to imply too close a connection between the Catholic Church and the Roman rite: it almost said that "there was no salvation outside of the Roman rite."

Bishop Franic of Split, Yugoslavia, stated that the Catholics of Yugoslavia lived in intimate association with the Orthodox of their country and hence they could venture to discuss the problem of reunion, not out of books but from life. As a number of Catholics had passed over to Orthodoxy for various reasons, a true dialogue with the Orthodox was absolutely necessary and should be conducted on a basis of regard for truth and mutual understanding, without any ambiguity, and with full recognition of the fact that an excessive zeal for Latinization of the Church was responsible for continuation of the separation.

Announcing himself as the voice of Syria, Bishop Hayek of Aleppo suggested that the schema should be entitled "Of the one flock and one shepherd," and that it should be directed to the "Oriental Churches," not to the "Oriental Church." He thought it was dangerous to speak of two parallel Churches, a notion voiced earlier in the debate, because it gave rise to an erroneous impression about one Eastern Church and all that this implied.

Archbishop Heenan of Liverpool put his finger on the crux of the matter when he spoke of the problem of authority as the real issue dividing the Churches, not doctrine as such. The difficulties to be overcome were very great. It would be a "miracle" if the Orthodox were to "submit to Rome." But there was no need to be discouraged. Hitler had forced the persecuted Christians of Central and Western Europe to unite; the Communists might bring about the same thing in Eastern Europe. He deplored the absence of representatives of the Ecumenical Patriarch of Constantinople, as well as any reference in the schema to Protestants and to the Anglicans in particular. Had not the latter always been the first to respond to ecumenical appeals? He was pleased, however, that the observer delegates no longer saw the Church as a monolith and that they would take home with them a more accurate view of the Church's diversity. It was a sign, he said, that Christians were drawing closer to each other and to Christ.

Toward the close a concrete suggestion was made by Bishop Olalia of the Philippines that, in the interests of reunion, the Congregation for the Oriental Churches ought to be abolished and the various Churches in question represented on the other Roman Congregations. Next Ruthenian Bishop Elko of Pittsburgh became involved in a long discussion about freedom of expression in the Church, as evidenced by the present Council and in contrast to the Orthodox view of papal infallibility, but he went well beyond the allotted time and had to be stopped by the President. He was followed by Bishop Bukatko, auxiliary of Belgrade, who brought the discussion to an end.

The following day the fathers were requested to vote on whether "this decree should form a single document with the decree on ecumenism prepared by the Secretariat for Promoting Christian Unity, and Chapter XI, also on the same subject, contained in the schema for a dogmatic constitution on the Church." The results were: 2,068 *placets;* 36 *non placets;* and 8 invalid votes. In spite of the carefully worded language of the official communiqué drawn up by the Secretariat for

Unity and the Commission for the Oriental Churches jointly, with a view to sparing the Secretary of State as President of the latter body any possible embarrassment, the schema on unity was in effect rejected.*

SUMMARY

November 26, 1962, Monday—27TH GENERAL CONGREGATION
PRESIDENT: Card. *Tisserant* (Curia). MASS: Celebrated by Archb. *Rosales* (Cebù, Philippines). PRESENT: 2,133 fathers.

At 11:15 A.M. the SG announces that the Council will take up the schema on Unity, the fathers having voted to conclude the morning's debate on the Communications schema.

SUBJECT: Schema *Ut unum sint* on reunion with Orthodox.
SPEAKERS: Card. *Cicognani* (President of Commission for Oriental Churches), and Fr. *A. Welykyj* (Secretary of Commission for Oriental Churches). Cards. *Liénart* (Lille), *Ruffini* (Palermo), *Browne* (Curia), and *Bacci* (Curia).

November 27, 1962, Tuesday—28TH GENERAL CONGREGATION
PRESIDENT: Card. *Liénart* (Lille). MASS: Celebrated by Archb. *Rodríguez Ballón* (Arequipa, Peru). PRESENT: 2,160 fathers.

Announcement by SG that the Holy Father had decided to postpone next session of Council to Sept. 8, 1963, instead of May 12.

Council is requested by SG to vote on 1) approving schema on Communications in principle; 2) proposal that it be referred to Commission for redrafting and shortening; 3) proposal that

* See *Irénikon,* 35 (1962) 530.

practical measures be incorporated in a pastoral instruction. Results: 2,138 votes in favor, 15 against, and 7 invalid.

SUBJECT: Schema *Ut unum sint*. SPEAKERS: Card. *De Barros Câmara* (Rio de Janeiro); Patr. *Maximos IV Saigh* (Antioch of the Melchites, Syria); Archbps. and Bps. *Principi* (Italy), *Pawlowski* (Wocawek, Poland), *Nabaa* (Beirut, Lebanon), *Parecattil* (Ernakulam, India), *Sapelak* (vis. of Ukrainians, Argentina), *Senyshyn* (Philadelphia for Ukrainians, USA), *Vuccino* (France), *Fernández* (Badajoz, Spain), *Edelby* (aux. Antioch of the Melchites), *Zoghby* (patr. vicar for Egypt), *Méndez* (Cuernavaca, Mexico), *Romero Menjíbar* (Jaén, Spain); Fr. *Hage* (Superior General of the Basilians, Lebanon).

November 28, 1962, Wednesday—29TH GENERAL CONGREGATION

PRESIDENT: Card. *Tappouni* (Antioch of the Syrians). MASS: According to Ethiopian rite, by Archb. *Yemmeru* (Addis Abeba) and students of Ethiopian College. PRESENT: 2,144 fathers. SUBJECT: Schema *Ut unum sint*.

SPEAKERS: Cards. *Tappouni, Spellman,* and *Ottaviani* (Curia); Patr. *Paul II Cheikho* (Babylon of the Chaldeans, Irak); Archbps. and Bps. *Tawil* (patr. vic. for Syrian Melchites), *Velasco* (Hsiamen, China), *Olaechea Loizaga* (Valencia, Spain), *Khoury* (Tyre of the Maronites, Lebanon), *Darmancier* (vic. ap. of Wallis Islands and Futuna, Oceania), *Hoang-van-Doan* (Vietnam), *Enrique y Tarancón* (Solsona, Spain), *Addazi* (Trani, Italy), *Scandar* (Assiut, Egypt), *Koestner* (Gurk, Austria), *Ancel* (aux. Lyons, France), *Assaf* (Petra, Jordan), and *Dwyer* (Leeds, England).

Revised text of Chapter I of Liturgy schema distributed to fathers to be voted on tomorrow.

Card. *Ottaviani,* in course of debate, suggests that Council next take up schema on Blessed Virgin rather than that on Church.

Meeting of Council of Cardinal Presidents at close of congregation.

Conference of Fr. *Dumont,* O.P. on ecumenism.

Conference of Dr. *Hans Küng* at St.-Louis-des-Francais.

November 29, 1962, Thursday

Announcement by OR of suspension since Tuesday of pope's special audiences on advice of physicians (Nov. 30, 1962).

Announcement of discussion by S. Congreg. of Rites of two miracles of the Ven. Mother Seton.

November 30, 1962, Friday—30TH GENERAL CONGREGATION

PRESIDENT: Card. *Spellman.* MASS: Celebrated by Bp. *Charue* (Namur, Belgium). PRESENT: 2,145 fathers.

Before the discussions, Council votes on Chapter I of Liturgy schema (9 amendments) and overwhelmingly approves changes, explained by Bp. *Martin* (Rouen).

SUBJECT: Schema *Ut unum sint* concluded.

SPEAKERS: Cards. *Wyszynski* (Warsaw) and *Bea* (Curia); Abps. and Bps. *Trinidade Salgueiro* (Evora, Portugal), *Hermaniuk* (Winnipeg for the Ukrainians, Canada), *Youakim* (Zahleh and Furzol of the Melchites, Lebanon), *Franić* (Split, Yugoslavia), *Vaz das Neves* (Bragança and Miranda, Portugal), *Sepinski,* O.F.M. (France), *Hayek* (Aleppo of the Syrians), *Heenan* (Liverpool, England), *Olalia* (Lipa, Philippines), *Pont y Gol* (Segorbe-Castellón de la Plana, Spain), *Staverman* (vic. ap. Hollandia, New Guinea), *Elko* (Ruthenian bp. of Pittsburgh, USA), *Bukatko* (coadj. Belgrade, Yugoslavia).

Publication by S. Congreg. of Rites of decree on insertion of name of St. Joseph in the canon of the mass.

VIII
The Debate on "The Church"

✠

THE SCHEMA *De Ecclesia* was taken up at the 31st General Congregation, on Saturday, Dec. 1. Cardinal Frings of Cologne was in the chair as President. After mass celebrated by Archbishop Grimshaw of Birmingham, the Secretary General made an announcement of great interest to all present. He reported that the Holy Father's health had materially improved and that he hoped to give his blessing from the window in his apartment and recite the *Angelus* with those assembled in St. Peter's Square. This news provoked loud applause.

At 10:45 A.M., as soon as the voting on the schema *Ut unum sint* had been completed, Cardinal Ottaviani, chairman of the

Theological Commission which had prepared the schema on the Church, took over the microphone to explain the project.

In his introductory talk, the cardinal again took an approach that had proved annoying to the opposition twice previously. While he appeared jovial and spoke pleasantly, he stressed the fact that the schema represented the work of some 70 learned and skilled theologians, and that it had the approbation of the Holy Father. Nevertheless it was submitted for the Council's examination and possible amendment. Asserting that it was both pastoral and biblical in its approach, he stated that great effort had been made to avoid even the appearance of scholastic formulations. But he could not resist the temptation to assert that, as usual, these seemed to be the main objections to all the Theological Commission's projects. Becoming somewhat jocose, he requested forbearance for the *relator,* Bishop Franič of Split, Yugoslavia, who, he said, would be very conscious of the need for brevity since he must feel, even before facing the fathers, that the lions were breathing down his neck: *"Tolle, tolle, subicite eum!"* "Down, down, take him away!" This observation was greeted with laughter and applause, and the cardinal left the microphone beaming.

Bishop Franič briefly outlined the 11 chapters dealing with the nature of the Church, its component parts, bishops, priests and laity, and its teaching power and authority.* He

* The schema was divided into 11 Chapters, as follows: 1. The nature of the Church Militant; 2. The members of the Church Militant and of the need for them to be saved; 3. The episcopate as the highest degree of the sacrament of order and of the priesthood; 4. Residential bishops; 5. States of evangelical perfection; 6. The laity; 7. The magisterium of the Church; 8. Authority and obedience in the Church; 9. The relations between Church and state; 10. The necessity of the Church to proclaim the Gospel to all peoples everywhere; 11. Ecumenism. The schema on the Blessed Virgin Mary, Mother of God and Mother of men, originally separate, was made an integral part of the schema on the Church, by decision of the Council on Nov. 26.

stated clearly that the sections treating of ecumenism, the
laity, and the religious were considered solely from a theological point of view.

Hardly had the *relator's* last words echoed though the hall
when Cardinal Liénart took the microphone. After a few
generous words for the labor involved in the schema, he said
he was glad to see that the Church was treated here as the
Mystical Body of Christ, which it was, solely and essentially.
But he felt that the schema failed to stress the conclusion
implicit in this fact—that the Church was therefore a Mystery.
As evidence of this failure, he cited article 7, in which the
Mystical Body was made to appear co-extensive with the
"Roman Church." Actually the Mystical Body and therefore
the Church was much greater, and truly includes—as every
Catholic schoolboy knew—the souls in purgatory as well as
the saints in heaven. What was more, could anyone really
deny that those separated from the Church, but who possessed
the faith, the sacraments, and remained in a state of grace
were not actually members of the Mystical Body and therefore the Church? It was obvious then that a too juridical
spirit animated the construction of this schema. Before de-
manding that the whole project be reworked, however, the
French cardinal observed that his remarks were not made in
a contentious spirit, but in an effort toward arriving at the
truth. *Amicus, Plato; sed magis amica, veritas!*

As in the debate on revelation, Cardinal Ruffini stood up
next to defend the schema "in its entirety." He admitted,
however, that there were corrections to be made, citing a few
of his own, and concluding with a caution regarding the sov-
ereign rights of the supreme pontiff. He was followed by the
Archbishop of Seville, Cardinal Bueno y Monreal, who insisted that the whole Church was to be identified with Christ's
Mystical Body and that, as a consequence, both the social and

mystical aspects of this doctrine should be dealt with in chapter 7. Finally he wanted to know whether the Council's approbation of any of these statements was an extraordinary act of the magisterium?

Cardinal Koenig of Vienna called for an abbreviation of the total schema. He then asked that instead of speaking of the Church's rights, more should be said about its duties, its obligation to preach and bring the Gospel to the whole of mankind so that modern man could realize that humanity, and not merely individual men, had been redeemed by Christ and could partake of His divine life. He noted the absence of any mention of freedom of conscience.

In these sentiments, he was echoed by Cardinal Ritter of St. Louis who insisted that the Church, by summoning the Council, was on parade before the world. The American cardinal made three particular points: 1. The holiness of the Church was not sufficiently emphasized in the schema; 2. The guardianship of the deposit of the faith was not the responsibility of the magisterium alone: all ranks in the Church shared in this in varying degrees; 3. As for the relations between Church and state, the schema should contain a clear statement about liberty of conscience. It should reflect the recent accomplishments in the field of ecclesiology and describe the Church in the light of these new, inspiring insights.

Bishop Bernacki, auxiliary of Gniezno, Poland, took exception to the fact that the primacy of the pope was not covered in a separate chapter—this central doctrine ought not be hidden under a bushel, at the risk of misleading the separated brethren. In fact so important was it, that he suggested changing the Creed to read: "I believe in the Holy, Catholic, and *Petrine* Church . . ." The President finally had to cut him off for overtime.

The speech by Bishop De Smedt of Bruges, Belgium, a

member of the Secretariat for Promoting Christian Unity, caused considerable comment, both within and without the Council, as did his intervention earlier in the debate on the sources of revelation. He said that while progress in theological thought about the nature of the Church in recent years was echoed to a certain extent in the schema, its presentation of the Church was faulty. He outlined three essential points:

(1) All species of "triumphalism" should be avoided in speaking of the Church. By that he meant the pompous and romantic style constantly used in *L'Osservatore Romano* and in the documents emanating from the Roman Curia. Thus the schema employed this style in speaking of the *Church Militant,* lining up its members as if in battle array. This approach had little if any relation to the sheepfold of which Christ spoke, nor did it reflect actuality, for today the Church was both persecuted and divided.

(2) The "clericalism" of the schema was equally offensive. The Church was not a pyramid of people, priests, and pope. The Church was essentially the People of God, and in them were to be found the rights and obligations of the Mystical Body. The hierarchy was much more a ministry or service, than a governing body. It was a particular continuation of Christ who came "not to be served, but to serve." Its function was to extend Christ by preaching the Word, and by offering His sanctifying grace to all mankind, the very opposite of any "hierarcholatria."

(3) Finally, in place of a juridical concept, the Church should be placed before the world as the Mother of mankind, for we were all reborn through her maternal action. Thus all mankind, as her sons, were brothers, both those within the family and those outside. "Reread pages 15 and 16 of this

document," he said, "and see to what misconceptions this legalistic spirit can give rise. No mother ever spoke thus."*

Bishop Lefebvre of Dakar proposed, as a compromise, that two different schemata be prepared for each treatise, one from a purely doctrinal and the other from a pastoral viewpoint. But this suggestion was answered immediately by Bishop Elchinger, coadjutor of Strasbourg, who pointed out that the pastoral spirit was not something added to the teaching of the faith, but an essential aspect of the Church. It was impossible to speak of the Church, he said, without considering it immediately from this point of view. Speaking as an auxiliary bishop, he was surprised to find nothing in the schema about their function, yet *all* bishops were the successors of the Apostles, whether residential, auxiliary, or titular.

Addressing the Council, once more, in the name of the bishops from the Congo, Bishop Van Cauwelaert stated that he and his colleagues had been disappointed by the schema. Expecting a joyful announcement of the good news that was the Church, they found themselves faced instead with a rather trite, juridical document. The Church was here described as a static entity, whereas it was a living body with an eschatological destiny. It was useless to proclaim the Catholic Church as the true Church of Christ, if it did not immediately present the face and spirit of Christ to the world. What was wanted was a return to the Church of Jerusalem—one heart, one mind in poverty and charity. The people of Africa were searching for a new manner of living together as a community—a new, solid, holy way of life. The Church could actually offer this to them, but certainly not as here represented.

Winding up the day's debate, Bishop Carli of Segni, Italy, who was considered by many as one of Cardinal Ottaviani's

* Cf. *Le Monde,* Dec. 4, 1962.

principal spokesmen, complained somewhat bitterly of the critical approach that many fathers had adopted toward this schema as well as the schema on Revelation. "We are dealing here with an internal matter regarding the Church," he said, "yet so many insist that we say nothing about those of our doctrines that could possibly offend Protestants. Thus it seems as though we cannot speak of the Blessed Virgin Mary, nor may we talk of the Church Militant. We dare not mention Communism. We can hardly mention ecumenism, and we will be outlawed if we bring up justice or chastity. Thus the Council is slowly petering out before a series of taboos." He was stopped by the President, and then hurriedly added his *placet* in favor of the schema as such. With applause for the presiding officer's intervention, the Council fathers joyfully departed.

The previous evening an article in *L'Osservatore Romano* took note of the anti-conciliar activities of certain politically (mainly rightist) groups in France and Italy. Recalling the Masonic attempt in 1869 to hold an Anti-Council while Vatican Council I was in session, and the several attempts of European governments to intervene in the debate on papal infallibility, Professor Alessandrini ["F. A."], admitted that the atmosphere today was totally different as regards the Church's reputation and position. While citing the worldwide news coverage and interest in the Council, he still felt that too many journalists were trying to report the Council as if it were some ordinary parliamentary meeting with its intrigues and counter-movements. The author was actually referring to a series of three articles published the previous week by Indro Montinelli in *Il Corriere della Serra* of Milan, in which this ordinarily "serious" journal allowed the writer to suggest that the pope, from his youth, was for all practical purposes a Modernist, and had called the Council in order to renounce papal infallibility. In the second article Cardinal

Tardini's truthfulness and loyalty to the pope were called into question. Finally, the third article judged almost all the protagonists of the Council as hopeless and misguided "revisionists."

Alessandrini likewise took note of an illustrated weekly that "alternated theological teaching with pornographic pictures" and accused the conciliar fathers of desiring to come to terms with Communism, sacrificing the persecuted to the persecutors. Finally, he mentioned the distortions of the Communist press only to complain of some journals, "even among our friends," who report the Council as "a more or less dramatic dialectic between 'conservatives' and 'liberals' as if in the great hall of St. Peter's, particular positions and persons were under discussion, and not the great truths of the faith." He commiserated with "the poor Curia, which is the practical expression of the central government of the Church," but which is under such continuous assault. "These are episodes that sadden Christians," the author asserted, "and little by little excite them to disdain."

While there was some truth in these observations of Alessandrini, particularly as regards the disdain or hatred which extreme rightist groups in north Italy feel for Pope John because of his teaching with regard to social and economic justice, the article in *L'Osservatore Romano* failed to put the finger precisely on this group, composed of powerful industrialists and corporation executives. Instead it chased after pseudo-masons, "laicists," and communists, not stopping to ask whether its own obviously ultra-conservative bias was not the occasion, perhaps even the cause, of much of the so-called controversy. Considering the tenor of the conciliar debates, it seemed less than honest to suggest that there were no disagreements.*

The morning's discussion on Monday, Dec. 3, in the 32nd

* *L'Osservatore Romano,* Dec. 1, 1962.

General Congregation with Cardinal Ruffini presiding, brought Cardinals Spellman, Siri, McIntyre, Gracias, Léger and Doepfner to the microphone. The first three had no particularly new light to shed on the subject under consideration, being out of touch with the newer theological thought appearing in central and northern Europe. Cardinal McIntyre did mention one obvious oversight, however, the failure to deal with the problem of infants who died without baptism.

Cardinal Gracias, on the other hand, spoke of the schema as offending against the true hospitality that ought to be the mark of the Church, and the bishops who pledge themselves to be "hospitable" in their consecration. He insisted that the missionary activity of the Church, particularly in a land such as his own, needed new orientation which could only come from a fundamental renewal of thinking in accordance with the will of the majority. He pointed out that Christians were prepared "to go so far as to shed their blood" for the faith was true enough, but insisted that it was not necessary to say things offensive or provoking to non-Christians, in the newer nations. Why say this then, when we were now aware that there were various ways of announcing the truth of the Gospel? He likewise suggested that more attention be paid to oriental philosophers, since the pagans were increasing rapidly in the Far East, and it was only by considering their true mentality that the Church could properly be preached to them.

For Cardinal Léger of Montreal, the schema "De Ecclesia" was the *cardo,* or hinge, of Vatican Council II. The two months of discussion thus far had at least one great benefit, he contended. They proved conclusively how correct Pope John had been in calling for a renewal of the Church through the Council.

Cardinal Doepfner of Munich likewise said that the present schema was of paramount importance both to the Council and to the Church. Hence he proposed a radical change in its structure that would bring out better the fundamental notion of the Church as the People of God, with pope, bishops and laity as coordinate members thereof. There was no particular connection between the different chapters. An insufficient, even superficial, use was made of Holy Scripture. Too much emphasis was placed on the juridical aspects of the Church. Whereas the collegiality of the bishops ought to have been stressed, this idea was merely noted; it was absurd to maintain that emphasis on the episcopate amounted to a downgrading of the papal primacy, since the pope or papacy was the crown of the episcopal order. Finally, the chapters on Church and state and the missions needed to be completely rethought. The revisions should be made by the Theological Commission on the basis of suggestions made in the Council, with the collaboration of the Commissions on the Laity, the Religious, and the Secretariat for Unity.

Of the speakers that followed, Archb. Marty of Rheims gave the clearest exposition of the Church as a Mystery. The bonds which united it were primarily of a spiritual nature, he said. Its nature as an institution, its hierarchy, its social aspects were definable, ultimately, only in terms of this Mystery, the mystery of the Mystical Body of Christ extended in the world for the salvation of mankind. The Church was the direct intervention of God in the affairs of the world, the chosen instrument by which He intended to redeem all mankind. And its principal function—that of both hierarchy and laity—was to bring knowledge of salvation and the means of achieving it to everyone on this earth. Hence to identify the Church too closely with its juridical or administrative aspects was to misrepresent it or lower it to the level of some earthly association.

While Bishops Gargitter of Bressanone, Italy, Huyghe of Arras, France, and Hurley of Durban, South Africa, rallied to the thesis favored by the majority, the Italian Bishops Barbetta and Musto kept hammering away at the line laid down by the Theological Commission. The true difficulty with the schema, said Bishop Rupp of Monaco, putting his finger on the crux of the matter, was that the authors had not had in view the same purpose or end desired by the pope and the Council. It was not calculated to bring about the reunion of Christians, or an *aggiornamento*. In fact it was rather scandalous to think that a part of the magisterium could have been capable of indulging in such exaggerations as the excessively juridical aspect of the Church presented by the schema. Bishop Musto, who followed, almost wept as he pleaded with the fathers not to destroy the Church by changing anything in it. His oratory made many of his hearers wonder why he thought the pope had summoned the Council. Finally, running overtime, he was stopped by the President.

The debate continued during the 33rd General Congregation on Tuesday, Dec. 4, under the presidency of Cardinal Caggiano of Buenos Aires. Cardinal Frings, speaking first in the name of all the German-language bishops, said that the present schema did not represent thinking about the nature of the Church as a whole, but merely a certain theology which did not go back more than a hundred years. There was nothing in it about what the Greek Fathers had to say on the subject, and very little about what the Latin Fathers had to say either. It would have to be completely rewritten to reflect the true catholicity of the Church's thought.

A much more cautious line was taken by Cardinal Godfrey of Westminster, whose remarks revealed that he was still influenced by the "siege mentality" which had characterized relations between the communions not so long ago. The situation in England today, he said, was confusing. It was difficult to know what members of the Church of England or the non-conformists believed. It was sometimes said that English Catholics were neither very enthusiastic Catholics nor very sympathetic toward the separated brethren. They were charitable and patient, however. The important thing was not to give the separated brethren any false ideas about concessions with regard to truth. *Magna est veritas et praevalebit.*

Discarding any such hesitant, fear-laden approach, the Archbishop of Malines-Brussels, Cardinal Suenens came out for a redrafting of the schema on an entirely new basis. As Vatican I was the Council of the Primacy, he suggested, so Vatican II should be the Council of the Church of Christ, the light of nations. He proposed that in keeping with Pope John's suggestions in his inaugural talk, the doctrine on the Church should be considered in two stages: *ad intra,* or the nature of the Church as the Mystical Body; and *ad extra,* with respect to its missions "to preach the Gospel to all nations." The latter obviously required a dialogue between the Church and the world today which was looking so desperately to the Church for a solution to its problems. Hence the Church must offer itself as the answer to: (1) All those questions having to do with the decency and dignity of the human person. This includes the problem of the population-explosion. (2) Everything having to do with social justice. This includes the sixth commandment (which, for all the books written about it, still lacks a proper orientation), private property, the poor. (3) The problem of winning the poor for the Church by teaching them to give themselves wholly to Christ in their homes as well as in foreign missions. (4) The problem of in-

ternal peace within nations, and the dangers of war. The
proper treatment of these subjects, he said, "involves us in a
triple dialogue: with the faithful, with our separated brethren, and with the world outside the Church. This analysis
will be seen to be nothing other than a reconsideration of
the opening discourse of Pope John."*

The discourse of Cardinal Suenens was greeted with long
applause by the fathers, so much so that it had to be choked
off by a reminder from the President, Cardinal Caggiano,
that such vociferous reactions were forbidden at the Council.

Cardinal Bea spoke in a similar vein, seconding the
thoughts of the preceding speakers. Although Cardinals Bacci
and Browne attempted to stem the tide by reiterating the
scholastic, juridical approach, Archbishop Blanchet of Paris,
Bishop Rabbani of Syria, Archbishop Guerry of Cambrai,
Bishop Holland of Portsmouth, and Bishop Hengsbach of
Essen, in quick succession, spoke out in favor of a radical
reworking of the schema. So did the Maronite Bishop Doumith of Lebanon. The last word of the day, however, was
spoken by Archbishop Descuffi of Smyrna and it was along a
more reactionary line. That evening *L'Osservatore Romano,*
for the first time, carried a much fuller account of what had
been said in the debate than usual, even admitting that such
themes as the collegiality of the bishops and the sacramental
nature of the episcopate had been discussed, and that the
juridical aspect of the schema had been criticized.

The intervention of Cardinal Suenens proved to be crucial.
At the 34th Congregation on Dec. 5, with Cardinal Alfrink
president, Cardinal Ruffini spoke in a conciliatory tone, reminding the fathers that, after all, their disagreements were

* Quoted at length in *Informations Catholiques Internationales,* Feb. 1,
1963, p. 6.

concerned with the manner of presenting the Church's doctrine, and not with the fundamentals of the faith itself. Whatever the purpose of this statement, Cardinal Montini next took the microphone and, to all intents and purposes, confirmed the suspicion that Cardinal Suenens had been speaking for the pope. Montini approved wholeheartedly of the Belgian Cardinal's approach. The Church, he said, was nothing by itself. It was not so much a society founded by Christ, but rather Christ himself using us as his instruments to bring salvation to all mankind.

The Cardinal of Milan went on to say that it was up to the fathers in Council, now, to restate the "mind and will of Christ" by defining the collegiality of the episcopate, by giving a truly ecumenical outlook to the Church, and by insisting that each bishop was "the image of the father and the image of Christ." The less we insisted on the rights of the Church, he said, the more chance we had of being heard, particularly in those parts of the world that were suspicious of the Church as a paternalistic or colonial-minded institution. Hence it was necessary to send this schema back to the Theological Commission and to the Secretariat for Unity so that it might be completely revised.

This was the first time that the Cardinal of Milan had spoken since the opening days of the Council. What made his intervention all the more significant was the fact that, over the weekend, in a letter to his diocese which he faithfully published every week, he was openly critical not only of those members of the Council who refused to follow the newer viewpoint, but he actually laid the blame for the Council's failure to make greater progress on those members of the Curia who had prevented cooperation between the various Commissions during the preparatory phase of the Council. They were obviously failing to follow the pope's lead, he said, as stated in his opening address. A discreet and prudent man such as the Cardinal of Milan would never have so revealed his true mind in this way, had he not been certain that he was expressing the thoughts of the Holy Father.*

Speaking the next day, Dec. 5, Patriarch Maximos IV Saigh, took a somewhat conciliatory line saying that it was not out of hostility or prejudice that the rejection of the schema was being proposed. Rather it was in the interests of the Church, which must put its best foot forward in the modern world. He pleaded that neither side in the debate should indulge in suspicions about the good faith of the other. He added that there was no need to insist on the primacy of the pope at this Council; it was a doctrine of faith, well appreciated everywhere. What was necessary was relieving the Church of the burden of legalism and a too cumbersome juridic background. Likewise it would be unjust to consider the desire to give an ecumenical turn to their deliberations as an attempt at attenuating the Church's doctrine. Neither Catholics nor Orthodox had any such desires. Citing several passages in a recently edited Italian work on the history of the Church, he remarked the lack of realism manifested on almost every page, stating that what was not real could not be theology. Then he called for the reworking of the schema with the assistance of a truly representative commission which would give proper weight to oriental theology.

Archbps. Ermenegildo Florit of Florence and Antonio Plaza of La Plata, and Bp. William Pluta of Poland returned to the Ottaviani line, but time was running out.

The question of the pope's health had become crucial during the final two weeks of the Council and rumors were rife, in Vatican circles, that soon after the close of the Council— on Dec. 10, it was said—Pope John would undergo surgery which his physician had been staving off for the past year or

---

* L'Italia (Milan), Dec. 2, 1962. See Herder-Korrespondenz, Feb. 1963, p. 247.

so. Word of this was published by a Netherlands newspaper in mid-November, then knowingly bruited about by some bishops and prelates. Finally, on Friday, Nov. 30, *L'Osservatore Romano* published a notice saying that the Holy Father was suffering from gastric trouble which had resulted in semi-severe anemia. Upon the insistence of his physician, he had cancelled all audiences from the 27th. No mention was made of a possible operation, but rumor again had it that the pope had had several gastric hemorrhages.

However, on Sunday, December 2, Pope John appeared at the open window of his private apartments in the Vatican at noon, and recited the *Angelus* with the immense crowd in the square below as was his custom—only this time they were reinforced by batteries of TV cameras—despite the fact that it was cold outside. Thanking the crowd for their solicitude and prayers for his health, he then rather casually informed them that "the good health, which threatened for a moment to absent itself, is now returning, has actually returned."

On Tuesday evening, the 4th, it was announced that the pontiff would bless the pilgrims from his window at mid-day on Wednesday instead of holding his usual audience for them and, by way of emphasizing his continued improvement, it was stated that he had received the Cardinal Secretary of State on both Monday and Tuesday.

Deciding to take advantage of the occasion, the fathers of the Council swarmed out of the basilica, on Wednesday, at 11:45, and joined the immense throngs of priests, nuns and laymen patiently waiting for the Holy Father to appear. Precisely at twelve noon, the papal window opened and the pope began to recite the *Angelus*. As he finished, the crowd broke into a tremendous roar, accompanied by the tooting of horns and the ringing of bells. The pope quickly signaled for silence. Obviously moved by the tribute, he said: "My sons, Divine Providence is with us. As you see, from one day to the next there is progress, not going down, but in coming up slowly—*piano, piano.* Sickness, then convalescence. Now we are convalescing. The satisfaction afforded us by this gathering is a reason for rejoicing. It is an augury of the strength and robustness which are coming back to us."

Gesturing majestically, he then continued: "What a spectacle we see before us today—the Church grouped together here in full representation: *ecco,* its bishops; *ecco,* its priests; *ecco,* its Christian people! A whole family here present, the family of Christ!"

Alluding to the fact that the Council was soon to close for a while, the pope then spoke of the pleasure it had afforded him thus far—not merely because of the obvious unity of clergy and people in the Church to which it attested, but because it represented all the races of the whole world, for all peoples everywhere had been redeemed by the Savior, Jesus Christ.

The 35th Congregation on Thursday, December 6, had Cardinal Tisserant as its President. The discussion was preceded by a statistical résumé of the Council's activities, presented by Archbishop Felici, indicating that since the opening day some 1,110 fathers had either spoken or presented their views in writing. Then Cardinal Lecaro of Bologna, initiating the day's debate, quickly put his stamp of approval on the Montini-Suenens thesis, and spoke eloquently of the Mystery of Christ in the Church of the poor. With an explicit reference to the pope's opening discourse, wherein he had cited the words of St. Peter: "Silver and gold I have none," the Cardinal of Bologna exhorted all in the Church to follow Christ truly "Who, though rich, became poor for us." His remarks were received with loud applause.*

*Cf. *La Documentation Catholique,* Jan. 6, 1963, p. 53–54, and Fr. R. Rouquette, S.J., in *Etudes,* Feb. 1963, p. 265.

The Secretary General then spoke, making a definitive announcement in the name of the Holy Father. This intervention on the part of the pope made it finally and unmistakably clear how he wanted the Council conducted. In the nine months between the adjournment of this first session of Vatican Council II and its second session, opening on September 8, 1963, all the schemata—particularly those discussed in Council—were to be reworked by mixed Commissions and sent to the bishops for their emendations and comment. The fathers were instructed to return these to the Secretariat as soon as possible. To coordinate the work of the collaborating Commissions, the Holy Father had decided to create a new committee under the presidency of Cardinal Cicognani.*

The rest of the debate was simply dénouement. The full significance of the papal intervention being comprehended, it was obvious that Pope John had remained on the "pastoral" side of the debate—as he had clearly asserted in his inaugural discourse—throughout the meetings of the Council.

This did not prevent several further statements on the opposite side, such as those by Bp. Compagnone of Anagni, Bp. Hervás y Benet of Ciudad Real, Spain, Bp. Fares of Catanzaro, and Archb. Stella of Aquila which reiterated the tried and not so true juridic themes. But the rest of the speakers, including Bp. Philbin of Down (one of the three Irish bishops who spoke in the Council) and Bp. Renard of Versailles, came out clearly for renovation and renewal.

---

* The names of the other members were not disclosed until over a week later, in the issue of *l'Osservatore Romano* for Dec. 17–18, 1962: namely, Cards. Liénart, Urbani, Spellman, Confalonieri, Döpfner and Suenens. Significant differences between the official Latin text of the norms and the translations prepared by the Press Office have been brought to light. Cf. *La Civiltà Cattolica*, Mar. 2, 1963, and *America*, Mar. 16, 1963. The popular versions glossed over the facts that the revised schemata are to be channeled through episcopal conferences, when "expeditious"; that general principles are to be treated, "above all," and that experts should be consulted on a wide scale, when necessary.

Father Joseph Buckley, the recently elected General of the Marist Order, with a good Massachusetts accent, then gave a fine discourse on the nature of obedience as it must be conceived in the context of the liberty enjoyed by the lay members of the Church in the world of today, and Bp. Hakim of Israel capped the day's discussion by reiterating the oriental approach.

The final general congregation, the 36th, was held on Friday, December 7, presided over by Cardinal Liénart. After the announcement that Pope John would arrive before midday to speak to the fathers, the President expressed his sentiments of joy and gratitude to all for the work and good spirit demonstrated by the Council. Cardinal Koenig in the first talk took the opportunity to correct a statement made a few days earlier by Bishop Griffiths, auxiliary of New York, who in his discourse had quoted the Gospel phrase, "Lord, we have labored the whole night long, and have taken nothing." Said the Cardinal of Vienna: "We have certainly not done everything, but in these two months we have accomplished great things. Within these halls by our exchange of viewpoints we have come to a much greater appreciation of the Church as it is in reality. Despite our differences, we have maintained the charity of Christ, and have prepared ourselves for the presentation to the world of the truth and love of Christ that we daily hope to accomplish in the next session."

Earlier, in a chronicle of the Council in the Paris journal Le Monde, the Auxiliary Bishop of New York had been bracketed with the Bishops of Salamanca and Trois Rivières (Canada) as among the more outstanding intransigents at the Council, because of his intelligence and extremely juridical outlook.

Cardinal Lefebvre of Bourges then gave a vivid but kindly discourse on charity as the heart and life of the Church. This was followed by a rambling, semi-hysterical discourse by Bp. Reyes of the Philippines who insisted on the royal character of the Church's rights, due to the kingship of Christ. Msgr. Isaac Ghattas, Coptic bishop of Thebes, brought the Council back to a balanced consideration of the true union in faith and love that should mark all the Christian Churches, while Bishop Ancel, auxiliary of Lyons, in reiterating the collegiality of the bishops in association with the pope, said there need be no conflict between the juridical and other aspects of the Church, so long as the former were seen as merely an accidental necessity, and not made the principal consideration of ecclesiastical thought and action. Bishop Silva of Concepción, Chile, struck a final blow on behalf of Cardinals Ruffini and Browne. The honor of the last word at the first session went to the Benedictine Abbot Butler.

At 11:15 the Holy Father arrived on foot, mounted the platform erected over the Confession of St. Peter and started reciting the *Angelus*. The fathers applauded his arrival, joined with him joyfully in prayer, and listened avidly as he thanked them for the work they had accomplished in their two months in Council. He indicated his pleasure at the unity and charity displayed, despite their divergences. Giving them his blessing, he then descended the platform unassisted, and left the basilica.

On Saturday morning, December 8 (feast of the Immaculate Conception), Cardinal Marella, the Archpriest of St. Peter's, chanted a solemn high mass that was sung in unison in Gregorian chant by all the bishops and faithful present in the basilica. At 10:15 Pope John arrived on foot, mounted the platform, and sat down. His appearance for the second consecutive day was not only reassuring, in view of the many rumors about his health, but many of the fathers pres-

ent were moved to tears of relief and admiration at the sight
of this portly figure, somewhat pale but vigorous in his movements, as he fished for his glasses and began to read his closing
address.

As he got absorbed in the reading, he became his old self
more and more. His voice was strong and he began to empha-
size points by quick movements of the paper in his hand, lift-
ing his head and peering over his glasses from time to time,
to note the effect of particular phrases. He admitted that the
Council had got off to a slow start, but it was necessary for
so many bishops from such diverse nations and cultures to
come to know and understand one another's points of view.
He touched lightly on the dissensions that had arisen during
the first session, indicating that they were both healthy and
necessary for the achievement of a holy liberty, in charity.
With a humorous allusion that seemed to escape many of his
listeners, he referred to the nine months' work ahead for the
conciliar Commissions, as a grave but important task "that
would be accomplished in silence!"

He indicated that there was no time to lose, with the world
as it is today. The Church must use all its resources—bishops,
priests, religious men and women, as well as the laity—in pursuing its mission to bring Christ to the world. He exhorted
the bishops to do their work by going over the schemas that
would be sent to them carefully in the light of what they
had learned at the Council, even though they would be absorbed in the pastoral cares of their dioceses. Reminding
them that they would all be back in September, Pope John
suggested that by bringing the Council to an end for Christmas 1963, they would be both satisfying the desires of the
peoples who are looking for concrete results from the Council, and at the same time be properly celebrating the four
hundredth anniversary of the closing of the Council of Trent.

With the help of God, he concluded, though the Council did not have directives to give to the world at this point, it had still achieved great things which should prove to be the seeding from which—not alone among Christians but among all men of good will—there would appear a reblossoming of the religious sense that is implicit even in the patrimony of secular cultures. He summoned the whole Church, its priests, religious and laity, to prepare to be the instruments for carrying the message of the Council to the world. In this way, he said, a new Pentecost will be effected, wherein the bond of charity will strengthen the reign of Christ on earth.

Obviously greatly moved by the occasion, Pope John imparted his blessing to the prelates and bishops, dismissing them with fond greetings for their flocks. Then as unostentatiously as he had appeared, he walked down from the platform, and out through a side door of the basilica.

SUMMARY

December 1, 1962, Saturday—31st GENERAL CONGREGATION
PRESIDENT: Card. *Frings* (Cologne). MASS: Celebrated by Archb. *Grimshaw* (Birmingham, England). PRESENT: 2,112 fathers.

Announcement by SG that pope's health is improving and that he hopes to give blessing from window of his apartment tomorrow at noon.

Voting on schema *Ut unum sint* as a whole and proposal that it should form one document with similar schemas prepared by Secretariat for Unity and Theological Commission. Results: 2,068 favorable votes, 36 against, and 8 invalid.

SUBJECT: General discussion of schema on the Church. SPEAKERS: Card. *Ottaviani* (President of Theological Commission) and Bp. *Franič* (Split, Yugoslavia). Cards. *Liénart, Ruffini, Bueno y Monreal* (Seville), *König, Alfrink, Ritter* (St. Louis); Abps. and Bps. *Bernacki* (aux. Gniezno, Poland), *De Smedt* (Bruges, Belgium), *Lefebvre* (Dakar, Africa), *Elchinger* (coadj. Strasbourg, France), *D'Avack* (Camerino, Italy), *Pawlowski* (Włocławek, Poland), *Van Cauwelaert* (Inongo, Congo) on behalf of African bishops, and *Carli* (Segni, Italy).

December 2, 1962, Sunday

Pope blesses crowds from window of his apartment at noon, says "Good health is returning."

December 3, 1962, Monday—32ND GENERAL CONGREGATION

PRESIDENT: Card. *Ruffini*. MASS: According to Malabar rite, celebrated by Archb. *Parecattil* (Ernakulam, India). PRESENT: 2,116 fathers.

Voting on amendment nos. 10 and 11 of Chapter I of Liturgy schema, explanation by Archb. *Grimshaw*. Overwhelmingly approved.

SUBJECT: General discussion of schema on the Church. SPEAKERS: Cards. *Spellman, Siri, McIntyre, Gracias, Léger,* and *Döpfner;* Archbps. and Bps. *Kominek* (Poland), *Marty* (Rheims, France), *Gargitter* (Bressanone, Italy), *Huyghe* (Arras, France), *Hurley* (Durban, South Africa), *Barbetta* (Italy), *Jubany* (aux. Barcelona, Spain), *Rupp* (Monaco), *Musto* (Aquino, Italy), *Kozlowiecki* (Lusaka, Northern Rhodesia).

Conference by Fr. Y. *Congar,* O.P. on tradition and the Church.

Conference by Card. *Bea* on missionary countries and ecumenism.

December 4, 1962, Tuesday—33RD GENERAL CONGREGATION

PRESIDENT: Card. *Caggiano*. MASS: Celebrated by Archb. *Rakotomalala* (Tananarive, Madagascar). PRESENT: 2,104 fathers.

Archb. *Seper* (Zagreb, Yugoslavia) spoke first of Council's devotion to Pope John and its hopes for his speedy recovery.

SUBJECT: General discussion of schema on Church continued.

SPEAKERS: Cards. *Frings, Godfrey, Suenens, Bea, Bacci, Browne;* Archbps. and Bps. *Seper, Blanchet* (France), *Rabbani* (Homs of the Syrians, Syria), *Gonzalez Moralejo* (aux. Valencia, Spain), *Guerry* (Cambrai, France), *Maccari* (Italy), *Holland* (coadj. Portsmouth, England), *De Voto* (Goya, Argentina), *Vairo* (Gravina and Irsina, Italy), *Hengsbach* (Essen, Germany), *Doumith* (Sarba of the Maronites, Lebanon), and *Descuffi* (Smyrna, Turkey).

Announcement pope would recite *Angelus* next day from window of his apartment.

December 5, 1962, Wednesday—34TH GENERAL CONGREGATION

PRESIDENT: Card. *Alfrink*. MASS: Celebrated by Archb. *da Silveira d'Elboux* (Curitba, Brazil). PRESENT: 2,114 fathers.

Booklet distributed to fathers containing titles of subjects which already have been or are to be discussed by Council. The 70 schemas originally prepared reduced to 20. Eleven amendments to Chapter I of Liturgy schema explained by Bp. *Calewaert;* voting on 8 of them, and results of 4 announced (nos. 12–15). Overwhelmingly approved.

SUBJECT: General discussion of schema on the Church continued. SPEAKERS: Cards. *Ruffini* and *Montini;* Patr. *Maximos IV Saigh;* Archbps. and Bps. *Florit* (Florence, Italy), *Plaza* (La Plata, Argentina), *Pluta* (Poland), *Fiordelli* (Prato, Italy), and *Mels* (Luluabourg, Congo).

Pope blesses crowds of fathers and pilgrims from window of apartment at noon.

December 6, 1962, Thursday—35TH GENERAL CONGREGATION

PRESIDENT: Card. *Tisserant*. MASS: Celebrated by Archb. *Gantin* (Cotonou, Dahomey). PRESENT: 2,082 fathers.

SG briefly summarizes work of Council thus far.

Announcement by SG that pope has granted bishops permission to impart apostolic benediction when they return to their sees and to say mass at any time of day or night on the day of their departure or arrival.

SUBJECT: General discussion of schema on the Church continued. SPEAKERS: Card. *Lercaro;* Archbps. and Bps. *Compagnone* (Anagni, Italy), *Hervás* (Ciudad Real, Spain), *Méndez* (Cuernavaca, Mexico), *Philbin* (Down and Connor, Ireland), *Renard* (Versailles, France), *Fares* (Catanzaro and Squillace, Italy), *Velasco* (Hsiamen, China), *Barrachina Estevan* (Orihuela-Alicante,

Spain); Fr. *Buckley* (Superior General of the Marists, USA); Bps. *Stella* (Aquila, Italy) and *Hakim* (Akka, Israel).

Voting on 3 remaining amendments (of 11 mentioned above) to Chapter I of Liturgy schema and on 2 additional amendments, explained by Archb. *Grimshaw*. Results of voting on amendments nos. 16–24 announced. Overwhelmingly approved.

Announcement by SG of norms laid down by Holy Father to govern work of Council during interval until Sept. 8, 1963. Appointment of a Coordinating Commission headed by Secretary of State, Card. *Cicognani*.

December 7, 1962, Friday—36TH GENERAL CONGREGATION

PRESIDENT: Card. *Liénart*. MASS: According to Chaldean rite, celebrated by Bp. *Ganni* (coadj. Beirut of the Chaldeans, Lebanon). PRESENT: 2,118 fathers.

Opening part of this congregation attended by about 100 journalists.

Announcement by SG that Holy Father would appear for closing of today's congregation.

Voting on revised Introduction and Chapter I of Liturgy schema as a whole. Results: 1,922 *Placets;* 11 *Non placets;* 180 *Placet iuxta modum;* and 5 invalid votes. Those marked *Placet iuxta modum* had to be submitted to SG for consideration by Dec. 31, 1962, otherwise the votes would be counted as *Placet*.

SUBJECT: General discussion of schema on the Church concluded, for this session. SPEAKERS: Cards. *König* and *Lefebvre;* Archbps. and Bps. *Reyes* (Borongan, Philippines), *De Bazelaire* (Chambéry, France), *Ghattas* (Thebes, Egypt), *Ancel* (aux. Lyons, France), *Silva Santiago* (Concepcion, Chile), *D'Souza* (Nagpur, India), *Volk* (Mainz, Germany); Abbot *Butler, O.S.B.* (Downside, England). The remaining 44 fathers who had asked to speak but were unable because of lack of time, were requested to submit their suggestions or amendments in writing to the SG by Feb. 28, 1963.

Pope arrives in conciliar hall and after reciting *Angelus* with fathers, delivers short talk, then blesses the assembly and departs, as the Council applauds.

December 8, 1962, Saturday—SOLEMN CLOSING OF THE FIRST SESSION

Pope addresses the Council.

Reception by Card. *Cicognani* for observer delegates, reply by Dr. Vischer.

December 9, 1962, Sunday

Canonization of 3 new saints in St. Peter's.

Reception by Diplomatic Corps for fathers of the Council.

IX

Pope John's "Revolution"

ANYTHING but a superficial evaluation of the first session of Vatican Council II at this time would be temerarious. The man in the best position to judge the Council's accomplishment was Pope John, and he expressed full satisfaction that the two months' work had been both constructive and epoch-making, despite the fact that no decrees could yet be published as an augury of the assembly's impact on the Church or the world. For the vast majority of the Council's participants, a revolution had been accomplished; it needed but the interval before the second session to clarify the details whereby all the world could see how the fathers had restored "the simple and pure lines that the face of the Church of Jesus had at its birth." As Pope John had made it clear from the start that "a holy liberty" was the prerogative of all men, he did nothing to force his opponents to see things his way.

The pope frequently speaks of himself as an optimist. In the case of the Council he realized from the beginning that it would be no easy task to get some three thousand bishops to settle down at once, and discuss the fundamental problems of the Church's business without argument or even heated debate. Remarking on this phase of conciliar activity he is reported to have asked: "What would you expect them to do, behave like a group of monks reciting the divine office in choir?" Some commentators have even wondered whether the original failure to supply a rule of cloture for cutting off debate on individual chapters of the schemata was not a deliberate calculation: if there were no way of getting off a particular topic, the conciliar fathers would be tempted to talk to each other about every subject under the sun. In actual fact, as the debate on the liturgy and more particularly on the use of Latin in the mass disclosed, something of this sort happened. In the first three weeks of discussion, they touched upon all the important questions of contemporary Catholic interest from the collegial character of the episcopate and the nature of divine revelation to the *intransigenza* of Curial procedure. Eventually the Holy Father did intervene, allowing the bishops by a standing vote to stop the debate on a particular issue. But by that time those who took an active part in the Council's debate had made up their minds to push ahead effectively. Once or twice, particularly in the discussion on the sources of revelation and in that on Christian unity, successive speakers directly contradicted those who had spoken before them. But on the whole the Council proved to be a vast educative procedure rather than an outright debate, for a large proportion of its members had come to Rome knowing little of the theological and scripture problems bothering Roman churchmen. Those who took the care to inform themselves on these grave matters left the Council with a thorough understanding of the Church's status in the modern world. Unfortunately a considerable number, particularly among the English-speaking bishops, seemed never to have caught on to what all the talking at the Council was about.

Despite the pope's optimism, there is still considerable concern behind the scenes. His health is a primary worry of course, for the work of the Council is only half done, and without his drive and paternal charity things could easily be brought to a standstill. While Pope John has accomplished something that will affect the course of the Catholic Church's history until the end of time, the spectrum of possibilities ranges from a miraculous renewal of its life and effectiveness in human affairs here and now, to a severe setback such as it received in the Protestant revolt and the age of the enlightenment. Meanwhile the administration of important church offices still appears to be in the hands of the ultra-conservatives and the signs of their continued power and methods are very much in evidence. *L'Osservatore Romano* in a special edition on December 9, on the second page immediately behind Pope John's quietly triumphal closing talk, ran an article on the "Work of the Council" by Fr. Ermenegildo Lio, O.F.M., a Defensor of the Bond in the Holy Office. In his article, omitting all reference to the sermon with which the Holy Father opened the Council and laid down directions for its pastoral orientation, the author stated that the Council must get round to condemnations—otherwise it would compromise the position taken by Pope John before the whole world (Fr. Lio said explicitly) in a radio message delivered last September. This article was then repeated verbatim in a regular issue on December 13. The

casual observer may well ask, who is really running the
Catholic Church—the pope and the majority of the bishops
in Council, or the advisors of the Holy Office?

Measured by the standards of modern "public relations,"
the Council was a huge success. It got more sustained publicity over a longer period of time than any other single
religious event. Over a thousand journalists covered the
opening session, and the effort they made to obtain authentic
and live information was in the end a tremendous education
for them, and through them, for the millions of people whom
the Church would perhaps never have reached without their
news stories. Ingenuity, a prime factor in the competence
of any journalist, was put to a severe test at Vatican Council
II. But day by day, in the more enterprising journals at least,
the news became more vivid and more accurate. The problems presented by the secrecy imposed on the conciliar fathers
and accepted most scrupulously by the observer delegates
proved a great hurdle. But each nation or language group,
after sufficient clamoring on the part of its reporters, finally
found a way to solve the difficulty. In the wake of each conciliar session, for example, groups of bishops and experts were
made available for questioning by the English, German and
Spanish speaking journalists, and these experts gave a sufficiently expanded account of the day's doings to satisfy
most newsgatherers. In the course of the fifth week, the
French Catholic daily, *La Croix,* feeling the competition
offered by the so-called "indiscretions" of the Italian press,
began to link the names of the conciliar speakers with the
general import of what they said. This move was certainly
known to the French episcopate, to the Secretary General of
the Council, and to its Committee for Extraordinary Affairs.
Yet nothing was done to stop it. Hence Father Antoine
Wenger, the editor, concluded that it was a tolerable way of

getting around the secrecy imposed on the conciliar fathers and theologians by the rules of the Council. Henry Fesquet, reporter for *Le Monde,* summed up the problem in the Christmas issue of *Témoinage Chrétien.* Though in the end he did not solve the dilemma posed by the necessity of secrecy in the debates to guarantee full freedom to the prelates in their observations, particularly on delicate or controversial matters, and the need of journalists to supply their readers with names and facts, he did think that a solution would be forthcoming before the next sessions.

In the past, particularly in Italy, the Church has generally had a bad press. This has prejudiced responsible Italian ecclesiastics against journalists generally.* In other parts of the world, complaints have been registered against religious reportage, indicating that Church news is not infrequently distorted or biased. On the whole this could not be said of the reporting of the Council. Some conservative-minded Catholics were disturbed by the airing of differences of opinion between certain prelates and the majority of cardinals and bishops who took the pope's opening address to heart. It is impossible, however, to have the advantage of great publicity without paying the price of honest reportage. As Pope

---

* Christopher Hollis, author, publisher, and former Member of Parliament, present at the opening session of the Council, had this to say: "The press relations (of the Council) were in the hands of Curial officials. It would perhaps be a discourteous exaggeration to say that this is as if one were to ask the prisoner in the dock to report on his own trial, but it is certainly true that what this first session of the Council revealed above all things—whatever may be its eventual outcome—is the existence among bishops of almost every country in the world of a vast mass of dissatisfaction with the lack of knowledge and imagination of the bureaucracy which has had in its hands the management of the administrative affairs of the Church. The strength of this dissatisfaction notoriously came as a total surprise to most of the officials. They cannot understand it, and therefore they are not the best people to interpret what they are the last people to understand. They try to perform their functions fairly enough, but they are not very competent." (*The Critic,* Chicago, Feb.–March, 1963.)

John himself said: "We have nothing to hide."*

In passing it might be noted that, at least for the English-speaking prelates, the first article in *The New Yorker* seemed in a literal sense to be "news" when it arrived in Rome. Before reading this article, which was mimeographed by some bishops and passed around quickly among American, English, Irish and Australian prelates, many of them had known nothing of the disputes going on in Rome between some Curial officials and the Biblical Institute, for example; nor had they any true notion of the reason for the pope's insistence on an *aggiornamento*.

In his summation of the first session, Pope John alluded to the remarkably good reception given to the conciliar fathers' activities by men of good will in many parts of the world. This is a fact whose appositeness can be appreciated only by comparison with the belligerently anti-Catholic atmosphere that surrounded Vatican Council I less than a hundred years ago. The Holy Father and the Church have good reason for continued optimism in this regard. In the secular press of the United States, Germany and Great Britain numerous attempts have been made to summarize the accomplishments of the Council; and while great attention has been focused on the differences and disputes, even they have been interpreted for the most part in a favorable light. There was universal acknowledgment of the fact that this was definitely Pope John's Council. The revolution in Catholic activity and thinking associated with the first session is recog-

---

* On November 24th a letter was addressed to Pope John by 19 cardinals, expressing their "disquietude over false doctrines" being aired at the Council (ICI, 15 March 1963). Mentioning articles in the *Revue Biblique* and the *Rivista Biblica*, and a book by Fr. Nierinck, theologian to the Bishop of Bruges, the letter was passed on to the Secretary of State and then to Cardinal Bea, whereupon 5 cardinals withdrew their signatures, leaving these 14 on the list: Pizzardo, Bacci, Marella, Traglia, Ruffini, Siri, Agagianian, Ottaviani, Browne, De Barros Camara, Santos, Godfrey, Bueno y Monreal and McIntyre.

nized as being due almost single-handedly to the pope's decision and his way of doing things.

Immediately before the Council opened Pope John remarked that Catholics in this world had no business acting as if the Church were a museum full of ancient artefacts. In his opening discourse he called for a new formulation of Catholic truths in such fashion that they would penetrate into the consciousness of modern man. He said explicitly that he was thinking of men of science, learning, labor, and industry who were responsible for the magnificent progress this world has made in material achievements. Since the Council, he has insisted repeatedly that he was an optimist who sees in the present age one of the most hopeful periods in human history, because it challenges the Church to show itself truly to be the Kingdom of God by reaching all mankind with its revolutionary message.

As far as the end results of the first session were concerned, it can be said without hesitation that Pope John turned the old guard's ways of doing things upside down. In this he has proved himself a supreme master. If thus far no one has really been hurt, it is owing to his great tact and kindness. Certainly under no other modern pontiff would such latitude have been allowed to men in high places whose minds were so obviously set against the Holy Father's wishes. The extremists are neither *vinti* nor *convinti*. As a matter of fact, after the first shock they have adopted two distinct lines of defense. The first maintains that the ultra-conservatives have actually been justified by the Council's course, the fact that no decrees were promulgated being proof that the Holy Father has been merely tolerating the show of independence and near rebellion on the part of radically-minded prelates from the north and east. These latter, they complain, received all the good publicity. But the tried and true doctrine was protected by the Holy Spirit, whose influence will certainly be much more manifest *on the right side* at the next session. Following another line, the less balanced group among them are somewhat bitter and unsubtle in their reactions. They refer to themselves as the "remnant of Israel," who have alone remained faithful to the traditional teaching of Holy Mother the Church. They compare themselves to the Macchabees being persecuted for the truth. What they can neither comprehend nor explain, however, is the position of Pope John. The more fanatic occasionally refer to him as a simpleton who has been hoodwinked by the scheming northerners. Meanwhile, they believe he is being used by Almighty God as a kind of scourge, requiring them to practice heroic forebearance, which they do for the good of the Church. One prominent U.S. monsignor goes about the campus of a Catholic University mumbling: "The damned Council!" His Italian counterparts have a phrase of similar significance though further removed from the blasphemous.*

What gives these men hope is the fact that in the meetings of the several sectors of the combined commission—Cardinal Ottaviani's Theological Commission and Cardinal Bea's Secretariat for Unity—which is currently dealing with the schema on revelation, the members of the Theological Commission have been able thus far to fight tooth and nail for the Ottaviani position. It is known, for example, that the first two or three sessions proved most difficult. Cardinal Bea was practically forced to agree to a vote on a statement of

* *Time's* "Man of the Year" article quotes the Holy Office consultor Msgr. Antonio Piolanti, who is Rector Magnificus of the Lateran University, as having warned his associates during the Council that "there are rationalist theologians going about Rome seducing innocent foreign bishops," and ominously telling one of his classes, "Remember, the pope can be deposed if he falls into heresy." This must have been said jokingly; whatever his ecclesiastical allegiance, the Rector Magnificus is too competent a theologian to have made the latter statement other than jocosely (*Time,* Jan. 4, 1963).

doctrine concerning the sources of revelation that was ambiguous, to say the least. The result of this vote was in the neighborhood of 19 in favor, as against 16 for rejecting the statement. Cardinal Ottaviani immediately claimed victory. But just as quickly it was pointed out that according to the rules of procedure under which the Council was operating, a majority of two-thirds was required. The matter finally had to be referred to the pope, who settled it summarily. The verdict was, stick to the agreed two-thirds rule.

They know likewise that *L'Osservatore Romano* is still under their control. If news is not to their liking, it is not news. On Jan. 13, 1963, for example, Cardinal Bea gave a revolutionary talk at Pro Deo University in Rome on the occasion of an annual *agapè* or fraternal celebration to which the representatives of various religious denominations in the Eternal City were invited. The cardinal spoke of liberty of conscience, stating that it was his intention to prepare a constitution on human freedom for presentation at the next session of the Council, in which the fathers would be asked to come out flatly with a public recognition of the inviolability of the human conscience as the final right of every man no matter what his religious beliefs or ideological allegiance. He stated further that the axiom "Error has no rights to exist," which is used so glibly by certain Catholic apologists, is sheer nonsense, for error is an abstract concept incapable of either rights or obligations. It is persons who have rights, and even when they are in error their right to freedom of conscience is absolute.* Cardinal Bea further con-

---

* Canon law has always proclaimed that "No one is to be forced against his will to embrace the Catholic faith" (Canon 1351 of the CIC). Despite the absoluteness of this statement, which proceeds from a principle of moral theology that in the end each person is responsible before God according to the dictates of his conscience, absolutist-minded ecclesiastics have frequently tried to force men either to profess a religious belief foreign to their thinking, or prevented them from exercising their contrary beliefs openly.

demned the religious wars of the Middle Ages as an obvious evil, despite the fact that many of them were waged by Catholic prelates and even by a few popes.*

In the mind of the Holy Office, these last two statements are so close to heresy that to this day no mention of this talk has been made in *L'Osservatore Romano,* even though it was the discourse of a cardinal closest to the Holy Father, and despite the fact that the Rome daily *Il Tempo* vigorously attacked Cardinal Bea's talk on the following Tuesday. Ordinarily, controversy concerning a cardinal that breaks out in the secular press is immediately smothered by indignant reaction in the columns of *L'Osservatore Romano* under the rubric "Ribalta dei fatti" or "In margine," in which every possible attempt is made to interpret the prince of the church's words or actions in a light most favorable to conservative Roman teaching. A cardinal's position in *L'Osservatore Romano* is to be defended at all costs. That this semi-official organ of the Vatican can have actually ignored the discourse of a cardinal of the Curia is simply incredible.

The Council has achieved thus far a major turn-over in Catholic thinking. Beginning with the discussion on the liturgy, slowly but with deliberate intent, a majority of the bishops, by a process resembling that of parliamentary debate, have begun gradually to strip the Roman Church of the juridical accumulations of centuries. In so doing, they have demonstrated that the essential fact about the Catholic faith was not a series of set formulas nor the bond of juridical unity; buts its dynamic participation in and witness to the living, redeeming and sanctifying presence of Christ in the world. They talked at first about the language and method of celebrating mass and dispensing the sacraments. But what they proved was that each age and clime has a right to clothe

* Text in *The Catholic Messenger,* Davenport, Iowa, Jan. 31, 1963.

these rites, essential to the well-being of the Christian, in a dress that fits the culture and intellectual pattern of the times. This was accomplished in a climate of free exchange, with an entrenched minority opposing every step of the way. When a rule of cloture was finally admitted, it was immediately employed by Cardinal Tisserant, with the rousing approval of the fathers who had been arguing liturgical reform for over three weeks. The final vote on acceptance of the liturgy schema as a whole is known to have heartened the Holy Father, who had become somewhat apprehensive over the apparent tenacity of the opposition. It shocked the ultraconservatives, however, for they immediately reacted by a feverish attempt to dominate the discussion of the next, and for them, crucial schema. Its title, "On the sources of revelation," at once betrayed its tendentious character. The Theological Commission that prepared the schema was controlled by the thinking of a small handful of theologians, all connected with the Roman universities, who had in common the belief that there was no other way of presenting the truths of the Catholic faith than by repeating the old and tried formulas and condemning all innovation. Hence their work on the draft decree was quickly labelled by various conciliar fathers as "excessively professorial and scholastic, not pastoral, incontinently rigid, theologically immature, incomprehensible, offensive to non-Catholics, unsympathetic to scientific research in theology and exegesis, and too evidently reflecting certain schools of thought." The resulting draft was far from what the pope had in mind as stated in his opening talk; nor was it in accordance with what the majority of the bishops felt was now necessary.

Evidently the ecclesiastical old guard had neither been heeding the signs of the times nor reading the theological output of their students, who had grown up and become

leaders in the Church at large. A good instance of this was
the pitiful appeal made by Archbishop Parente to the native
African bishops during the third week of the Council. Most
of these Negro bishops had been trained at the Propaganda
University in Rome. Msgr. Parente, therefore, accused them
of showing gross ingratitude toward their former teachers by
siding with the northern European bishops. But the Africans
were actually giving a magnificent lesson to the Council and
to the Church as a whole. They had come back to Rome to
learn what the Holy Father had in mind with respect to
progress for their countries. They took their cue from some
forty-two episcopal conferences or organized groups of
bishops in different countries or regions, who met regularly,
with executive committees for *ad hoc* activities, and attempted to attain local uniformity of ecclesiastical policy and
action. These groupings achieved a special consciousness of
themselves at the Council, and may prove part of the answer
to the widespread call for a decentralization of the Roman
Curia. It was truly amazing to witness all through the Council the cohesion demonstrated by the 292 African bishops,*
who organized a secretariat to represent their nine regional
groups in Rome on a permanent basis. Of equal significance
is the slowly emerging unity of the South American bishops
(some 600 all told) who, thanks in particular to the concern
of Rome for the fate of Catholicism in that area, the generous
assistance of North American bishops, and their own theological centers, particularly in Chile and Buenos Aires, are
gradually witnessing a renewal of Catholic thought along
social, economic, spiritual and religious lines, which can
alone save the continent from the grasp of communism.

From the theological point of view, this episcopal collabo-

* The bishops from Mozambique and the near-by islands raised the number
from 262 to 292.

ration according to natural human groupings, may prove to be one of the most important accomplishments of the Council, for it marks a return to recognition of the collegial pattern of government and the practice of the early Church as reflected in the letters of the second-century bishop and martyr St. Ignatius of Antioch and the third-century bishop of Carthage, St. Cyprian. In defining the relations between the bishops and the pope, as the Council must do when it deals with the structure of the Church, most informed observers in Rome believe that this truly hierarchical development will receive canonical sanction. It will likewise automatically settle the disputed question of the power and position of apostolic delegates and nuncios.

The Council's overwhelming acceptance of the first chapter of the schema on liturgy was a truly revolutionary step, though the fact is only slowly beginning to dawn on observers here. An article by the noted Benedictine professor of Liturgy, Father Cipriano Vagaggini, published in *L'Osservatore Romano* for December 8, spells out the significance of the principles established in this conciliar document. The Church's sacramental and prayer life is now acknowledged to be at the very heart of all its activities. It is the substance of the Catholic faith in action. Hence there can be no question of depriving the people of their proper part in the mass and sacraments—and that participation means an intimate sharing of these ceremonies and sacred actions. In seminaries and schools there must be a new reorientation designed to make the students at once both liturgical- and pastoral-minded. In each country, or cultural area, the local episcopate is to determine how much national custom or native tradition can be legitimately utilized in the Church's ceremonies, while preserving of course the basic meaning and structure of the mass and sacraments, and referring to the Holy See for final directions. This implicitly establishes the principle of the collegiality of the episcopate as a complement to the pope's position as primate, and recognizes the responsibility of episcopal conferences or groupings as units in dealing with the Holy Father and the Church. The question of the use of Latin in the Western Church is thereby reduced to a matter of minor importance; although it was on this point that the fathers-in-opposition, at the beginning, chose to make their stand.

It is known here that when the Secretary General of the Council saw Fr. Vagaggini's article, he was outraged. For use had been made of material covered by the secrecy of the Council, and it had not been cleared through him. He was informed however that clearance had been obtained through the Cardinal Secretary of State, the article having been "inspired" by an editor of *L'Osservatore Romano* on word from above.

Meanwhile Protestant reaction was on the whole favorable to the Council. Although a group of 150 French, Swiss and Belgian evangelical pastors meeting in Nogent-sur-Marne, two days after the Council's adjournment, were severe in their attitude: "A few liturgical *aménagements*," said their spokesman, "and even the rediscovery of certain New Testament truths are not sufficient to have us recognize the Roman Church as a sister in the Christian community, and much less a Mother and Teacher," the reaction of most "disjointed"—the new term utilized by a conciliar father to replace the outmoded "separated"—brethren was both pleasant and hopeful. The delegate of the World Council, Pastor Luke Vischer, addressing Cardinal Cicognani who received the observers on the eve of their departure instead of the pope, whose strength was not fully returned, said that he and his colleagues simply did not know how to thank the Holy Father sufficiently for the truly fraternal reception that they had been given in Rome. Referring to the obvious importance which John XXIII gave to their presence at the Council, he wanted to reassure the pope that because of the confidence placed in them by the free access to all the Council's doings, they felt that every effort was being made by the Catholic Church to comprehend their difficulties and religious convictions. "It is true, of course," he admitted, "that what separates us has not been disposed of in one quick move. But at least we ourselves now understand better just how great a task it will be to give new expression to the unity called for by Christ . . . We do not see how all this will end . . . but we are convinced now that we can make a common effort to come together."

Even more positive was the reaction of the Orthodox lay theologian, President Tadros, a counsellor in the Court of Appeals at Alexandria. He testified that of all the ecumenical meetings he had attended as observer or participant, Vatican Council II was the most satisfying. "I have been at Rhodes and New Delhi," he stated, "but all records have been broken here in Rome. We were well received in Rhodes, but excluded from a number of sessions; at New Delhi we were treated with the ecumenical spirit . . . but here in Rome the pope treated us as brothers, so that we felt that for all practical purposes we were fathers of the Council since we were given the schemata and had access to all the conciliar secrets . . . Nor was there any attempt to conciliate us or palliate the Catholic position on the papacy. This is our primary difficulty. But we were made to face up to it squarely. This is what I would call a true diplomacy—a Christian diplomacy made up of goodness, patience and theological competence."

Both the Soviet *Literary Gazette* and TASS agreed that the universal interest shown for the Council was more than justified. They cheered the pope's "unequivocal appeals for peace." Apparently by way of concretizing this approval, the

two Russian observers called on the Cardinal of Poland before departing for Moscow, and on taking leave of his eminence, kissed his ring. Even if this represents merely one more
move in the intricate political program of the Soviets, its
effect on Christians behind the Iron Curtain is bound to be
hopeful.

The Council has had a decided effect on the collective consciousness of the bishops themselves. The entire episcopate
has begun to realize what is implied by its collegial character. It has begun to see itself in the mirror of its true catholicity or universality. As Pope John said on December 8,
"Each man must feel in his heart the beat of his brother's
heart. [In the Council] there was thus need for a realization of diverse experiences, for an exchange of reflections,
and a mutual encouragement in our pastoral apostolate."
The bishops have begun to understand that it is not sufficient to await passively for a charismatic inspiration, or to
repeat the formulas of the scholastic manuals. They must
take cognizance of the fact that they are the free instruments
used by the Holy Spirit as the proponents of the faith in their
divine mission, and that they are given an immense task
which they must accept with humility and courage. They had
no right to think, in coming to the Council, as Bishop Sheen
observed in a sermon to the journalists, that a Council made
up of 3,000 fallible bishops would become infallible without
excruciating effort.

One thing is certain. The Bishops quickly realized the full
significance of their responsibility and of their liberty. On
December 8 Pope John told them: "These providential debates have brought out the truth and have let the whole
world see the holy liberty of the children of God such as it
is embodied in the Church."

What was also evident is that there are no true heresies

menacing the Church today other than fear of speaking the plain truth. Father J. van Kilsdonk, S.J., university chaplain to the Catholic students of Amsterdam, on September 30 last year, delivered an address before the St. Adalbert Society of Dutch Catholic intellectuals, in which he said that the nature of the Roman Curia was such that it frequently hampered the freedom of the pope, and dominated the bishops. He maintained that criticizing the Church could be "a holy duty like practising charity," adding that for the most part the Curia was controlled by "aged men who were conservative and incomprehensible to young people." On October 6, just before departing for the Council, Cardinal Alfrink of Holland gave a talk in which, while he did not mention Father van Kilsdonk by name, he said that public criticism of the Church was often not wise as it tended to stir up unrest without providing improvement. In December, immediately after the Council, Bishop van Dodewaard of Haarlem was admonished by the Holy Office not to keep this priest in his position as university chaplain. The Catholic daily *De Tijd-De Maasbode* of Amsterdam editorialized: "Any disciplinary measure against Fr. van Kilsdonk would make a bad impression on Dutch Catholics with their sensitive love of freedom . . . A sanction against this speaker, whom the Council demonstrated not to have been wholly in the wrong, would give offense to Dutch Catholics . . . who speak with great enthusiasm about their chaplain, and not only because of his outspokenness." Discussions were then inaugurated between Bishop van Dodewaard and Cardinal Alfrink with the Holy Office, the result of which were published by the Bishop of Haarlem in an official statement: "The Holy Office maintains its objections against the way in which Fr. van Kilsdonk adopted a position in regard to the Roman Curia. But, taking into account the steps taken by the Dutch

Church authorities in regard to reaction to the address, the Holy Office also leaves eventual measures to the local Ordinary. The Bishop of Haarlem will not dismiss Fr. van Kilsdonk from his post as chaplain to students." What conscientious Catholics object to is the fact that, with the Holy Father daily speaking of a fearless approach to the world, and of a "holy liberty" that befits the children of the Church, one of the offices of the Roman Curia still attempts to stifle even the mildest criticisms of its actions, and more particularly of its personnel.

As R. Rouquette points out in *Études* (Jan. 1963, p. 110) the serious theological opposition to the Council's accomplishment thus far came mainly from men who are devoted to the Church and its traditions, but who have unfortunately come to identify the present Roman Curial system with the divine right of the papacy. They believed themselves in some way as sharing in papal infallibility. It is said of one noted Jesuit theologian that he had his first doubt about infallibility the day he discovered that the reigning pontiff disagreed with one of his opinions.

As regards the Council, these men seem to forget that the episcopate in session in a Council is an instrument of the Holy Spirit. It is thus that an American ecclesiologist, in a ponderous attempt to defend his good friend Cardinal Ottaviani from the "drum-fire of journalistic attacks against the cardinal" . . . in articles "remarkably alike for inaccuracy of observation and for pure malevolence" that are to be found in "the Italian communist press, *Time* . . . *Newsweek*," etc.,* fails himself to distinguish between the Cardinal's function as Secretary of the Holy Office and his position in the Council as a bishop and as chairman of the Theological Commis-

* *Amer. Ecclesiastical Review*, Jan. 1963, p. 44.

sion.* In the latter two capacities, the Cardinal needs no defense. He is entitled to his opinions and has a right to express them as he pleases in Council or outside it. In actual fact as chairman of the Theological Commission he even had an obligation to fight for the retention of the schemata prepared by the committees under his control. But what *Time* and *Newsweek* in particular objected to were the methods the Cardinal used both before and after the Council to intimidate and even silence sincere and orthodox men who did not hold his opinions. His American defender says nothing of this accusation.

Since at this junction a theologian considered it necessary to defend the Cardinal's right to his opinion, by the same token, he might have thought it necessary to point out that journalists were free to make informed judgments about the figure made by the Cardinal as a leader of what quickly came to be the opposition at the Council; and that theologians are likewise free to criticize his theological opinions and preferences. That the Cardinal gave the impression that he was functioning at the Council as head of the Holy Office was unfortunate. For Pope John had made it absolutely clear— as does canon law (canon 222)—that the Roman Curia has nothing to do with a Council. That he likewise appeared to be using that same office to intimidate theologians brought to Rome by the bishops to assist them in understanding the work of the Council made it appear that he was hardly playing the game squarely. It is on this score that the main bulk of criticism was levelled against Cardinal Ottaviani in the reports on the Council. On this plane he had to run the risk that every prominent man is exposed to in a free society.

---

* "In the light of true history it will be seen that the mission of the Cardinal Secretary of the Holy Office at this latest Ecumenical Council of the Catholic Church has been truly providential." (*Amer. Ecclesiastical Review,* Jan. 1963, p. 53.)

He was expressing a viewpoint and attempting to act upon it. He could hardly expect those who disagreed with the propriety of his words and actions not to say so. It is certain that the Cardinal is used to this kind of give and take. It is his overzealous supporters who have actually given rise to most of the exaggeration in the estimates of his actions, and who have thus cast a shadow on his intentions.

Pope John said, "The Council is an act of faith in God, of obedience to His laws, of sincere effort to correspond with the plan of redemption according to which the Word has become flesh." That these men should be upset by an expression of this truth, which is not what they had expected, should be comprehended with patience and sympathy. But it is also highly desirable that they use other means of expressing their opposition. The oblique, hidden maneuvers which they often employ have profoundly astonished and indisposed a great part of the bishops on the "periphery," and in particular the North American bishops, who have been badly impressed by a certain lack of fair play. Americans who have come to the Council as neutrals, have departed transformed in good part because of these maneuvers. It would hardly be beside the point had the commentator remarked that thus God would seem "to have brought great good out of evil."*

In the encyclical epistle, *Mirabilis ille,* which Pope John sent to the bishops of the whole world (dated Jan. 6, published Feb. 7) concerning their work in the Council, he said: "We, the bishops of the Church of the Savior, must awaken our consciences to the grave responsibilities we have with regard to our participation in the world-wide apostolate. To have remained and to remain faithful to the purity of Catholic doctrine according to the teaching of the Gospel, of tradition, of the fathers and the Roman pontiffs is surely a

* *Etudes,* Jan. 1963.

great grace, a title for merit and honor. But this does not suffice for accomplishing the command of the Savior when he tells us: 'Go and teach all nations!' (Mt 28:19) or even for that passage from the Old Testament: 'He has confided to each the care of his neighbor' (Eccl 17:21).''

To journalists, on the feast of St. Francis de Sales (January 27, 1963), he claimed: ''The fact of the Council has caused a great echo in the world. You must certainly ask yourselves what such a lively interest, such a widespread attention, really means? First of all, we can eliminate the interest evoked by the external splendor of the ceremonial . . . It is caused, thanks be to God, by other things. It seems to us proper to say that the fact of the Council itself has been understood. It is recognized as a striking personification of the Christian message in its entirety, adapted to the exigencies of our times . . .''

In a recent summation,* Pope John claimed:

The experience of the first two months of Vatican Council II has enabled us, with God's help, to contribute something to the progressive march of the great assembly and to give it clarity and useful direction.

It is not an easy task which opens before us in this phase . . . following the line which the Saviour has inspired in us in convoking the Council. We are committed to a general and more ardent renewal of the life of the Church, and to a new and vigorous showering of the Gospel on the whole world through the Holy Church . . . This renewed pastoral *élan* is the constant care of our heart. It is the aim of the Ecumenical Council to see that our contemporaries are kept *au courant* of the maternal action of the Church for the spiritual elevation and even the material betterment of all humanity.

Let us be permitted to restate here, for the direction and encouragement of all, . . . what we wished to express with simplicity and clarity in our introductory discourse on October 11th

* Dec. 23, 1962.

last, at the solemn and splendid inauguration of the Council. We said then to the immense throng of venerable brothers in the episcopate, reunited for the first time in so remarkable a number . . . that, as regards the Council, it is committed by fidelity to the basic doctrines of Christ, which give it authority and which are immutable in the sacred deposit of faith . . .

We added immediately that our sacred obligation is not only to take care of this precious treasure, as if we had only to worry about the past, but we must also devote ourselves with joy and without fear to the work of giving this ancient and eternal doctrine a relevancy corresponding to the conditions of our era.

The character of John XXIII is so genuinely unpretentious that one hesitates to call him the hero of the Council to date, yet the ovations that greeted him on every occasion left no doubt that the majority of the conciliar fathers consider him so. It is no small achievement to have launched the Catholic Church into a new era. The reform and renewal of the most ancient continuous institution of Western civilization were not simple matters to initiate. No one believed that the *aggiornamento,* or modernization, that Pope John worked for so strenuously from the first months of his pontificate had been accomplished in this first session—a mere eight weeks could hardly do that—and the repercussions of much that has happened will not be felt for some time. But the process had been started. In the pope's words, this first session was "a good beginning." An American bishop has predicted that when the sessions are resumed the Council will have shifted "from low gear into high." While this remains to be seen, one thing is certain: the pope, on the very first day of the assembly, handed the bishops a Magna Carta whose full revolutionary import is only gradually being realized by the Council and by the world at large.

Appendix I

Toward Christian Unity

(*The address of Pope John XXIII at the solemn opening of the Vatican Council II, October 11, 1962.*)

Mother Church rejoices that, by the singular gift of Divine Providence, the longed-for day has finally dawned when—under the auspices of the Virgin Mother of God, whose maternal dignity is commemorated on this feast—the Second Vatican Ecumenical Council is being solemnly opened here beside St. Peter's tomb.

The Councils—both the 20 ecumenical ones and the numberless others, also important, of a provincial or regional character which have been held down through the years—all prove clearly the vigor of the Catholic Church and are recorded as shining lights in her annals.

In calling this vast assembly of bishops, the latest and humble successor of the Prince of the Apostles who is addressing you intended to assert once again the Church's *magisterium* [teaching authority], which is unfailing and perdures until the end of time, in order that this *magisterium,* taking into account the errors, the requirements and the opportunities of our time, might be presented in exceptional form to all men throughout the world.

It is natural that, in opening this universal council, we should like to look to the past and to listen to its voices, whose echo we like to hear in the memories and the merits of the more recent and ancient pontiffs, our predecessors. These are solemn and venerable voices, throughout the East and the West, from the fourth century to the Middle Ages, and from there to modern times, which have handed down their witness to those councils. They are voices which proclaim in perennial fervor the triumph of that divine and human institution, the Church of Christ, which from Jesus takes its name, its grace and its meaning.

Side by side with these motives for spiritual joy, however, there has also been for more than 19 centuries a cloud of sorrows and of trials. Not without reason did the ancient Simeon announce to Mary, the mother of Jesus, that prophecy which has been and still is true: "Behold this child is set for the fall and the resurrection of many in Israel, and for a sign which shall be contradicted" (*Luke 2:34*). And Jesus Himself, when He grew up, clearly outlined the manner in which the world would treat His person down through the succeeding centuries with the mysterious words: "He who hears you, hears me" (*Ibid. 10:16*), and with those others that the same Evangelist relates: "He who is not with me is against me and he who does not gather with me scatters" (*Ibid. 11:23*).

The great problem confronting the world after almost two thousand years remains unchanged. Christ is ever resplendent as the center of history and of life. Men are either with Him and His Church, and then they enjoy light, goodness, order and peace. Or else they are without Him, or against Him, and deliberately opposed to His Church, and then they give rise to confusion, to bitterness in human relations, and to the constant danger of fratricidal wars.

Ecumenical Councils, whenever they are assembled, are a solemn celebration of the union of Christ and His Church and hence lead to the universal radiation of truth, to the proper guidance of individuals in domestic and social life, to the strengthening of spiritual energies for a perennial uplift towards real and everlasting goodness.

The testimony of this extraordinary *magisterium* of the Church in the succeeding epochs of these 20 centuries of Christian history stands before us collected in numerous and imposing volumes, which are the sacred patrimony of our ecclesiastical archives, here in Rome and in the more noted libraries of the entire world.

As regards the initiative for the great event which gathers us here, it will suffice to repeat as historical documentation our personal account of the first sudden welling up in our heart and lips of the simple words, "Ecumenical Council." We uttered those words in the presence of the Sacred College of Cardinals on that memorable January 25, 1959, the feast of the Conversion of St. Paul, in the basilica dedicated to him. It was completely unexpected, like a flash of heavenly light, shedding sweetness in eyes and hearts. And, at the same time, it gave rise to a great fervor throughout the word in expectation of the holding of the Council.

There have elapsed three years of laborious preparation, during which a wide and profound examination was made regarding modern conditions of faith and religious practice, and of Christian, and especially Catholic, vitality. These years have seemed to us a first sign, an initial gift of celestial grace.

Illuminated by the light of this Council, the Church—we confidently trust—will become greater in spiritual riches and, gaining the strength of new energies therefrom, She will look to the future without fear. In fact, by bringing herself up to date where required, and by the wise organization of mutual cooperation, the Church will make men, families and peoples really turn their minds to heavenly things.

And thus the holding of the Council becomes a motive for

wholehearted thanksgiving to the Giver of every good gift, in order to celebrate with joyous canticles the glory of Christ Our Lord, the glorious and immortal King of ages and of peoples.

The opportuneness of holding the Council is, moreover, Venerable Brothers, another subject which it is useful to propose for your consideration. Namely, in order to render our joy more complete, we wish to narrate before this great assembly our assessment of the happy circumstances under which the Ecumenical Council commences.

In the daily exercise of our pastoral office, we sometimes have to listen, much to our regret, to voices of persons who, though burning with zeal, are not endowed with too much sense of discretion or measure. In these modern times they can see nothing but prevarication and ruin. They say that our era, in comparison with past eras, is getting worse and they behave as though they had learned nothing from history, which is, none the less, the teacher of life. They behave as though at the time of former Councils everything was a full triumph for the Christian idea and life and for proper religious liberty.

We feel we must disagree with these prophets of doom who are always forecasting disaster, as though the end of the world were at hand.

In the present order of things, Divine Providence is leading us to a new order of human relations which, by men's own efforts and even beyond their very expectations, are directed toward the fulfillment of God's superior and inscrutable designs. And everything, even human differences, leads to the greater good of the Church.

It is easy to discern this reality if we consider attentively the world of today, which is so busy with politics and controversies in the economic order that it does not find time to attend to the care of spiritual reality, with which the Church's *magisterium* is concerned. Such a way of acting is certainly not right, and must justly be disapproved. It cannot be denied, however, that these new conditions of modern life have at least the advantage of having eliminated those innumerable obstacles by which at one time the sons of this world impeded the free action of the Church. In fact, it suffices to leaf even cursorily through the pages of ecclesiastical history to note clearly how the Ecumenical Councils themselves, while constituting a series of true glories for the Catholic Church, were often held to the accompaniment of most serious difficulties and sufferings because of the undue interference of civil authorities. The princes of this world, indeed, sometimes in all sincerity, intended thus to the protect the Church. But more frequently this occurred not without spiritual damage and danger, since their interest therein was guided by the views of a selfish and perilous policy.

In this regard, we confess to you that we feel most poignant sorrow over the fact that very many bishops, so dear to us, are noticeable here today by their absence, because they are imprisoned for their faithfulness to Christ, or impeded by other restraints. The thought of them impels us to raise most fervent prayer to God. Nevertheless, we see today, not without great hopes and to our immense consolation, that the Church, finally freed from so many obstacles of a profane nature such as trammeled her in the past, can from this Vatican basilica, as if from a second Apostolic cenacle, and through your intermediary, raise her voice resonant with majesty and greatness.

The greatest concern of the Ecumenical Council is this: that the sacred deposit of Christian doctrine should be guarded and taught more efficaciously. That doctrine embraces the whole of man, composed as he is of body and soul. And, since he is a pilgrim on this earth, it commands him to tend always toward Heaven.

This demonstrates how our mortal life is to be ordered in such a way as to fulfill our duties as citizens of earth and of heaven, and thus to attain the aim of life as established by God. That is, all men, whether taken singly or as united in society, today have the duty of tending ceaselessly during their lifetime toward the attainment of heavenly things and to use only for this purpose the earthly goods, the employment of which must not prejudice their eternal happiness.

The Lord has said: "Seek first the kingdom of God and his justice" (*Matt. 6:33*). The word "first" expresses the direction in which our thoughts and energies must move. We must not, however, neglect the other words of this exhortation of Our Lord, namely: "And all these things shall be given you besides" (*Ibid.*). In reality, there always have been in the Church, and there are still today, those who, while seeking the practice of evangelical perfection with all their might, do not fail to make themselves useful to society. Indeed, it is from their constant example of life and their charitable undertakings that all that is highest and noblest in human society takes its strength and growth.

In order, however, that this doctrine may influence the numerous fields of human activity, with reference to individuals, to families and to social life, it is necessary first of all that the Church should never depart from the sacred patrimony of truth received from the Fathers. But at the same time she must ever look to the present, to the new conditions and new forms of life introduced into the modern world which have opened new avenues to the Catholic apostolate.

For this reason, the Church has not watched inertly the marvelous progress of the discoveries of human genius and has not been backward in evaluating them rightly. But, while following these developments, she does not neglect to admonish men so that, over and above what is perceived by the senses, they may raise their eyes to God, the Source of all wisdom and all beauty. And may they never forget the most serious command: "The Lord thy God shalt thou worship, and Him only shalt thou serve" (*Matt. 4:10; Lk. 4:8*), so that it may not happen that the fleeting fascination of visible things should impede true progress.

The manner in which sacred doctrine is spread thus having been established, it becomes clear how much is expected from the Council in regard to doctrine. That is, the 21st Ecumenical Council, which will draw upon the effective and important wealth of juridical, liturgical, apostolic and administrative experiences, wishes to transmit the doctrine, pure and integral, without any attenuation or distortion, which throughout 20 centuries, notwithstanding difficulties and contrasts, has become the common patrimony of men. It is a patrimony not well received by all, but always a rich treasure available to men of good will.

Our duty is not only to guard this precious treasure, as if we were concerned only with the past, but to dedicate ourselves with an earnest will and without fear to that work which our era demands of us, pursuing thus the path which the Church has followed for 20 centuries.

The salient point of this Council is not, therefore, a discussion of one article or another of the fundamental doctrine of the Church which has repeatedly been taught by the Fathers and by ancient and modern theologians, and which is presumed to be well known and familiar to all.

For this, a Council was not necessary. But from the renewed, serene and tranquil adherence to all the teaching of the Church in its entirety and preciseness, as it still shines forth in the acts of the Council of Trent and First Vatican Council, the Christian, Catholic and apostolic spirit of the whole world expects a step forward toward a doctrinal penetration and a formation of consciences in faithful and perfect conformity to the authentic doctrine which, however, should be studied and expounded through the methods of research and through the literary forms of modern thought. The substance of the ancient doctrine of the Deposit of Faith is one thing, and the way in which it is presented is another. And it is the latter that must be taken into great consideration, with patience if necessary, everything being measured in the forms and proportions of a *magisterium* which is predominantly pastoral in character.

At the outset of the Second Vatican Council, it is evident, as always, that the truth of the Lord will remain forever. We see, in fact, as one age succeeds another, that the opinions of men follow one another and exclude each other. And often errors vanish as quickly as they arise, like fog before the sun.

The Church has always opposed these errors. Frequently she has condemned them with the greatest severity. Nowadays, however, the spouse of Christ prefers to make use of the medicine of mercy rather than that of severity. She considers that she meets the needs of the present day by demonstrating the validity of her teaching rather than by condemnations. Not, certainly, that there is a lack of fallacious teaching, opinions and dangerous concepts to be guarded against and dissipated. But these are so obviously in contrast with the right norm of honesty, and have produced such lethal fruits, that by now it would seem that men of themselves are inclined to condemn them, particularly those ways of life which despise God and His law, or place excessive confidence in technical progress and a well-being based exclusively on the comforts of life. They are ever more deeply convinced of the paramount dignity of the human person and of his perfecting, as well as of the duties which that implies. Even more important, experience has taught men that violence inflicted on others, the might of arms and political domination, are of no help at all in finding a happy solution to the grave problems which afflict them.

That being so, the Catholic Church, raising the torch of religious truth by means of this Ecumenical Council, desires to show herself to be the loving mother of all, benign, patient, full of mercy and goodness toward the children separated from her. To the human race, oppressed by so many difficulties, she says like Peter of old to the poor man who begged alms from him: "Silver and gold I have none; but what I have, that I give thee. In the name of Jesus Christ of Nazareth, arise and walk" (*Acts 3:6*). In other words, the Church does not offer to the men of today riches that pass, nor does she promise them a merely earthly happiness. But she distributes to them the goods of divine grace which, raising men to the dignity of sons of God, are the most efficacious safeguards and aids toward a more human life. She opens the fountain of her life-giving doctrine which allows men, enlightened by the light of Christ, to understand well what they really are, what their lofty dignity and their purpose are, and, finally, through her children, she spreads everywhere the fullness of Christian charity, than which nothing is more effective in eradicating the seeds of discord, nothing more efficacious in promoting concord, just peace and the brotherly unity of all.

The Church's solicitude to promote and defend truth derives from the fact that, according to the plan of God, "who wills all men to be saved and to come to the knowledge of the truth" (*I Tim. 2:4*), men without the assistance of the whole of revealed doctrine cannot reach a complete and firm unity of minds, with which are associated true peace and eternal salvation.

Unfortunately, the entire Christian family has not yet fully attained to this visible unity in truth.

The Catholic Church, therefore, considers it her duty to work actively so that there may be fulfilled the great mystery of that unity, which Jesus Christ invoked with fervent prayer from His Heavenly Father on the eve of His sacrifice, She rejoices in peace, knowing well that she is intimately associated with that prayer, and then exults greatly at seeing that invocation extend its efficacy with salutary fruit even among those who are outside her fold.

Indeed, if one considers well this same unity which Christ implored for His Church, it seems to shine, as it were, with a triple ray of beneficent supernal light: namely, the unity of Catholics among themselves, which must always be kept exemplary and most firm; the unity of prayers and ardent desires with which those Christians separated from this Apostolic See aspire to be united with us: and the unity in esteem and respect for the Catholic Church which animates those who follow non-Christian religions.

In this regard, it is a source of considerable sorrow to see that the greater part of the human race—although all men who are born were redeemed by the blood of Christ—does not yet participate in those sources of divine grace which exist in the Catholic Church. Hence the Church, whose light illumines all, whose strength of supernatural unity redounds to the advantage of all humanity, is rightly described in these beautiful words of St. Cyprian: "The Church, surrounded by divine light, spreads her rays over the entire earth. This light, however, is one and unique, and shines everywhere without causing any separation in the unity of the body. She extends her branches over the whole world. By her fruitfulness she sends ever farther afield her rivulets. Nevertheless, the head is always one, the origin one, for she is the one mother, abundantly fruitful. We are born of her, are nourished by her milk, we live of her spirit" (*De Catholicae Ecclesiae Unitate, 5*).

Venerable Brothers, such is the aim of the Second Vatican Ecumenical Council, which, while bringing together the Church's best energies and striving to have men welcome more favorably the good tidings of salvation, prepares, as it were, and consolidates the path toward that unity of mankind which is required as a necessary foundation in order that the earthly city may be brought to the resemblance of that heavenly city "where truth reigns, charity is the law, and whose extent is eternity" (Cf. St. Augustine, *Epistle 138, 3*).

Now, "our voice is directed to you" (*2 Cor. 6:11*), Venerable Brothers in the episcopate. Behold we are gathered together in this Vatican basilica, upon which hinges the history of the Church where heaven and earth are closely joined, here near the tomb of Peter and near so many of the tombs of our holy predecessors, whose ashes in this solemn hour seem to thrill in mystic exultation.

The Council now beginning rises in the Church like daybreak, a forerunner of most splendid light. It is now only dawn. And already at this first announcement of the rising day, how much sweetness fills our heart. Everything here breathes sanctity and arouses great joy. Let us contemplate the stars, which with their brightness augment the majesty of this temple. These stars, according to the testimony of the Apostle John (*Apoc. 1:20*), are you, and with you we see shining around the tomb of the Prince of the Apostles, the golden candelabra—that is, the churches confided to you (*Ibid.*).

We see here with you important personalities, present in an attitude of great respect and cordial expectation, having come together in Rome from the five continents to represent the nations of the world.

We might say that Heaven and earth are united in the holding of the Council—the saints of Heaven to protect our work, the faithful of the earth continuing in prayer to the Lord, and you, seconding the inspiration of the Holy Spirit, in order that the work of all may correspond to the modern expectations and needs of the various peoples of the world.

This requires of you serenity of mind, brotherly concord, moderation in proposals, dignity in discussion and wisdom of deliberation.

God grant that your labors and your work, toward which the eyes of all peoples and the hopes of the entire world are turned, may abundantly fulfill the aspirations of all.

Almighty God! In Thee we place all our confidence, not trusting in our own strength. Look down benignly upon these pastors of Thy Church. May the light of Thy supernal grace aid us in taking decisions and in making laws. Graciously hear the prayers which we pour forth to Thee in unanimity of faith, of voice and of mind.

O Mary, Help of Christians, Help of Bishops, of whose love we have recently had particular proof in thy temple of Loreto,

where we venerated the mystery of the Incarnation, dispose all
things for a happy and propitious outcome and, with thy spouse,
Saint Joseph, the Holy Apostles Peter and Paul, Saint John the
Baptist and Saint John the Evangelist, intercede for us to God.

To Jesus Christ, our most amiable Redeemer, immortal King
of peoples and of times, be love, power and glory for ever and
ever. Amen.

Appendix II

The First Session of Vatican II

✠

(The address delivered by Pope John XXIII, on December 8, 1962, at the formal closing of the first session of the Second Vatican Council.)

The first session of the work of the Council, begun on the Feast of the Divine Motherhood of Mary, comes to an end on today's Feast of the Immaculate Conception in the radiance of the grace of her who is God's Mother and our own.

She provides the mystic link between today's ceremony and that of the splendid opening of the Council on October 11, while her two feasts sound the keynote of our prayer of thanksgiving.

The deep significance of these two feasts is all the more striking when one reflects that our predecessor, Pius IX, the Pope of the Immaculate Conception, inaugurated the First Vatican

Council on this same feast day of our Lady. It is good to commemorate these happy coincidences which, in the light of history, help one to recognize how many of the Church's great events take place in Mary's presence, in testimony and assurance of her motherly protection.

The Council, in its reality, is an act of faith in God, of obedience to His laws, of sincere endeavor to correspond with the plan of redemption according to which the Word was made flesh of the Virgin Mary. And as today we pay reverence to the most pure stem of the root of Jesse from which the flower has sprung—"The flower from his root shall rise up"—our hearts are filled with a joy that is all the greater in that we see this flower blossoming in the season of Advent.

Now that the bishops of the five continents are returning from this hall to their beloved dioceses to continue the pastoral service and guidance of their flocks, we should like to dwell a little on what has been done so far and, encouraged and enlightened by this, to map out the future while waiting for the fulfillment of what yet remains to be done to bring the great enterprise to a happy conclusion.

We will consider these three points: the beginning of the Ecumenical Council; its continuance; and the fruits which are expected of it in the way of spreading faith and holiness and apostolic activity in the Church and in modern society.

The opening of the Ecumenical Council is still vivid in our minds—the vast assembly of bishops of the entire Catholic world, a gathering unique in history. The one, holy, catholic and apostolic Church was revealed to all humanity in the splendor of her perennial mission, in the solidity of her organization, in the persuasiveness and attractiveness of her teaching. Furthermore it is with pleasure that we recall the delegations from various nations representing their governments in the solemn inauguration of the Council. On this subject we would once again like to express our thanks for the way in which the whole world has been an admiring witness of these events and for the reports that have come to us from all over the world in expressions of respect, esteem and gratitude.

Since this is the end of the first phase of the work begun on that memorable day, October 11, it is only fitting to reflect on what has been accomplished.

The first session was like a slow and solemn introduction to the great work of the Council—a generous willingness to enter into the heart and substance of Our Lord's plan. It was necessary for brothers, gathered together from afar around a common hearth, to make each other's closer acquaintance; it was necessary for them to look at each other squarely in order to understand each other's hearts; they had necessarily to describe their own experiences, reflecting the conditions of the apostolate under the most varied climates and circumstances, in order that there should be a thoughtful and profitable interchange of views on pastoral matters.

In such a vast gathering, it is understandable that a few days were needed to arrive at an agreement on a matter on which, in all charity, there existed with good reason sharply divergent views. But even this has a providential place in the triumph of truth, for it has shown to all the world the holy liberty that the sons of God enjoy in the Church.

It was not by chance that the first schema to be considered was on the sacred liturgy, which defines the relationship between man and God. Since it is the highest form of relationship, it must be based on the solid foundation of revelation and the apostolic teaching, so as to proceed for the good of souls with broadness of vision, free from the superficiality and haste which sometimes characterize the relationship between men.

And then five more schemata were presented, a fact which alone makes one realize the extent of the work thus far completed. Indeed, it is right to conclude that a good beginning has been made.

It will, then, be a question of extending to all departments of the life of the Church, social questions included, whatever the Conciliar Assembly may decide, and applying its norms to them with "generous assent and prompt fulfillment" (Prayer for the Ecumenical Council). This most important phase will see pastors united in a gigantic effort of preaching sound doctrine and applying the law, which they themselves desire, and for this task will be called forth the collaboration of the forces of the diocesan and regular clergy, of the congregations of religious women, of the Catholic laity with all its attributes and potential, in order that the acts of the Fathers be seconded by a joyous and faithful response.

It will be a "new Pentecost" indeed, which will cause the Church to renew her interior riches and to extend her maternal care in every sphere of human activity. It will be a new advance of the Kingdom of Christ in the world, an elevated and persuasive reaffirmation of the good news of redemption, a clarion call of God's kingship, of the brotherhood of men in charity, of the peace promised on earth to men of good will in accordance with God's good pleasure.

These, Venerable Brethren, are the feelings of our heart, which issue in hope and prayer. Now that the labors of this first session of the Council are over, you are going back to your own countries and to the precious flocks committed to your care. As we now wish you "Godspeed," we desire that you should be our faithful messengers in expressing to your priests and people the greatness of our affection.

On this occasion there come to mind the words of greeting and hope which Pius IX addressed, one day, to the bishops of the First Vatican Council: "See brethren, what a blessed and joyful thing it is to go forward in harmony in the house of God. May you always so progress. And as Our Lord Jesus Christ gave peace to His Apostles, so I also, His unworthy vicar, give you peace in His name. Peace, as you know, casts out fear; peace shuts its ears to what is said without real knowledge. May this peace be yours all the days of your life."

In the past months of companionship here together, we have experienced the savor of these words of Pius IX. There is much yet to be done, but you know that the Supreme Shepherd will have loving care of you in the pastoral activity which you exercise in your own dioceses, an activity which will not be dissociated from the preoccupations of the Council.

In drawing your attention to the threefold activity, which is the task of all, it was our intention to stir up your enthusiasm. The glorious opening of the Council provided the first introduction to the great enterprise. In the coming months the work

will go on unflaggingly, as also will the earnest reflection, so
that the Ecumenical Council may be able to bestow upon the
family of mankind those fruits of faith, hope and charity which
are so ardently expected from it. This threefold character clearly
shows the unique importance of the Council.

A heavy responsibility, therefore, rests upon our shoulders, but
God Himself will sustain us on the way.

May the Immaculate Virgin be with us always; may Joseph,
her most chaste spouse, patron of the Ecumenical Council, whose
name, from today, shines in the canon of the Mass all over the
world, accompany us on our journey in the same way that he
accompanied the Holy Family with his support in accordance
with God's will. And with them Saints Peter and Paul and all
the apostles with John the Baptist, and all the popes, bishops,
and doctors of God's Church.

And now, Venerable Brethren, one's glance turns trustingly to
that phase of the work, seemingly silent, but none the less important, which opens up during these nine months of interval
after your return to your sees.

Meanwhile, it pleases us to contemplate each of you in your
separate diocese, and a deep satisfaction fills our heart, for we
know that, returning from Rome, you bring to your Christian
peoples the shining torch of confidence and of charity, and that
you will remain united with us in fervent prayer.

This calls to mind the words of Ecclesiasticus, referring to the
high priest Simon: ". . . He himself stood by the altar, and about
him was the ring of his brethren" (*Ecclus. 50:13*). It is thus that
our activity continues now, in this mutual blending of prayers
and wills.

Today's celebration does not bring the work to an end; rather,
the work that awaits all of us is of the greatest importance, which
certainly was not the case during the recesses of previous Councils. The conditions of modern life, however, make it easy to
have rapid communications on all types of business, personal
and apostolic.

That activity will continue is made clear by the institution of
a new commission composed of members of the Sacred College

and of the episcopate and representing the universal Church. This commission's duty is to pursue and direct the work during these months and, along with the various conciliar commissions, to lay the firm foundations for the happy final outcome of the ecumenical sessions. Thus the Council really remains open during the next nine months of suspension of the ecumenical sessions properly so called.

Each bishop, although preoccupied with his pastoral administration, should continue to study and investigate the schemata provided and whatever else may be sent later. In this way, the session which will begin in the month of September of next year—at the new hoped-for meeting in Rome of all the Fathers of the Church of God—will proceed more surely, more steadily and with greater speed, thanks to the experience of these two months of 1962, so that there is hope that the conclusion awaited by all our faithful children may be reached in the glory of the incarnate Son of God in the joy of Christmas in the centenary year of the Council of Trent.

The vision of this grand prospect, which reveals the whole course of the coming year so rich in promise, stirs up in the heart a more ardent hope for the realization of the great goals for which we have convoked the Council: namely that "the Church founded on faith, strengthened in hope and more ardent in charity, may flourish with new and youthful vigor, and, fortified by holy ordinances, may be more energetic and swift to spread the Kingdom of Christ" (papal letter to the German episcopate, January 11, 1961).

Even if the stage of putting the Council into effect is not imminent—for that we must wait until the work of the Council is over—it is none the less consoling to turn one's gaze toward the benefits that are anticipated: benefits for the Catholic Church; renewed attention on the part of all those countless children of ancient and glorious civilizations, which the light of Christianity does not desire to destroy, but in which she could—as has happened at other times in history—develop the richest seeds of religious vigor and human progress.

Our heart casts its glance in that direction, Venerable Brethren, and we know also that your heart has the same solicitude as our own.

We are, in this Basilica of St. Peter, in the center of Christianity, at the tomb of the Prince of the Apostles. But we recall with pleasure that the cathedral of the Diocese of Rome is the Lateran Basilica, the mother and foundation of all churches, dedicated to Christ, the divine Saviour. To Him, therefore, Who is the immortal and invisible King of all ages and all peoples, be glory and power forever (cf. *1 Tim. 1:17; Apoc. 1:6*).

In this hour of heartfelt joy, it is as if the heavens are opened above our heads and the splendor of the heavenly court shines out upon us, filling us with superhuman certainty and a supernatural spirit of faith, joy and profound peace. In this light, as we look forward to your return, we salute all of you, Venerable Brothers, "with a holy kiss" (cf. *Rom. 16:16*), while at the same time we call down upon you the most abundant blessings of our Lord, of which the apostolic blessing is the pledge and promise.

Index of Names

✠

Vosté, J. M., O.P., 151
Vuccino, A. G., Abp., 198, 212

Weber, C., Bp., 132
Weber, J. J., Bp., 63, 134, 136, 137
Welykyj, A. G., Rev., 42, 43, 90, 192, 211
Wenger, A., A.A., 142, 243
Willebrands, J., Msgr., 42, 77, 80, 90, 186
Williams, G. H., Rev. Dr., 81
Wijtyla, K., Bp., 136, 173
Wright, J. J., Bp., 63, 119
Wronka, A., Bp., 136
Wyszynski, S., Card., 66, 94, 137, 180, 186, 207, 213

Xenopulos, G., Bp., 135

Yago, B., Abp., 137
Yamaguchi, P. A., Abp., 133

Yemmeru, A. M., Abp., 201, 212
Yoshigoro Taguchi, P., Bp., 139
Youakim, E., Bp., 213
Yougbare, D., Bp., 131
Young, G., Bp., 130
Yü Pin, P., Abp., 135

Zak, F., Bp., 135
Zakka B. Iwas, R., Rev., 80
Zanini, L., Abp., 131
Zarranz y Pueyo, J. P., Bp., 187
Zauner, F., Bp., 135
Zazinovic, C., Bp., 118, 133
Zazpe, V., Bp., 186
Zerwick, M., S.J., 53
Zilianti, P. R. M., Abbot, O.S.B., 139
Zizola, G., 156
Zoa, J. B., Abp., 158, 171
Zoghby, E., Bp., 199, 212
Zohrabian, C. J., Bp., 67, 132, 134, 138
Zougrana, P., Bp., 65